Heritage of Sea Power

By the same author

The British Submarine
Up She Rises   (with John Davies)

H.M.S. *Victory*

Heritage
of Sea Power

The story of Portsmouth

by F. W. Lipscomb

Hutchinson of London

HUTCHINSON & CO *(Publishers)* LTD
178–202 Great Portland Street, London W1

London Melbourne Sydney
Auckland Bombay Toronto
Johannesburg New York

★

First published 1967

*This book has been set in Baskerville, printed in Great Britain
on Antique Wove paper by Anchor Press, and
bound by Wm. Brendon, both of Tiptree, Essex*

*To my Wife
for all the help she has given me
in writing this book*

Contents

Illustrations

PLANS

The pen sketches at the heads of chapters were specially drawn by John Ross

ERRATUM

Captions to line drawings on pages 110 and 141
should read: chapter 6 *The Royal Charles*, not
The Ipswich; chapter 7 *The Ipswich* not *The
Royal Charles*.

Foreword

The Island of Portsea and its Naval Dockyard has played a permanent part in the history of England throughout the ages. Though historians have recorded these events, either in general works on British Naval History or in single episodes, there has been no co-ordinated account of the history of Portsmouth from the maritime aspect.

I have endeavoured to fill this gap within the limitations of a single book, which I hope will serve to remind citizens and friends of Portsmouth of the great heritage of this Naval City.

I myself have known Portsmouth from my early Naval Cadet days, and later have lived here with my family for the past twenty-two years. My direct ancestor, Richard Lipscomb, was christened and married at the Parish Church of St. Thomas à Becket (now the Cathedral), in the seventeenth century, and my mother's great-grandfather, Henry Peake, Surveyor of the Navy, was knighted by the Prince Regent at the Governor's House, Portsmouth, on the occasion the of visit of the Allied Sovereigns in 1814. These personal connections with the City have given me an added interest in writing this book.

F.W.L.

Hanaker, Craneswater Park, Southsea, Portsmouth

ACKNOWLEDGEMENTS

In writing this book, which has taken some five years to complete, I have received help from so many people that it is not possible to thank them all in person, and I must ask for the understanding of those whose names do not appear in these acknowledgements.

I am specially indebted to the staff of the Portsmouth City Library under the able and experienced direction of Mr. H. Sargeant, F.L.A., until recently Librarian and Curator, who has given much time and careful consideration to the many questions posed. In the early stages I was assisted by Mr. J. A. J. Munro, A.L.A., the then Head of the Reference Department, and latterly by Mrs. M. J. Guy, A.L.A., to whom I am greatly indebted for all the work she has done, for the personal interest she has taken, and for so kindly devoting periods of her spare time checking information and dates. Among other members of the Corporation staff who have kindly assisted me are Mr. A. Corney, Curator of Antiquities, and Mr. B. F. Jeffrey, of the Photographic Department. Again, in the early stages Miss J. R. Masters, B.A., the then City Archivist, assisted me with notes and papers relating to a series of lectures, given over a period of six months, on Corporation History. Her successor, Mr. M. J. W. Willis-Fear, B.A., has continued this help in the final stages of the book.

I have to thank Councillor F. A. Emery-Wallis for his interest and ready assistance whenever I turned to him for advice from his vast knowledge of the history of Portsmouth. Also, I am indebted to the late Mr. J. C. V. Lovatt, who advised on Social History.

On the naval side I wish to thank successive Commanders-in-Chief and Admirals Superintendent of the Dockyard, who gave me the facilities necessary in writing such a book and advised in many ways. I should like to thank Mr. R. S. Horne, I.R.I.B.A., of H.M. Dockyard, for helping me with certain parts of the history of the Dockyard, and the Commanding Officers of H.M.S. *Excellent* and H.M.S. *Vernon* for helping me with the history of their respective establishments. Also, I am grateful to the Curator of the Royal Marine Museum, for allowing me to extract information from historical accounts in the files of the museum.

My warmest thanks are due to Professor Christopher Lloyd, C.B.E., M.A., late Professor of History at the Royal Naval College, Greenwich, for reading the manuscript and advising generally on the naval history; to Mr. Alan Ivimey, Editor and Author, for his expert advice on the presentation of the book as a whole; and to my brother, J. F. Lipscomb, for his expert and knowledgeable assistance in checking the page proofs.

I should like to record my thanks to Mr. A. W. H. Pearsall, M.A., together with Lieutenant-Commander A. H. Waite, R.N.R., of the National Maritime Museum, Greenwich, for their ready assistance. For the drawings of the ships at the head of each of the chapters my special thanks are due to Mr. John Ross, who kindly undertook the task in spite of many urgent calls on his time. Also, I am most grateful to Mrs. St. George Saunders and the staff of her Writers' and Speakers' Research Organisation for much expert work and personal interest. My thanks are due as well to Mr. L. S. Baynton-Williams, 70 Brompton Road, London, S.W.7, for his permission to use his print of the view of Portsmouth for the centre spread illustration.

In order to write the Epilogue it was necessary to visit Portsmouth, Virginia, and Portsmouth, New Hampshire. In both these cities I received abundant help on all sides for which I am most grateful. At Portsmouth, Virginia, Marshall Butt, Curator of the Norfolk Shipyard Museum, besides giving me much of his valuable time, permitted me to quote liberally from his own writings, and for all this I am extremely grateful. Again, I wish to record my sincere thanks to Captain Carl Johnson, U.S.N.(Retd.), late Commanding Officer of the Naval Shipyard, Portsmouth, New Hampshire, and now Director of the Strawbery Banke Organisation, for his enthusiastic help on all matters relating to the port.

Finally, I have to thank Mrs. Phillips of Southsea for much typing and retyping, often carried out late at night and at weekends.

PRINCIPAL DATES

501 Saxon landing.
979 Portsea Island raided by Danes.
1066 Harold cruises off the Isle of Wight.
1194 Charter granted by King Richard I.
1196 Churchyard and two side altars of the Church of St. Thomas à Becket consecrated by Godfrey de Lucy, Bishop of Winchester.
1212 King John orders the building of Portsmouth's first dock.
1213 King John sails to France to re-establish his Angevin possessions.
1346 King Edward III's expedition to France. (Fights the battle of Crecy.)
1415 King Henry V's expedition to France. (Fights the battle of Agincourt.)
1445 Landing of Margaret of Anjou.
1450 Murder of Bishop Molyens. Portsmouth excommunicated.
1495 Henry VII orders the building of the first graving dock in northern waters.
1497 The building of the *Sweepstake*.
1509 The building of the *Peter Pomegranate*—the first man-of-war built in the dockyard.
1513 The building of the *Mary Rose*—the first battleship to be built in the dockyard.
1538 The beginning of Southsea Castle.
1545 The sinking of the *Mary Rose*.
1563 The Plague in Portsmouth.
1591 Queen Elizabeth I visits Portsmouth.
1600 The granting of the First Charter of Incorporation.
1623 King James I visits Portsmouth.
1628 Murder of the Duke of Buckingham.
1629 John Mason founds New Hampshire in America.
1634 Death of John Mason.
1642 (August.) Civil War. Colonel Goring declares for the King. (September.) Portsmouth capitulates to Parliamentary forces.
1650 Launch of the first *Portsmouth*.
1662 Landing of Catherine of Braganza and her marriage to King Charles II.
1672 Visit of the French Fleet under Admiral d'Estres.
1687 King James II opens the King James's Gate and touches for the King's Evil.

1688	The revolt of the six Portsmouth Captains.
1689	Visit of King William III.
1698	Visit of the Tsar of Russia.
1702	Founding of the town of Portsea.
1703	The great storm.
1710	Construction of the dockyard wall.
1747	Founding of the *Portsmouth and Gosport Gazette*.
1757	Execution of Admiral Byng.
1759	Body of General Wolfe landed at Portsmouth.
1779	Court martial of Admiral Keppel.
1782	Sinking of the *Royal George*.
1788	Founding of Sydney, Australia, by Portsmouth Marines.
1792	Court martial of mutineers of the *Bounty*.
1794	Lord Howe enters Spithead with prizes after the battle of the 'Glorious First of June'.
1797	Mutiny in the Fleet at Spithead.
1805	Lord Nelson joins the *Victory* before the battle of Trafalgar.
1814	Visit of the Allied Sovereigns.
1822	Opening of the first stage of the Portsmouth–Arundel canal.
1842	Queen Victoria visits Portsmouth for the first time.
1844	Visit of Louis Philippe, King of France.
1901	Funeral of Queen Victoria.
1906	Launch of H.M.S. *Dreadnought*.
1926	Portsmouth raised to the status of a City.
1928	H.M.S. *Victory* granted permanent resting place in the dockyard.
1936	King Edward VIII leaves Portsmouth for France after abdication.
1941	Portsmouth attacked by enemy bombers.
1944	'D' Day.
1965	Freedom of the City conferred on the Portsmouth Naval Command.

1

The Haven

Seal of Portsmouth

A scene to marvel at is the panorama viewed from the Portsdown Hills which overlook the island of Portsea. Standing on
this high ground, by one of the old defensive forts, the view on
a clear day spans the coast of Hampshire from Selsey Bill to
Southampton and the New Forest.

To the left and east of Portsea can be seen the expanse of
Langstone Harbour, with Hayling Island beyond. To the
right and west lies the harbour of Portsmouth itself, with its
many creeks leading a few miles inland towards Fareham. On
a spit of land at the head of the harbour stand the ruins of the
Roman castle of Portchester. Now looking due south and
immediately below one, the two main bridges from the mainland to Portsea can be clearly seen. The principal road, coming
from London, crosses the Portsbridge and runs southwards
within one hundred yards of the original course along which,
throughout the ages, successions of kings, their knights and
armies, have come to embark on expeditions.

Further south across the water, beyond the dockyard with
its massive cranes and the masts of Nelson's *Victory*, lies the
Isle of Wight, forming a perfect shelter for the famous Spithead

B

anchorage, with more defensive forts rising out of the water in splendid isolation.

At night the panorama is transformed into a fairylike scene which has no match in England. Thousands of lights glitter as far as the eye can see. This brilliance spills itself into the narrow strip of coastal water, to be picked up again on the opposite side by the lights of the town of Ryde in the Isle of Wight.

*   *   *   *   *

In 1944 a mighty army under General Montgomery left Portsmouth to land on the beaches of Normandy. Six hundred years earlier, in 1346, twenty thousand men, under Edward III, left Portsmouth for those same beaches. During this six hundred years the story of Portsmouth is in many respects the naval story of England. But the full story goes back to the fifth millennium B.C., when nature separated Britain from Europe, and the Isle of Wight from the mainland, leaving a piece of land some four miles long and three miles wide, itself divided from the mainland proper by a narrow channel. This is the island of Portsea on which now stands the city of Portsmouth.

This vast geographical change provided one of the finest natural harbours in northern European waters and heralded the influence of sea power in our island history.

In the latter part of the third century the Romans built a chain of forts around the coast from the Wash to Southampton. One of these was built at Portchester on the northern shore of Portsmouth harbour. Most of them were placed under the command of a high officer known as the Count of the Saxon Shore. His duty was to keep the channel free of Saxon raiders, using ships based on Portchester. Thus Portsmouth harbour entered naval history. Nor was the mercantile aspect neglected, as the first trading in hides, wool and corn was begun by the Romans with Honfleur in Normandy. From these beginnings the sea was to be used and understood.

Towards the end of several hundred years of gradually declining Roman occupation the Saxon Porth made a landing in A.D. 501, and began to colonise the area. A hundred years later, at the beginning of the seventh century, Britain was invaded and overrun by the Teutonic Saxons, of whom it was written by a Roman poet: 'The sea is their school of war and the storm their friend.'

Some settled on Portsea Island, thus bringing it on to the scene for the first time.

While St. Augustine and his monks made good progress elsewhere converting Anglo-Saxon Britain to the Christian faith, according to the Venerable Bede, the Hampshire dwellers remained pagan, until the sea intervened and washed up St. Wilfred on to the shore at Bosham. Not long afterwards Portsea Islanders accepted his preaching.

The successful invader must look for tranquillity to land his forces, and by now the unique feature of Spithead and the Solent had become well known to dwellers on the northern shores of the Continent. The Danes, seeking new realms to plunder, swept up Southampton Water in 838, but Hampshire men turned them back. However, twenty years later a stronger force broke through to Winchester. Alfred, now King of Wessex, looked for a solution, and turned to sea power. He met the invaders at sea in his own ships, built and manned locally, and for the first time British oak, which was to play such a vital part in naval warfare in the years to come, was put to the test and found to be superior to its European counterpart.

The effect of Alfred's policy lasted until 979 when, under Ethelred, who had no ships, Hampshire and Portsea Island in particular suffered devastating raids from the Danes, culminating in Canute usurping the kingship.

For a time peace came to the shores of Britain, but towards the end of the reign of Edward the Confessor the Norman threat from across the Channel faced members of the House of Godwin with the same problems as their predecessors had forced on the Anglo-Saxons. Harold understood the importance of sea power and his fleet cruised off the Isle of Wight all through the summer of 1066. No invasion came and when, in the autumn, he laid up his ships, partly because of false intelligence and the onset of the bad weather and also because of lack of food, he made his great mistake. History would have been very different if he had made the effort to keep his ships in readiness.

England and Normandy were now one kingdom and Portsea and the surrounding waters the centre of the sea communications between the two. The Domesday Survey of 1085–6 shows increasing development. Numerous new manors were described with names familiar today on the island of Portsea and the hinterland, such as Froddington (Fratton), Copenore (Copnor), Coseham (Cosham), Wineringes (Wymering) and Bocheland (Buckland). In 1066 Portchester, as in Roman times, and later Southampton, with Honfleur and Barfleur, were bases for trade, gradually rising throughout Norman times to equal importance with the Cinque Ports and their trade with Boulogne and northern France. But Portchester and Southampton could not stand by themselves throughout the 138 years of rising maritime activity across the Channel, and Portsmouth took its place with them in history whenever sea power became the overriding influence in the minds of kings, queens and military commanders.

Henry I used Portsmouth on his frequent journeys to Normandy, and later Matilda entered the country here to conduct her civil war against Stephen.

Henry II embarked and landed from Portsea Island at least ten times, and at the height of his power left England for the last time from Portsmouth. Legend says he made his will on these very shores.

The hundred or more years of Norman reign established Portsmouth in the minds of seafaring men as the springboard of maritime power in the south and, of necessity, the once little hamlet had grown.

With the death of Henry II his son Richard returned to England, landing at Portsmouth. After only a few months he set out on a crusade, but with his capture by Leopold, the Austrian duke, he was prevented from returning until five years later. Immediately he set foot on English soil for the second time he called together a fleet at Portsmouth, having vowed his intention of punishing the French king for betraying him to his Austrian captor. For this task he needed money and among the places which, as a consequence, received their first charter was Portsmouth. Firstly, he took over the settlement from John de Gisors, and in the words of the Curia Regis Rolls: 'It pleased the Lord King Richard to build the town of Portsmouth.'

Next, he gave the town its charter. Dated 1194, it begins:

Richard, by the Grace of God, King of England, Duke of Normandy and Aquitane, Earl of Anjou, to the Archbishops, Bishops, Abbots, Earls, Barons, Sheriffs, Bailiffs, Ministers and all faithful people of all his realms,—Greeting: Know ye that we have recovered into our hands our Burgh of Portsmouth.

Now the burgesses were given the right to run the town. Among various privileges, they could keep the trade fees for the good of the community, set up local courts instead of going to the hundred or shire, and devise their own seal and coat of arms.[1]

Richard built a hall for himself and granted plots of land to others on which to build. The charter also granted permission for Portsmouth to hold a fair each year, lasting a fortnight.

The fair, known as the Free Mart Fair, was begun at once. It was held for fifteen days as a 'Free Mart for all people, natives or foreigners, to enter the Kingdom, be exempt from dues, impositions or tolls, not to be arrested for debt, or oppressed in any way.'

A large open hand was displayed during the period of the fair, this being the Norman emblem of justice. The fair was held in the High Street, and very soon became important for the sale of wool, many Frenchmen coming over from Normandy and Dutch traders making visits.

Richard sailed for France, never to return, but by his last act in this country he had established Portsmouth as a small borough.

A traveller approaching the town from the north and over the Portsdown Hills would see the island of Portsea almost entirely cultivated. Immediately below him lay the Ports-bridge, a semi-fortified bridge which had accommodation for a few soldiers in an emergency, and which at that time afforded the only crossing to Portsea Island and its manors. There was open country as far as the church of St. Mary, Kingston, and beyond that lay the more heavily cultivated approach to Portsmouth itself, then a little town with a few hundred inhabitants.

In those days Portsmouth had no defences, not even a wall

---

1. It is widely held that the city's coat of arms, with the emblems of the star and crescent, derives from King Richard's seal, used to seal the charter in 1194. The charter was 'given by the hand of William de Longchamps, Bishop of Ely, our Chancellor, at Portsmouth'. De Longchamps' seal also had a crescent and eight-pointed star, but both the Bishop and the town may have taken their emblems from that of the King. The star and crescent was a widely used device at the time, and no documentary proof exists as to the truth of the matter.

or a ditch, and no mounted archers or spearmen to keep a look-out. In the town there were only two streets worthy of the name. These were the High Street and St. Thomas's Street, both of which ran down to the Camber, a small inner harbour close to the entrance to the main harbour. One of the more impressive houses was the King's Hall standing at the north end of the High Street. All the houses were of wood and thatch.

Nearer the Camber, on an acre of open grassland, stood the church of St. Thomas. This was a place of worship for pilgrims from the Isle of Wight and from France on their way to Canterbury, Winchester and St. Albans. John de Gisors, the rich descendant of the Norman invaders from whom Richard I had taken over the town, bought the acre in 1180 and endowed the church. By 1188 work on the chapel was sufficiently advanced for Bishop Toclive of Winchester to consecrate it. Building was continued and on Tuesday the 12th of March 1196 the churchyard and two side altars were consecrated by Godfrey de Lucy, also Bishop of Winchester.[1] To the eastward of the church stood the foundations of the Domus Dei or Hospital of St. Nicholas. Here Peter de Rupibus had bought a very large plot of land and was building Portsmouth's first hospital. It was here the pilgrims would rest before proceeding on their journeys.

To the east of the town there was an area of marsh known as the little morass. This separated the town from common land known as Froddington Heath. Further east there was a great morass extending towards Lumps Farm and then more heath as far as Eastney Farm on the Langstone harbour side of the island.

In the harbour the tides run very strongly, both through the narrows of the entrance and in the harbour itself, making the handling of vessels difficult, particularly on the ebb tide, when the many long tidal creeks empty themselves completely in the space of two or three hours.

In those days the first of the creeks on the eastern side of the harbour was called the Pond of the Abbess, there being halfway along its southern shore a windmill which was owned by the Abbess of Frontevrault. This creek lay no more than a quarter of a mile from the town, and ran inland for a mile or so.

1. Documentary evidence of the consecration of the chapel no longer exists.

It was here that the principal shipping of the port anchored after discharging cargo at the Camber, or before making a voyage. In addition, the mud flats on either side of the creek were suitable for hauling vessels out clear of the water, for repair or cleaning.

There might be as many as fifty ships lying in the Pond, and as many again hauled out on the mud. There would be galleys, some the King's own ships, and others the property of barons and knights. They usually had a single mast with a square sail made from flax or animal skins. Each of them carried a ship-man, a steersman, a crew of about twenty mariners, and some-times three boys, the latter being considered equal to one man.

No doubt there would be some merchant vessels in the Pond too, some afloat, and some hauled out. These were round ships, not much longer than they were broad, and they 'spread' so much at the water-line that they looked like swans. Like the galleys, they had only one mast, and set a square sail on a yard, which meant they could do little more than blow before the wind.

It was in the early summer of the year 1212, when King John had been on the throne of England for thirteen years, that the first really significant maritime development in Portsmouth's history occurred. It was then that the Sheriff of Southampton received the following royal command:

The King to the Sheriff of Southampton. We order you without delay by view of lawful men, to cause our docks at Portsmouth to be enclosed with a Good and Strong Wall in such a manner as our beloved and faithful William, Archdeacon of Taunton, will tell you for the preservation of our ships and galleys, and likewise to cause penthouses to be made to the same Walls as the Archdeacon will also tell you, in which all our ships' tackle may be safely kept, and use as much despatch as you can, in order that the same may be completed this summer, lest in the ensuing winter our Ships and Galleys and their rigging should incur any damage by your default; and when we know the cost it shall be accounted to you.

Portsmouth's first dock—the first permanent dock in the history of England—was about to be built.

The edict was addressed to the Sheriff of Southampton because in those days Portsmouth came within his jurisdiction, and William de Wrotham, Archdeacon of Taunton, was charged with carrying out the work because, in addition to his position and duties in the Church, he held the appointment of 'Keeper of the King's Ships'. He had received this appointment simply because of his learning in an age when few men could read or write. Such men as he were in great demand and many of the dignitaries of the Church performed very practical secular functions as well.

At this time the King had three fleets, totalling many hundred ships in all. The eastern fleet was based on London and ports on the east Kent coast as far as Sandwich. The southern fleet was based on Rye, Winchelsea, Shoreham, Portsmouth, Southampton and Exmouth. The western fleet operated from Bristol and neighbouring harbours.

The construction of the dock at Portsmouth was very much the Archdeacon's business. He was particularly interested in this project because he was ambitious to acquire land for himself, and the King had promised him a piece in Westminster in return for ensuring the safe-keeping of the royal ships.

The Archdeacon was soon active in Portsmouth, directing the construction of the dock on the site of the Pond of the Abbess, along its southern shore. The dock walls were to be made of mud and clay reinforced with brushwood and rushes. There were to be penthouses of brick and wood, with shelves for sails and ships' tackle. Special lockers were to be provided for navigational instruments—such as compasses (very recently invented), and sounding leads. Every shipman of a king's ship was to have his specially appointed space for storage. A time limit was set. Everything must be completed by the autumn of that year.

With the starting of the dock, Portsmouth began to come into its own. In commerce the town had always been over-shadowed by Southampton, which had far better communications. The building of the dock afforded some compensation for the lack of commercial activity.

Workmen flocked into the area. Throughout the summer many hundreds of labourers were camped on Froddington Heath. They came from towns and hamlets as distant as Southampton and Chichester, and their presence stimulated business, particularly during the week of Portsmouth's Free Mart Fair.

All the summer the work of levelling the mud flats, building the surrounding sea wall and constructing the penthouses went on, until the day came when there was nothing left to do except seal the entrance. The labour camp broke up, and the Archdeacon, who had paid periodical visits to Portsmouth to inspect the work, went up to London to report to the King and receive his coveted piece of land.

The primary importance of Portsmouth at this time was as a port of embarkation for operations against France, and, by the time of the building of the dock, English possessions were sadly diminished. When King John came to the throne in 1199 he had received from his brother, King Richard, a continental dominion stretching from the northern seaboard of France to the Pyrenees, but in the short space of five years all Normandy had been lost, together with much of Maine, Anjou and Poitou. Only La Rochelle, with the hinterland in the west, and Gascony, with the important port of Bordeaux, were still loyal to the English throne.

It was at Portsmouth that King John's first effort to recover his lost possessions was mounted, in 1205, but proved abortive. The Archbishop of Canterbury, the Earl of Pembroke, and others in the name of the Pope, forbade him to proceed, and many of the earls and barons refused on their own account to follow him. The Fleet put to sea for a few days, but, although the fourteen thousand sailors manning the ships were loyal, the King realised that he had insufficient support from his nobles and reluctantly landed, disappointed, at Wareham. He set out the following year, again from Portsmouth, but then a two years' peace was arranged with King Philip of France before any hostilities commenced.

For the next six years King John never abandoned the hope that he might one day lead another expedition to La Rochelle or Bordeaux.

His chance came a year after the completion of the dock at Portsmouth, in which his ships had wintered safely. In May 1213 news was received that France was mounting an invasion of England. The King acted quickly. He despatched a fleet under the Earl of Salisbury to Damne, which caught the French fleet unawares and destroyed more than four hundred ships.

With the danger at home diminished, John decided to counter-attack at two points. While an army under the Earl of Salisbury was despatched to Flanders to aid his ally, the Emperor Otto IV, the King himself prepared to go to Poitou.

With these plans made, the Portsbridge once more felt the heavy tread of men-at-arms and horses, and the rumble of ox-carts, all heading for the high ground to the east of Portsmouth. Here, that autumn, a vast camp was pitched. It was so big that the little township was completely dwarfed by it.

As this great concourse of men assembled—nearly thirty thousand of them in all—tents in their thousands, and pavilions, many of them coloured, and with flags flying from their centre-posts, added their gaiety to the great encampment.

Provisions from Southampton, which came regularly by ox-cart and boat, were stored under cover. Large tubs of fresh water were placed at intervals throughout the camp. Stables and forges were erected, and armourers and farriers were kept busy well into the night. Lighting was supplied by torches and candles. Men-at-arms, mounted archers, cooks, scullions, hangers-on, beggars and pages hurried here and there about their various occupations, while barons, knights and other commanders rode to meet each other and co-ordinate their forces.

The English army which now covered the common outside Portsmouth brought mixed blessings to the town. On the one hand their custom was welcomed by local merchants, but, on the other, the presence so close to the town of such a horde of men whose normal life was one of fighting and pillage gave rise to anxiety.

All the autumn, while his forces were gathering on the common, King John refused to say when he intended to sail for France. The delay, added to the rigours of camp life in increasingly bad weather, produced its expected grumbles from the rank and file, which their commanders, already incensed by the King's indecision, did not trouble to subdue. Some of the barons and knights themselves returned to their castles and manors.

As Keeper of the King's Ships, the Archdeacon of Taunton was particularly concerned to know the sailing date, and at last he managed to extract one from the King. It was to be February 2nd, 1214. The Army was told this just before Christmas and was elated, not realising what a sea voyage at this time of year might mean. The seamen in Portsmouth were dismayed. They knew only too well what might be in store for them, and wanted to know what the new dock was for, if it was not for protecting the King's ships during the winter.

Despite these grumbles, and the fact that there was a good deal of sickness in the camp, the Archdeacon, having extracted a date from the King, would not hear of a postponement. Himself an experienced sailor, he judged that it ought to be possible to pick about six fine days in February to make a series of short passages to the Biscay ports. He had already sent messengers to the barons of the Cinque Ports instructing them to bring their ships to Portsmouth by mid-January. The sheriffs of all the southern counties had been instructed to order the bailiffs in their various ports to arrest appropriate shipping for the expedition and send it fully manned to Portsmouth by the same date.

Thus the great concentration began, and mounted until there were over a thousand ships at Portsmouth and in the harbours and creeks of the Solent and the Isle of Wight. They were a mixed assortment. There were the King's own galleys, and his yacht, or *esnecca* (a royal pleasure-vessel capable of being used as a transport), which was equipped to be propelled by a hundred and thirty oarsmen, in addition to having a large mast taking a square sail, and which in design was reminiscent of the 'long ships' of the Vikings. There were also the galleys of the barons and knights. There were *cogs*, which were sailing vessels manned by about forty seamen under a coxswain, specially constructed for carrying troops; *huissiers*, equipped to transport twenty-five horses each; *buses* (cargo vessels with large stowage space) for carrying stores and fighting equipment, and a large number of 'round' ships. This vast fleet was manned by well over ten thousand mariners.

The King arrived in Portsmouth in late January. The expedition was ready to leave, but on the evening of his arrival the weather deteriorated. Soon a full gale was blowing, with lashing rain which turned the camp on the common into a quagmire, and the shipmen anxiously had to put out extra anchors to hold their ships.

For the next seven days the wind blew strongly out of the south-west. Though the assembled fleet suffered no appreciable harm, the King and his army had to bear the enforced inactivity and frustration. Then the gale dropped, and was replaced by a gentle breeze from the north. A fair wind.

This was what the Keeper of the King's ships had been waiting for, and he now gave the order for embarkation. At once all was activity. Every ship in the harbour began to stir.

By midday hundreds were beached or lying off, ready to take on board the army which had lived for so long on the common.

The embarkation took four days. By evening on the fourth day, when the tide began to fall, all the ships were loaded. Now the royal standard, which was on wheels so that it could follow the Army everywhere with comparative ease, was moved up to the ramp of the King's ship, safely embarked and placed amidships. At a command from the King the standard was hoisted, the royal retinue boarded the vessel, and a great cheer went up from the whole armada.

Slowly the sail in the King's great ship was hoisted, and this was the signal for the rest of the fleet to make sail too. In the evening light, with a favourable breeze off the shore, the whole magnificent array of ships gradually crossed Spithead and the Solent to Yarmouth, in the Isle of Wight, where final preparations were to be made before the dangerous passage of the open sea.

Now the only occupants of the camp on the common would be beggars, scroungers and dogs, and by morning nothing would be left, as these camp-followers would have removed everything, down to the last tattered rag and meatless bone. Then the wifflers (police) would come out from the town and drive them across the island, over the Portsbridge and into the countryside beyond.

From Yarmouth the fleet set sail and Portsmouth, like the rest of England, awaited the outcome of the venture. Throughout the summer, news of varying fortunes trickled back, brought by ships returning from La Rochelle and Bordeaux.

King John's campaign did not go well and he was glad to be able to arrange a comparatively favourable peace with King Philip's son, Louis. Another inconclusive essay at arms was over.

By the autumn, the dock at Portsmouth was once more full of ships and the King was back in England with a domestic crisis on his hands which was to lead to Magna Carta, and no prospect of further expeditions. The men of Portsmouth returned, for the time being, to their modest share of the wool trade, and to local agriculture.

In 1216 King John died and during the minority of Henry III no matter of any great military or maritime moment disturbed the life of the town.

This state of calm was fostered by a decision which affected the maritime life of the Town.

The position selected for King John's dock was not a good one, because it was exposed to the force of the winds and the strength of the tides. When the moon is new or full and the spring tides run, besides a great volume of water passing through the narrow harbour entrance, the height of the water is such that the land on the western side no longer affords protection from the prevailing south-west wind. In turn this wind pushes the tide even higher and causes rough seas inside the harbour.

The Pond of the Abbess, lying immediately inside the entrance on the eastern side, was so placed as to receive the full force of these acts of nature, which are very violent when all happen to be acting together.

No doubt the seamen were aware of these dangers and the periods in the calendar when they were likely to occur, but it appears from the Close Roll of 1228 that matters had reached a point when a decision had to be made regarding the future of the dock, because of the repeated damage to it and to the ships inside.

In this year King Henry III made a gift of tree trunks and brushwood from the Forest of Bere to the Abbess of Fronte-vrault, to 'block up the locks which King John had made in the tidal marshes'. The Roll goes on to say that a causeway should be built. The King instructed the Constable of Portchester to see that the Prior of Letton, who was evidently the Abbess's business agent in this country, received the trees and brush-wood. The order to the Constable speaks of storm and flood which had broken down the dock. Some time in this year a full south-westerly gale must have coincided with an exceptionally high spring tide and, not for the first time, the dock had been very considerably damaged.

Great care was taken to see that all concerned with a decision of this nature were fully informed, and the Sheriff of South-ampton, whose predecessor had brought the order from King John to build the dock, was instructed to allow the Abbess to 'block up the locks' and to see that the causeway was built.

At this time Henry III may have had little reason to keep the dock in active use. No doubt the refined and cultured builder of Westminster Abbey had many other matters closer to his interests in mind. The fact is that nothing more is heard of this dock from that date, which must have been a serious blow to the town which now had nowhere in its vicinity to lay up ships in the winter.

Since those early days, the fourteenth-century kings and queens always made their docks and built their storehouses further up harbour, evidently having learned their lesson from what happened to King John's dock.

2

Gateway to Normandy

Fourteenth-century ship

The filling in of Portsmouth's first dock put an end to the
naval development of the port for the rest of King Henry III's
reign, but during these years the Domus Dei, or Hospital of
St. Nicholas, was completed. This building, which had been
started during King John's reign, was an inspiring place. Its
dedication to St. Nicholas was apt, for he was the special
guardian of sailors and those who travelled on the high seas,
and the hospital did much good work.

The buildings consisted of a gatehouse with lodgings, a
church, an armoury, a smith's forge, a pay chamber, a captain's
chamber, a guest chamber, a dining chamber, a pigeon house,
a kitchen and larder, a bakehouse, a stable, and a nursery.
The hospital received its income from a variety of endow-
ments of land, rentals and levies, chiefly in Hampshire, but
some further afield, and was under the direct patronage of the
King. It was administered by a master, sometimes called the
prior, or warden, or custos, with six monks and six nuns. For
three hundred years it cared for wayfarers and the sick, and
received pilgrims and strangers on passage through the port.
When Portsmouth suffered its worst devastations, either at the

hands of the enemy, or from disease or natural hazards, it was often the only source of comfort. At one time its influence even began to overshadow that of the church of St. Thomas but happily an arrangement was arrived at which prevented any usurpation by the hospital of the place of the parish church.

Associated with it there was, on the Portsmouth road at the head of the Pond of the Abbess, a Home of Public Assistance, which also cared for wayfarers and the sick.

In spite of the filling in of the dock, expeditions still left Portsmouth from time to time, and some of these were on quite a grand scale. Henry III embarked there for France at least three times, and on one of these occasions was accompanied by his queen. None of the purely military ventures of these years achieved anything of note.

By the time of King Henry III's death in 1272 the export of wool and grain had steadily increased, in spite of the rivalry of neighbouring Southampton, but shortly after Edward I succeeded Henry III he issued the Statute of Westminster, which put a tax on wool. This tax was controlled by the commercial port of Southampton and thereby diverted the major part of the trade to that town. The Hundred Rolls records of Portsmouth at that time:

There are few houses which could be called large and nearly all are of wood. They are scattered around the Church of St. Thomas and the Camber. There are no well-defined streets; one main road, the High Street, and several side lanes and alleys comprise the Town proper. Scattered homesteads in large plots of ground extend on all sides. To the east, stretch the common fields of the townsfolk; for although the trade of the port is growing, agriculture is still the main occupation of the people. In times of distress the town is sometimes comparatively deserted.

Part of the reign of King Edward I was absorbed in the endeavour to subdue the Scots. In the latter campaign the King based his southern fleet on Portsmouth to prevent an assault by the French in his rear. This fleet was under the command of Sir William Leybourne and its presence undoubtedly made the French hesitate before coming to the aid of the Scots. This new importance promised better times for Portsmouth, whose inhabitants were understandably encouraged when Sir William assumed the title of admiral, one of the first to be so named in this country. But this promise was not maintained. From 1307, when Edward I died, until 1330, when Edward III assumed full powers at the age of seventeen, maritime affairs in Portsmouth were sadly neglected, so much so that when Edward III went to war with France in 1338 (and thus contributed further to the causes of the Hundred Years War), a Frenchman, Sir Nicholas Béhuchet, sailed over with a small fleet to plunder Portsmouth and Southampton.

The French ships came over flying English flags, and naturally the people of Portsmouth thought it was their own fleet. Most of the enemy had landed on the common before anyone realised they were hostile. The port had no trained guards, and consequently no one to give the alarm. With appalling swiftness and brutality, Portsmouth was razed to the ground. Only the church of St. Thomas and the Domus Dei were left standing. Women and children kneeling in the streets begging for mercy were cut down, all livestock was slaughtered, and every dwelling place set on fire and pulled down.

All that year and the next the French did much as they pleased in the Channel, destroying many of our seaport towns, even the Cinque Ports. Our ships had no haven of refuge, and ceased to operate as a fleet. But the King, having now learned the lesson, that to invade France successfully the French fleet must first be defeated, determined to re-form his own fleet, and gave orders for the ships to be refitted, whatever the condition of the ports.

Somehow Portsmouth struggled to life again, if only in a small way, and in secret, for the Isle of Wight was occupied by the French for some of the time.

The spirit of Portsmouth was emulated all along the south coast, and it was a marvel how the fleet was refitted and finally concentrated.

In 1340 the new fleet destroyed the French at Sluys. Portsmouth seamen returned jubilant, carrying with them a number of French knights, who were paraded in the streets before being sent to Portchester Castle to await their ransom.

Interest in Portsmouth was stimulated again when the King ordered a supply of men-at-arms and archers for the town. Unfortunately, it was discovered that this force would consist of only one man-at-arms and two archers, so the town protested to the King in such terms that he issued a royal mandate 'for enclosing with walls and paving with stone our town of Portsmouth'.

C

This mandate instructed the bailiffs and honest men of the town to collect a tax on merchandise entering the port during the next eight years in order to raise money for the project. A farthing was to be taken for every horse load of corn, a halfpenny for every horse or cow sold, and twopence for every tun of wine. Unhappily, the King did not appreciate that there were very few people in the town and that trade was slight. In addition, all Customs dues were still collected by the authorities from Southampton, with the result that traders found they were paying double taxation, and avoided Portsmouth altogether.

The scheme was therefore dropped. Enough was collected to erect some very inadequate mud and timber walls, which had to suffice for the next forty-five years.

After the destruction of the French fleet at Sluys in 1340, more ships were built and manned from the King's exchequer, and he felt an increasing need for a purely military port where he could concentrate his armies and his ships for a major attack on France. Portsmouth was the obvious choice, not only from the geographical position it commanded, and the fine enclosed harbour, but because the common provided an admirable camping ground for the largest armies, which could be embarked in tranquil waters from the three miles of gently sloping beach. Moreover, being on an island, entry and departure could be controlled on the landward side with comparative ease. Even the lack of trade, so greatly regretted by the inhabitants, was an advantage in that it enabled the military commanders to concentrate without hindrance on matters of war. Thus, Portsmouth once again was singled out as a place of embarkation when in 1346 King Edward III decided to invade France and to leave from Portsea Island.

The King made meticulous preparations for his campaign, using both Portchester Castle and the priory of Southwick (situated a little north of the Portsdown Hills) as his headquarters. Next he succeeded in gaining the confidence of a dissatisfied French nobleman, and, from intelligence thus gained, decided that he would land on the Normandy coast. He also learned of the number of rivers and bridges that he would have to cross to get to Calais, so made arrangements to embark carpenters, miners and shipwrights. He understood he might have difficulty in taking Caen, where in fact he was held up for some days.

Portsmouth played its part by the refitting of ships, supplying materials, and in providing sixteen thousand cleys[1] for the embarkation of horses in transports for France. Some twenty thousand men-at-arms were first encamped on the common, which, as in the days of King John's expedition, was a mass of tents and pavilions, more effectively hidden from prying French eyes than if the base had been at Dover or Margate.

During May and June strong south-westerly winds prevented Edward sailing. Eventually on July 5th embarkation began, but the Fleet got no further than St. Helens, off the Isle of Wight, when the seven hundred vessels which had been gathered to transport the Army were forced to anchor due to further gales. At length, on July 11th, conditions were set fair and the expedition left for the Normandy beaches on the Cotentin peninsula, carrying with it a few bombards, the first time cannon had been taken to the field of battle.[2]

Then followed the great Battle of Crécy and the prizes of victory were great. Not only were many high-born Frenchmen brought to the town and imprisoned at Portchester, but spoils of all kinds found their way to many houses, including gold vases, silks and tapestries and many trophies of silver.

Two years later the Black Death[3] struck the luckless town just at the moment when it might have been established as the greatest military port in the kingdom. For two years Portsmouth suffered, and whole families were wiped out, leaving voids in certain trades vital to military needs. Fishermen, ropemakers, sailmakers, shipwrights and painters perished, and their skills with them. In the town itself only a few able-bodied men survived, while many of the neighbouring districts, such as Hayling Island, suffered complete annihilation.

In spite of the great toll of the Black Death, the King's eldest son was able to win the Battle of Poitiers in 1356, but this victory did not benefit Portsmouth. Confident in his strength in France, the King ordered his ships to be hauled above the high-water mark, where they could be kept cleaned, and much

1. Baulks of timber used on the beach to facilitate embarking.
2. The presence of guns at Crécy is one of the best established facts of the Hundred Years War.
3. Bubonic plague was primarily spread by rats, but was further disseminated by uncleanliness.

money saved for the exchequer. The French, quick to take advantage of the situation, came over again in 1369, with the result that the spirit of the inhabitants was now almost broken. Matters did not improve even when King Richard II came to the throne in 1377, for the town was burnt again that very year. In 1380, when the French returned to repeat the destruction, not only was the town burnt, but not a man opposed the enemy.

Yet incredibly, only five years later, Portsmouth had fitted out her own squadron of ships and when in the spring of 1385 the confident French approached yet again they were met at sea by the men of Portsmouth in their own ships. Remembering their previous easy invasions, the French were not prepared for a fight at sea and were utterly defeated.

The following year a commission was appointed by the King to survey the town. A wall and ditch were constructed for its defence, this time paid for from the exchequer. It would have been preferable if the wall had been made of stone instead of mud, but this was still the best defence the town had had so far.

Within a year confidence in the port had grown and the powerful Duke of Lancaster chose Portsmouth to embark for Spain. He took with him his wife, Constantia of Castille, and their two daughters, Philippa and Catherina. What was more, King Richard II and his queen accompanied them to Portsmouth to wish them a successful voyage.

Throughout his reign Richard II worked for peace with France, and in 1396 he achieved it. There was then no encouragement for the development of a seaport, and the century ended much as it had began.

Henry IV, the first Lancastrian king, was too occupied at home to turn his mind to foreign wars, and the French on their part made no trouble. So followed a quiet period of about fourteen years for Portsmouth until the advent of King Henry V on the throne in 1413. This energetic young king decided, like so many other monarchs, that his best course would be to divert attention from home affairs to matters overseas. And, as always in those days, this meant France.

It meant, too, a time of great activity for the regarders and verderers of the great oak forests. The King had rights in all the forests, employing his own regarders. These men had no easy task. Not until each load of trees was safely at its destination could they be free of anxiety. Beaulieu and Lymington were kept busy shipping trees from the New Forest to Portsmouth, and when good stern posts and keels were in short supply, the King's Regarder used his authority to draw on the Hampshire forest of Alice Holt. Sometimes he looked with envious eyes on the groves of Surrey, Kent and Sussex, where the clay soil was perfect for forestry, but the power of the Cinque Ports was still felt, and it was seldom a good stern post could be diverted to Portsmouth.

Apart from marauders along the route from the forest to the port, when trees could so easily be stolen, and even changed for less good specimens, skill was required in selection. In all there were twenty-seven common defects in standing oak which had to be assessed, and thirty-eight more after felling.

For the next eighteen months the building ports named by the King strained to complete the programme ordered, and the regarders drove their teams of men in the forests and groves to breaking-point.

By late July King Henry was in Winchester, sending the last of the French ambassadors on their way. This done, he came to Portchester Castle to make his final preparations. Soon all was ready for embarkation at Southampton, and at his order six thousand men-at-arms, twenty-four thousand archers, twenty thousand common soldiers, together with the carts, waggons, horses, smiths, masons, farriers, and all the variety of men and materials which formed the army of that day, boarded the ships.

On Wednesday, 7th August, the King left the castle of Portchester in a rowing boat and embarked in his ship *La Trinitée*, which was waiting for him at Portsmouth. The master immediately set sail, and the King directed him to proceed to the waters between Portsmouth and Southampton, where he sailed round the thousand ships awaiting him there. Of special interest was the great ship *Le Saint Esprit*. On board her were the first units of a medical service ever to accompany the forces on an overseas expedition. The physician, Nicholas Olnet, and the surgeon, Thomas Morstede, were known to King Henry, so they, too, had come under the King's orders, and after some considerable negotiations regarding their retinue, wages and transport, found themselves members of this great company of invaders.

There were great ships, cogs, carracks, ships, barges, ballingers, galleys, galleons and drommons. Suddenly a sheet of flame shot skywards from one of the larger ships. Immediately, two more caught fire, while the remainder in the vicinity drew off for fear of becoming victims themselves. Such an event was enough to shake the determination of the superstitious sailors, and over one hundred vessels shortened sail and lagged behind. However, there was seen off Bembridge a large flock of swans, and this favourable omen clearly outweighed the disaster of the burning ships, so all except the timid hundred pressed on after their king into the Channel.

Three months later the Battle of Agincourt was fought and the news rejoiced the hearts of all Portsmuthians. Very many of the ships which had carried the successful army to France had been fitted out in the harbour, and the great commander himself had embarked in his flagship *La Trinitée* only a stone's throw from their town. Portsmouth now would surely be remembered and recognised.

It was a proud moment for the inhabitants, therefore, when a King's Messenger arrived, with personal instructions from the King. First, a Round Tower was to be built on the point opposite the Blockhouse, to begin the stone defences of the port; secondly, the land up harbour from the Pond of the Abbess, which the King had earmarked for possible purchase by the Crown, would be bought at once, and was to be called 'The King's Dock'.

When Henry returned to England in 1420 with Catherine, daughter of King Charles VI, as his bride, a period of peace and quiet was generally forecast among the common people. Traders had long since recovered their ships, and commerce was once again passing through Portsmouth. This period, however, was short-lived. Thomas, Duke of Clarence, the eldest of King Henry's three brothers, who had been left in charge of the new conquests, was attacked by followers of the Dauphin and defeated at Beauge. The Duke lost his life in the battle, and, on hearing the news, King Henry hurried back to France.

Within a year the King had died in France, exhausted by his exertions, only to be followed to the grave two months later by his mad father-in-law. The year 1422 might have been a time of much prosperity for England and Portsmouth, but the death of these two kings had changed the situation.

The heir to the two kingdoms of England and France was a

boy not one year old, the son of King Henry V and Queen Catherine, and with the confusion at home which this inevitably caused, few reinforcement were sent to the English army in France, and very few ships were needed. In France, in spite of the able efforts of King Henry V's second brother, the Duke of Bedford, the Army could not be rallied against the French, now inspired by Joan of Arc.

Meanwhile, at Portsmouth there were upwards of forty ships of four to six hundred tons owned by the Crown lying on the flats near the new dock. No orders for their future had been received. Eventually an order came from the Regency Council under King Henry V's third brother, the Duke of Gloucester, commanding the sale of all the King's ships to merchants. Sadly the men of Portsmouth and the mariners prepared the ships for sale, and stowed the remaining gear in shelters erected on the land recently bought by King Henry V for his dock. For the next four years the only military progress made was the completion of the Round Tower, but there was little of military value to defend.

When Henry VI was twenty-three a marriage was arranged with Margaret of Anjou. The price was the surrender of Maine to her uncle, King Charles VII. No marriage could have been more unsuitable, for the young king was simple and religious, while Margaret was vivacious, quick-tempered and dashing. The young future bride disembarked in 1445 on the beach at Portsmouth near the Round Tower and from there, with her royal retinue, set out on her journey to the priory of Titchfield for her marriage.

In January 1450 Portsmouth suffered a public disgrace. Bishop Moleyns, Bishop of Chichester, came to Portsmouth under the King's instructions to pay the sailors of the Fleet the money that was owing to them. The men knew that until recently the Bishop had been one of the leaders at court, and Lord Privy Seal. They felt he had been to blame for the defeats abroad and the lack of action at home in sending sufficient aid. When the men were paid they received less than they expected and blamed the unpopular bishop for this as well.

These idle and discontented men were driven to desperation. They sought him out from the chapel of the Domus Dei and murdered him.

The Pope then placed the town under the Greater Ex-

communication.[1] This meant the prohibition of the celebration
of Mass and all other liturgical ceremonies, the ringing of
bells, the public administration of the sacraments and solemn
burial.

1. This censure on a population, town, province or region is sometimes
referred to as an interdict. Examples of interdicts exist as early as the
ninth century under the name of excommunication. The whole of the
kingdom of England was placed under an interdict in a limited form in
1208 to support the election of Stephen Langton to the See of Canterbury,
which lasted until the submission of King John in 1213 (Chapter 1 refers.)

3

Battleships and Broadsides

The Great Harry

The Battle of Bosworth was as much a turning-point in the history of Portsmouth as it was for the country as a whole. Not only did that year, 1485, bring to England the first of the Tudors on the throne, it also heralded a great and continuing rise in maritime interest.

When King Henry VII came to the throne world conditions were ripe for great changes. People had begun to think that the world was round, and that England might not, after all, be on the perimeter. Portuguese navigators had opened up the coast of Africa as far south as Cape Verde. Two years later, in 1487, Bartholomew Diaz rounded the Cape of Good Hope, and in 1492 Christopher Columbus crossed the Atlantic, which brought Spain into the field of discovery.

These events meant increased trade, and it was with some feeling of frustration that King Henry heard, in 1493, that the Pope had issued a Bull dividing, by a line drawn north and south a hundred miles west of the Azores, the eastern trade to Portugal and the western to Spain. It was a tragedy that Columbus's offer to sail under an English flag was not accepted.

King Henry VII was at heart a merchant. From the very

beginning of his reign his mind was primarily concerned with trade. The King's ships were used for trade, he built larger and better ships, and gave every encouragement to his subjects to follow his example. No ships had yet been built as fighting ships only, and the King did not pioneer this idea; but, like his predecessors, he knew that well-constructed merchant ships could be turned into fighting ships if required.

King Henry's immediate view across the Channel was of a hostile coast, except for Calais, and he wisely looked around the south coast of England for a suitable port which would serve as a naval base, if need be. The Cinque Ports were too small for this man with grand designs, and the length of hostile coast required a base more to the westward.

Remembering the constant use of Portsea Island by his predecessors, Henry devised a scheme for a fortified arsenal, and chose Portsmouth as the place for it. First, in 1494, the fortifications were improved to seaward of the Round Tower by the completion of a Square Tower and Platform (begun in the reign of King Edward IV, and continued during King Richard III's short reign). The Round Tower, originally built mostly of wood, was now reconstructed entirely of stone.

Next, in 1495, King Henry made a decision which was to influence naval affairs in Portsmouth for the next four hundred years. He ordered the building of the first graving dock to be constructed in this country.

The idea was not exactly original, as there had already been some talk of such a thing on the Continent, but there is no reason to suppose that Henry knew very much about the details. He was, however, virtually forced into thinking along these lines by the size of the ships he was building which were larger than had hitherto been attempted, the latest of these being the *Regent* and the *Sovereign*. These two ships were too deep draught to be floated high up on mud flats at spring tides for cleaning and repairs. The answer lay in a graving dock at Portsmouth, to be constructed on the land acquired by Henry V.

On the 1st May 1495 Robert Brygandine took up his duties as Clerk of the King's Ships, and in June work on the dock was begun. In this, Brygandine was advised by Sir Reginald Bray, His Majesty's principal architect and the builder of Windsor Chapel.

A period of twenty-four weeks, from 14th June to 29th November, was taken up with digging out the dock and fixing the sides, which were backed by stone and lined with wood, one hundred and fifty-eight loads of timber being used. Brygandine then suspended work during the winter months, but suddenly decided in February 1496 to go on without waiting for the spring. Between then and the 17th April the gates were constructed. These were made from one hundred and thirteen loads of timber, which were sawn into 4,524 feet of planking. On the 8th July he announced that the dock gates were to be fortified with clay, stones and gravel, in order to withstand the pressure of water from outside.

Eleven weeks later the first dry dock in England was completed. To pump the water out of the dock, Brygandine supplied an 'ingyn',[1] and he provided a storehouse, a smithy and a forge. He kept full details of this. While making the dock, he accounted for every payment 'made by the said Robert Brygandine, as well as the wages and victuals of divers and sundry carpenters, sawyers, smiths, labourers, carters with their horses, and for provision of timber, stones, clay and other stuff for the work'. This he found cost £193 0s. 6¾d. Then he made an inventory, including smithy bellows, lanterns, caulking irons, chains, pick-axes and all that remained for the operation of the dock.[2]

The next large undertaking was the docking of 'the Kynge's Ship the *Souveraigne*'. The ship was hauled into the dock in May 1496, and remained there until 31st January 1497. The business of docking was not difficult, and the filling in of the area between the dock gates was soon done. But when the ship left, twenty men were at work for twenty-nine days at every tide, both day and night, removing the piles and shores, and digging out the clay, stones and gravel from between the dock gates.

As soon as the *Sovereign* was out, the *Regent* went in. The long docking of the *Sovereign* cost five hundred pounds, and this was in part due to the rearming of the vessel. Gunpowder was now in general use, and small guns called 'serpentines' were fitted on the poop and the forecastle. They were installed athwart ships, but were not heavy enough to damage the

1. A pump.
2. To gather some idea of the real value of wages and prices of those days, in 1506 the Salters Company of London sat down to a meal of which the bill survives. They paid twopence for fifty eggs and four-and-sixpence for thirty-six chickens.

thick wooden sides of an enemy ship, and were intended only to bring down the rigging and sails. The serpentines were not considered to be the main armament, and when ready for war, the ship carried two hundred bows and eight hundred sheaves of arrows. The other reason for the long docking was simply that the vessel would in any case have remained idle for this time unless the King had hired her out as a merchant ship.

Labour was short in Portsmouth, and Brygandine had to ride as far as Kent to get all the carpenters and smiths he needed, which is not surprising, since so much ship construction and repair work was the province of Kent and the Cinque Ports. These men he paid according to their skill, twopence to sixpence a day and their travelling expenses, together with their food, which consisted chiefly of bread, beer and salted fish. None of them would come to Portsmouth until they had secured the contract for their travelling expenses. Brygandine himself got twelvepence a day, with threepence a day for his travelling expenses, the number of days he claimed having been verified on oath.

Although accurate with his accounts, Brygandine was not the only responsible person in Portsmouth who kept his books well. Indeed, all in authority were required to do so, including the constables, one of whom at this time sent in a bill to the Mayor 'For whipping two women and a lame man and taking all to Gosport, 2/-d.'

While other southern ports prospered in the trade of wool and coal, the inhabitants of Portsea Island had no new employment other than the work in the dock. Then, in 1497, the King ordered the building of a ship at Portsmouth to be used solely for war. It was now realised that protection must be given beyond that of the merchant ship's own armament. She was a very small ship, but was none the less important for that, as she enjoyed the privilege of being the first ship to be built in the dockyard. Her name was the *Sweepstake*. She was still a round ship, and could have been used for trading, but in her design she was more of a fighting ship than any of the King's previous ships. She was much longer in relation to her beam than her predecessors, and the castles at either end, which were fitted to carry serpentines, were considerably stronger. In spite of her smallness she had three masts, but the sail these carried was not considered sufficient for mobility, so fittings were provided for eighty oars. Robert Brygandine noted that the cost of the *Sweepstake* was £120 3s. 2d.

By 1508, fifty-eight years had passed since the Bishop of Chichester, 'the Lord Adam Moleyns of honoured memory underwent temporal death at the hands of the men of Portsmouth'. The people felt that the stagnation of their merchant trade dated from that event, and accordingly they petitioned for the removal of the excommunication. Proceedings took place on Thursday, 6th April 1508. The church of St. Thomas was locked and barred. Judges assembled in the Domus Dei, and Robert Adam, the Vicar, and his parishioners, were herded to the site of the crime. Then, barefooted and singing psalms, they moved to the church. All knocked and craved admittance. The judges and commissioners of the church, using purifying vapour, cleansed the people. The doors were opened, High Mass was sung, and the crowd chanted praises through the streets. That evening was laid the first stone of the chapel which was to be built on the spot where the Bishop had been killed.

The people hoped that prosperity would follow. They expected it through trade, but it came to them from a different source.

One year after the removal of the excommunication, Henry VII, by one of the last acts of his reign, ordered another ship to be built in the dockyard. This ship was no round ship; she was long and manœuvrable under sail. Moreover, she was four hundred and fifty tons and, above all, a fighting ship. Henry did not live to give her a name, but this was chosen by his son Henry VIII, who named her the *Peter Pomegranate*, in celebration of the destruction of the Moorish kingdom of Granada by the Spaniards, an event which was loudly applauded by all Christendom. The *Pomegranate* was part of the arms of the city of Granada, and it was a touch which people thought appropriate with the arrival of Katharine of Aragon in England.

With the building of both the *Sweepstake* and the *Pomegranate* lay the future of Portsmouth and the dockyard, and the beginning of the British Navy proper.

An air of hope, confidence and brightness pervaded the whole country when the young King Henry VIII succeeded his father in 1509. This spirit communicated itself to Portsmouth more than to any other seaport town in the realm, and there was every justification for this attitude.

Basically antagonistic to France and Scotland, and with the

traditional bias towards waging a successful war, King Henry's policy was one which was bound to affect Portsmouth strongly. The town became prominent as the new naval arsenal. Added to this, the King realised, more than any previous king, the value of a fleet as the practical instrument of his policy. All his life he devoted himself to augmenting the Navy, thereby laying the foundation of England's greatness at sea.

There were additional reasons for the King's maritime interest. King James IV of Scotland was busy creating a fleet, and already had between sixteen and twenty men-of-war Also, from across the water came stories of the fortifying of Le Havre, and of King Louis XII's encouraging the Breton sailors to contest the command of the Channel. Spain, too, had progressed in the art of shipbuilding under the stimulus of her interests in the New World. She was building very large ships to stand the hazardous journey across the ocean, and her seamen were rapidly gaining in knowledge and experience. Finally, in southern ports, and particularly in Portsmouth, foreign ships were always to be seen, although they were only merchant ships, and it was evident from their design that England could not at this time fall behind in maritime development without jeopardising her trade and security.

The new king designed his own ships, and throughout his reign, in spite of his battles with the Pope, and his matrimonial difficulties, he never wavered from his keen and most knowledgeable interest in maritime, and especially naval, affairs. Not only did he spend a great deal of his father's fortune on the Navy, but some of the revenue accruing from the dissolution of the monasteries was spent on building men-of-war.

These ships, the King realised, would need administering, together with his dockyards, arsenals and storehouses, so he formed a committee, known as the Principal Officers of the Navy, and later the Navy Board, to set these matters in order.

It was not long before King Henry put his foreign policy into effect. Spurred on by Katharine of Aragon and the energetic Wolsey, he joined with King Ferdinand of Spain 'to defend the Church against all aggression and make war against the aggressor'. In June 1512 an expedition left Southampton for the Biscay coast, but, on landing, the Earl of Dorset, the military commander, found that the Spaniards had not come to meet them, and the Lord Admiral, Lord Edward Howard, could find nothing of them along the coast.

The next decision was made by the soldiers and not by their commander; they mutinied and demanded to return home. Mutinies were most uncommon in those days, and it was thought best to come to the arsenal of Portsmouth to sort out matters and to refit the ships.

It was not surprising that, after the necessary repairs had been effected, the King came to Portsmouth to see the state of affairs for himself. He left London on 31st July 1512, and arrived at Portsmouth on the 2nd August.

In the fleet which King Henry came to see there were seventeen English ships, including Portsmouth's own *Peter Pomegranate*, and some forty others hired or bought from Italy or the Hanseatic League, but these were not so strong or well armed as the ships built in England. The King first rode to the Round Tower, from where he could view the ships anchored in the harbour. Although the *Gabriel Royal* and the *Kateryn Fortileza*, two of the foreign purchases, were the largest, both being over seven hundred tons, the English ships *Regent* and *Sovereign* stood out for their appearance of strength and for their revolutionary armament. Gunpowder and heavy guns were already in general use on land, but hitherto the latter had not been embarked in ships. The *Sovereign*, however, rebuilt in 1509, had four whole and three half curtalls of brass, three culverins, two falcons, and eleven heavy iron guns among her total of seventy-one. The *Regent* was similarly armed. These heavy guns were placed on the broadside amidships, thus making the ships true men-of-war, there being no longer any space for cargo.

King Henry wished this fleet to sail again to the Bay of Biscay under the Lord Admiral, Lord Edward Howard, but it was first necessary to appoint captains, so he repaired to the Square Tower, where he gave a banquet. The Square Tower, not being appointed on the lines of a royal palace, gave the King the excuse to dress like the seamen of the day, which he much enjoyed, and was fully justified in doing, both because of his knowledge of ships, and because he saw to it that his sailors, for whom a vague sort of uniform had been slowly evolving during the two previous reigns, were all properly supplied with blue jackets and white gaberdines, with the Tudor Rose on the breast and back. Nevertheless, it was not the clothes which King Henry specially treasured, but his whistle and chain, which he proudly displayed, this being the hallmark of the seaman, and the precursor of the boatswain's pipe.

The captains he appointed were selected from his household, and, being a prudent man, he chose two each for the larger ships, and gave them a dozen or more of his bodyguard to sail with them. Of the two most important commands Sir Thomas Knevet, Master of his Horse, and Sir John Carew, were given the *Regent*, and Sir Charles Brandon and Sir Henry Guildford took the *Sovereign*.

Next morning, the King set off on the London road to Croydon, while the ships 'with great minstrelsie' sailed for the Bay of Biscay.

By now the ships engaged in the war carried a fair number of Portsmouth men, so the outcome of any major battle was awaited with some anxiety by the town. When, therefore, a galley returned to Portsmouth with the news that the *Regent* had blown up, an air of horror and incredulity spread over the town. This disaster was described by Wolsey in a letter to the Bishop of Worcester:

To ascertaine yow of the lamentabyll and sorowfull tydyngs and chance wych hath fortuned by the sea. Our folks, on Tuesday the 14th August, met twenty one gret shyppes of Frawnce, the best with sayle and furnyshed with artyllery and men that ever was seyn.

After innumerabyll shotyng of gunnys at the last the *Regent* most valyently bordyd the great caryke of Brest, wherin wer four lords, three hundred gentlemen, eight hundred soldiers and maryners, four hundred crossbowmen, one hundred gunners, two hundred tonnes of wyne, one hundred pypes of befe, sixty barells of gonepowder, a marvelose nombyr of shot and other gunys of every sorte.

Sodenly the caryke was one flamyng fyre and lykewise the *Regent* within the turnyng of one hand. Sir Thomas Knyvet was slain with one gonne. Sir Thomas Carewe with diverse other whos namys be not yet knowne be lykewise slayne.

Loss of their menfolk at sea was not unknown to Portsmouth women, but the blowing up of the *Regent* was unprecedented. It was the recent invention of gunpowder which had been the cause. The fact that the French flagship *La Cordeiliere* had also blown up, and that the whole action had been called off by both sides, showed that man had invented something which for the time being he could not control, and people began to wonder where in the world anyone could be safe again.

Meanwhile, the picture on the Continent changed with the death of King Ferdinand of Spain, who was succeeded by his grandson, the Emperor Charles V, while in France the death of King Louis XII brought to the throne the equally young King Francis I. This set Wolsey's active mind to work, and he quickly saw that King Henry could, by offering his support to one or the other, have a controlling influence on all European affairs. While diplomacy, therefore, held the major field, the instrument of policy, namely the Navy, was steadily built up. Nor was this relaxed at all during King Henry's reign, in spite of his other preoccupations.

The spate of maritime activity was almost too great for the dockyards of England to meet even the repair programme, and in Portsmouth, the chief of them all, men toiled ceaselessly to keep pace. In addition, considerable new construction was put in hand, and from the dockyard at Portsmouth there was launched the flower of them all, the *Mary Rose*, named after the King's sister, Mary Tudor. This ship was a considerable advance on the *Peter Pomegranate*, for whereas the latter was still chiefly armed with serpentines, the *Mary Rose* had seventy-nine guns, of which only thirty-three were serpentines, the remaining forty-six being larger, and on the broadsides.

On 22nd March 1513 Sir Henry Howard reported by letter to the King in answer to a royal command to report on the Fleet.

'The *Kateryn Fortileza*,' he wrote, 'sails very well, but the *Mary Rose* is your good ship, the flower I trow of all the ships that ever sailed.'

About this time a Frenchman, who had assumed the name of Jack Tarratt, was building ships for King James IV of Scotland. He had designed the *Great Michael*, which was said to be the wonder of all mankind in northern latitudes, and reputed to be the biggest ship afloat. When Lord Darcy informed King Henry of what was happening he immediately ordered the building of a ship which was to be the greatest of all. With the success of the *Mary Rose*, it would have seemed reasonable for this honour to be given to Portsmouth, but by now Henry had become fond of Greenwich, and, wishing to keep in touch with the building of this ship, he suggested it should be laid down on the Thames.

To this his advisers readily agreed, because they were already finding difficulty in keeping Portsmouth supplied with men and

D

materials. They had to recruit many skilled men from Kent, (they were descendants of the shipbuilders from the Cinque Ports), and these demanded heavy travelling expenses for going to Portsmouth. London, too, could supply so many of the materials ships needed, such as pitch, tar, oakum and iron-work, without a long haul across Hampshire, and trees could be brought down the Thames without difficulty. Thus, the building of the *Henry Grace à Dieu* went to Woolwich, and, as a result, Woolwich, Deptford and Erith gradually increased in favour as building yards.

Some thought, however, was given to the defences of Ports-mouth, and over a period of twenty-one years the mud wall was improved and strengthened with great baulks of timber. Guns were placed along this formidable structure to defend the town from all sides; some were made of iron and others of brass. Small towers were built at strategic corners. Visitors to the town were much impressed with this array of ordnance, but it was not impressive to those who understood these things. The walls were not firm, and the cannon had no proper foundation. Every spell of wet weather loosened the mud, some of which fell into the ditch, while children made paths and hideouts in the soft earth.

The King's mind also turned to the safety of his ships in Portsmouth, and in 1522 a great chain of iron was made which stretched from the Round Tower across the harbour to Block-house. The links were three feet nine inches in length and three inches in diameter. This chain was supported by lighters, and could be raised and lowered by means of capstans. There is no doubt that it could stop any sailing ship trying to enter the harbour.

Meanwhile, King Henry was intent on using Portsmouth for the fleet of great ships he was creating, and as these had to be supplied with beer, he ordered four great brewing houses to be built on the north-east side of the town, close to a suitable fresh spring. They were named 'Lyon', 'Dragon', 'White Hart' and 'Rose'. At the same time he increased the bakeries. 'The Anchor', a bakehouse and brewhouse at the corner of St. Thomas's Street and St. Mary's Street, was considerably enlarged, and another bakery was built on piles near the Camber and called 'Ye Swan'.

In 1523 it was decided that the *Henry Grace à Dieu*, England's first line-of-battle ship, built at Woolwich, must be dry-docked. The easiest solution was to enlarge the dock at Portsmouth and accommodate the ship there.

It was as well that the timely measure of building brewhouses was taken, because over one thousand men were employed in this business, and consumed every day four tuns of beer and forty-two dozen loaves of bread.

The entry of the *Henry Grace à Dieu* to Portsmouth was conducted with much ceremony. The ship had been built by Brygandine, so the occasion was one well worthy of special attention. Not only was it a great honour to Portsmouth, but Brygandine was, of course, well known to the inhabitants.

The ship itself cost £8,708 5s. 3d., and three thousand seven hundred and twenty-three tons of timber were used. A quarter of the money had been given by private persons, peers and religious bodies, representatives of whom came to see the *Henry* docked.

As this mighty ship slowly approached the great chain, she hoisted the red-and-white flag calling for a pilot, and was taken in tow by row-barges. She was certainly a sight to behold. Although carving, gilding and painting were not much in evidence, she made up for this by banners and flags. Streamers floated in the breeze from her four masts. Two from the mainmast were fifty-one and forty feet long, one from the foremast thirty-six feet, and one from the mizzen twenty-eight feet. Everywhere there were banners; of the *Portcullis*, indicating the control of the Strait of Dover; of the *Pomegranate*, referring to Katharine of Aragon; of St. George and the Dragon, and of St. Anne. Many were white and green with a Tudor Rose, and surmounting all was the great banner of England.

Most of her company had collected on deck. Two hundred and sixty sailors and forty gunners normally manned the armament, and over half of these men came round from the Thames with the ship.

Protruding from the lofty forecastle and poop, serpentine and smaller ordnance were clearly visible from the shore, and in the waist amidships could be seen the muzzles of half a dozen of the new heavy guns.

Inboard, pointing down on to the waist from the forecastle and poop, murderous pieces projected, ready to repel boarders should they gain the centre of the ship in close battle. Stowed inside the huge bulging hull were two thousand bows, five thousand bowstrings, four thousand sheaves of arrows, one thousand five hundred bills,[1] two thousand stakes, five lasts of gunpowder, and five hundred suits of harness for use by the bowmen.

The arrival of the *Henry* had been timed for one hour before high water, so that the ship could have all the depth of water possible and enter the harbour on the last of the flood stream. It was a calm morning, with the green of the Isle of Wight as a backcloth to the scene as viewed from the Square Tower and the beach, where hundreds of the inhabitants had gathered to see the flagship of the King's Fleet.

To complete the docking and carry out the necessary repairs, gentlemen, yeomen and mariners all played their part. There was no great resident population of shipwrights and other skilled trades, and to augment the men already employed in the yard, artisans were brought from Plymouth, Dartmouth and other towns in the west, and from Ipswich, Yarmouth and Hull in the east. These men received a halfpenny a mile and a shilling a day travelling expenses. The one hundred and forty-one carpenters were supplied with coats, entirely free, which cost the Crown two shillings and fivepence each. Special cooks under a chamberlain were brought to provide cod, hake, herring and oatmeal. Beds were provided under rough shelters, each bed being made to hold two or three persons, but these were insufficient, and sometimes ten men had to share one bed. The overall average wage was ninepence a day.

It did not take long to float the ship carefully into the dock, but the filling up of the dockhead and pumping out the water was a matter of days. This strenuous work placed a great strain on the brewing houses so thoughtfully built to meet such a situation.

By now the dockyard could not hold all the ships building and under repair, so an extension had to be made. In 1527 nine acres were purchased at twenty shillings an acre. This was a splendid sign for Portsmouth, but elsewhere things were moving just as quickly. Deptford, Woolwich and Erith were also extended, and there was talk of Chatham being opened up as a major base. Against this competition Portsmouth could not compete. With the attractions of London on the Thames, labour began to drift away, and Portsmouth was unable to accept some of the orders offered. Nevertheless, the value of the dockyard had increased to such a degree that it was thought prudent to build a fortification on the shore, a mile to the eastward of the Round Tower. The work was entrusted to Anthony Knyvet who, with the help of the Dean of Chichester and John Chaderton, built a castle which they generously said was 'of His Majesty's own device'.[1] Clearing of the site began in 1538, and six years later, Knyvet reported to the King:

It may please Your Most Excellent Majesty to be so good Lord unto me to give me licence to come see Your Majesty, the which shall comfort me of all things under the Heavens and so to inform Your Majesty of the state of the new fortress here, the which may be called a Castle, both for the compass, strength and beauty, and the device and fashion thereof is strange and marvellously praised of all men that have seen it, with the commodious and profitable situation thereof, as well for the defence of this Your Majesty's town and haven, as of the country thereabouts, the like is not within the realm.

In addition, yet more attention had been paid to the town's defences, and among the improvements was the first wooden bastillion at the Landport Gate, possibly the first of its kind in England.

King Henry's money from the dissolution of the monasteries served the security of his state here, as elsewhere. Part of the money came from the surrender of the Domus Dei. At the same time as the castle was being built, commissioners arrived, acting on the orders of the Chancellor of the Court of Augmentations, and on 2nd June 1540 the hospital, with all its lands and rights, not only in Portsmouth, but in Hampshire and Wiltshire, was surrendered to the King by the Warden, John Incent, on behalf of himself and the brethren and sisters. Two days later John Incent was rewarded with the Deanery of St. Paul's Cathedral. From that time, for the next twenty years, the hospital of St. Nicholas in the Domus Dei ceased to function, and wayfarers, the sick and the homeless had to seek sanctuary elsewhere.

The civic life of the town was increasing in importance, and though Portsmouth had long ago risen to the status of having a mayor and burgesses, there was no Town Hall. About this

1. In 1559 Chaderton's son wrote of 'the Castle called Chaderton Castle and sometimes Southsea Castle'. This may have been the first use of the name of Southsea.

time, Leyland, a traveller, wrote in his notes: 'One Carpenter, a rich man, made of late time in the middle of the High Street a Town House.'

Carpenter had served as mayor in 1531 and 1537, and had felt the need for such a building. Already in the High Street, which was wider than most streets of those times, there was a Shambles, or butchery and fish market. Carpenter erected the Town House at the southern end of the Shambles, blocking the street, and having only just enough room for a cart to pass on either side.

In 1543, after years of intrigues and plotting, Henry made a treaty with the Emperor Charles of Spain, 'to attack France within the next two years'. The Emperor, though, deserted him and left him to fight by himself. Fearful that he might lose Boulogne, early in 1545 King Henry despatched Lord de Lisle with a fleet to the mouth of the Seine, where an indecisive action was fought with two hundred French ships, and de Lisle was driven back to Portsmouth by the weather. Although King Francis was determined to lay siege to Boulogne, he put this project aside for the moment, and in July sent his fleet under Admiral d'Annebault to Portsmouth.

Anthony Knyvet had completed his work just in time. News reached the King that the French had mustered an invasion fleet greater than any expedition since William the Conqueror. Indeed, it was said that some three hundred ships with twenty thousand men had been collected at Le Havre and surrounding ports, and that this armada had sailed on the 6th July.

Messengers were immediately despatched to Portsmouth to warn Lord de Lisle in his flagship, the *Henry Grace à Dieu*. Soldiers were gathered from Hampshire and Sussex and encamped on Southsea Common, and the ordnance surrounding the town brought to the ready. Much confidence was placed in the guns of Southsea Castle.

The King left Greenwich on the 12th July, and by the 17th July, a Friday, the whole of the King's retinue had arrived, and were billeted in the town or under canvas on the common. The King himself was on board his flagship, the *Henry Grace à Dieu*.

Sunday, the 19th, was one of those breathless mornings, with the sun blazing down and the sea a flat calm. King Henry's great ships were anchored inside the protection of the Spit

Sands, and at midday he was entertaining Lord de Lisle, the naval Commander-in-Chief; Sir George Carewe, the second-in-command, whose flagship was the *Mary Rose*; Sir Gawen Carewe, and a young man, Peter Carewe. On hearing rumours of some foreign ships approaching, Henry told Peter Carewe to climb up a mast and see if he could spot any ships coming round Bembridge Point. At first, Peter Carewe called out that the ships were merchant vessels, but very soon afterwards changed his mind and said that there were a large number and they were warships. Henry immediately ordered beacons to be lit to warn the country, and was rowed ashore. Meanwhile, Sir George Carewe and the other officers returned to their respective ships. The French, under Admiral d'Annebault, began their attack in the afternoon, using about thirty oared galleys, each carrying one large gun in the bow. To counter these, Admiral de Lisle ordered his forward ships to try and lure the enemy under the powerful guns of the newly built castle. Sir George Carewe in the *Mary Rose*, with her excellent sailing qualities, was soon out ahead of the others and, turning to tack, to the consternation of all in the English fleet and the spectators on the shore, including the King, she rolled on her side and sank. Sir Gavin Carewe said that he had called out to his brother to ask him how he was getting on and Sir George had replied that 'he had got too many knowledgeable mariners on board, who all though they knew what was best', but it appears that the broadside gun ports, which were, after all, a very new innovation, were only about eighteen inches above the water-level, and that these ports were not closed when the *Mary Rose* tacked. It would not have taken more than a very small list in this situation to let the water in by the ports and sink the ship. The French, on the other hand, naturally claimed that they had sunk her by their gun-fire, while the Spanish Ambassador, who wished to ingratiate his country with both sides, told a colourful story of how the *Mary Rose* fired a broad-side and, turning to fire another, heeled over rather sharply and sank. He thought it was the effect of the broadside which might have caused the disaster.

By this time fortunately a number of row-barges had come out from Portsmouth inner harbour and inflicted such damage on the French oared galleys that they retired.

The awful tragedy of the *Mary Rose* now filled everyone's mind. Only about twenty-five sailors and a few personal servants of the knights had survived, over five hundred of her company being lost.

The King sent for some of the survivors. From them he heard that when the ship had turned to fire her second broadside the ports on the side which had just fired were still open, and when the ship heeled over, the water came in and she sank at once. They added that the ship was in shallow water, and they thought she could be raised.

Next day the French landed on the Isle of Wight, but the local army, augmented from the mainland during the preceding week, were not dismayed. After plundering only a few villages the enemy withdrew to their ships. Afloat, firing went on all day, but lack of wind prevented a general action.

The Spanish Ambassador attempted to persuade King Henry to make terms with King Francis I, but, as the King pointed out, now that a battle was actually in progress on the very shores of England, this was hardly the time to discuss such a thing. Moreover, there were eight thousand men on the common, and many more were coming. With his fleet and a well-equipped army opposing the enemy, the King felt that the main danger had been warded off, and in this he was absolutely correct. That night the French admiral decided that he was confronted by too great a force to continue the invasion, and withdrew to carry out the long deferred siege of Boulogne.

Great relief, coupled with pride in their fleet, spread through Portsmouth and the countryside. The people felt strong, and equipped with a fleet able to defend them against all comers. Nevertheless, for Portsmouth the loss of the *Mary Rose* was a tragedy never to be forgotten.

Peace was concluded, and Admiral d'Annebault came over with a large retinue, landed at the Tower of London with full military honours, and proceeded to the King at Hampton Court, where he solemnly swore to keep the peace.

When King Henry VIII died in 1547 he left England with an efficient fleet which had repulsed a most serious attempt at invasion. He also left a great administration for the fleet and the dockyards on the Thames and at Portsmouth, sufficient for the country's maritime needs.[1]

From Portsmouth's point of view, there were two clouds in

1. By ensuring that there would be for all time a permanent maritime fighting force, Henry VIII can be said to be the true founder of the Navy.

The English fleet engaging the French fleet off Portsmouth,
July 1545, at the time of the sinking of the *Mary Rose*. Picture
shows Henry VIII on horseback witnessing the scene from the
shore near Southsea Castle.

Southsea Castle in 1720

Above left Lord Anson
Above right Lord Keppel
Left The Hon. John Byng
Right Sir George Rooke

Portsmouth Dockyard in 1772

an otherwise clear sky. One was the growing preference of the Fleet for the Thames dockyards, and the other was the increasing erosion in the town's defence walls, large pieces of which were constantly falling into the ditch. Besides, the gates were rotten, particularly the one at Point, opening on to the Camber and the Round Tower (see map 2) which Edward Langham, Captain of Portsmouth, said was so weak that four or five men with a piece of timber could lay it on the ground with one good blow. Henry Huttoft, writing in 1547, describes Portsmouth as 'utterly decayed and no man comes here with victuals or merchandise'.

With the accession of Edward VI, England once again found herself with a minor on the throne, a frail and precocious boy of ten. Taking advantage of a second Protestant accession, the Duke of Somerset, then Protector, introduced the first English Prayer Book, copies of which were distributed in St. Thomas's Church, Portsmouth. In the West Country the arrival of the Prayer Book caused a rebellion, but in Portsmouth this great treasure of the English language was accepted by the Catholics without any great show of antagonism.

Two years earlier, after peaceful methods had failed, the Protector invaded Scotland to try and unite the two kingdoms through the marriage of King Edward VI to Mary Queen of Scots. The expedition aroused some interest in Portsmouth in case the Fleet were called upon to help, but the campaign was short and fruitless, and the mariners relapsed into a life of comparative leisure.

There were few alarms at this time, and the only noteworthy one occurred on the morning of 5th November 1551, when the first full gale of winter was blowing.

Sir Richard Wingfield, Captain of Southsea Castle and the Arsenal of Portsmouth, was preparing to set out to ride the bounds as usual, and, glancing towards the Isle of Wight from his upper room in the castle, he quickly made up his mind that no one would be fool enough to put to sea this day. Even with the protection of the island, the waves were lashing against the castle, heavy squalls whipped the sea into a fury, and the driving rain added a final touch to this uninviting picture.

At this moment the watch blew his horn, which brought Sir Richard instantly to the battlements. The watch, whom he could now see, was pointing seawards to the south-east. At

first Sir Richard could see nothing, but then he made out a
sail or two. It looked as if some merchant ships were running
for shelter under the lee of Bembridge, though their masts
were more like those of men-of-war.

Before long at least a dozen ships were in sight, driving along
under the gale towards Spithead. Sir Richard had to act.
First of all, messengers were sent to the dockyard to warn the
ships, and to the Mayor, Henry Byckeley, to have the defences
manned.

After the first alarm the tension eased. It was evident, as
there were no transports with the men-of-war, there was not
going to be another invasion. Though these ships looked like
Frenchmen, they could only be running for shelter.

Shortly, the leading ships were clearly visible, and one of
them was flying from the top of her mainmast a very large
flag which looked like a royal standard. The ships were now
lowering all sail and coming to anchor, as well they might in
such a gale. Whoever they were, nothing could be done until
the wind went down and boats could put to sea.

All day the gale blew, but by evening the wind began to
fall, the rain stopped, and the citizens of Portsmouth crowded
on to the platform and beach to have a look at the visitors.

A boat was coming in. It was flying a very large flag similar
to the one at the masthead of the flagship. As the boat approached the narrow harbour entrance the occupants could be
clearly seen. They were Frenchmen, but the flag was the royal
banner of Scotland.

Excitement at the Camber was immense. Sir Richard had
mustered two companies of the guard, who cleared a space at
the landing-stage. Immediately the boat came alongside, a
courier jumped ashore and handed a letter to Sir Richard.
He and the Mayor conferred briefly. Both looked worried, for
they found themselves in a very difficult position. Her Majesty,
Mary Guise, Queen Dowager of Scotland, wished to land and
craved safe conduct.

The situation posed many problems. Mary Guise had refused
to let her daughter marry the King of England and, taking her
to France, had married her to the Dauphin. Also, Mary Guise
had been doing her best to foment discord between France and
England. Mary was therefore scarcely a welcome visitor, nor
was she a voluntary one. Before setting out for France from
Scotland, she had been wise enough to ask for safe conduct

'in case she should by stress of weather be driven into any English port', and this is what had now happened.[1]

Sir Richard decided on his course of action. He wrote a message, which the boat took back to the squadron, in which he welcomed the Queen and the French ships, and begged them to wait until he had had word from London.

Instructions arrived from the King. Sir Richard was to wait upon Her Majesty and ascertain whether she intended to continue her journey by sea or land. He left Southsea Castle at once and boarded the French flagship. Here he learned from the Queen that she had had enough of travel by sea, and hoped she might continue the rest of the way by land.

Once again messengers rode at full speed to Hampton Court, and this time brought back orders that the Queen should be received with all hospitality. The message added that the King hoped she would be his guest at Hampton.

On learning this, Mayor Byckeley told Sir Richard that there was no suitable house in Portsmouth in which the Queen could possibly lodge. This was only too true. The castle was too primitive, and most of the Domus Dei was used as an ammunition dump. Even the church was filled with such things as sails and falcons,[2] iron shot and coils of rope. There were culverins in the hall, and the vestry housed an assortment of stores, saltpetre, pitch, tar, turpentine and linseed oil. Sir Richard therefore suggested Mr. White's house at Southwick. Mr. White was the Treasurer of Portsmouth.

1. James V of Scotland married Mary of Guise. Their daughter was born on the 8th December 1542 and became queen by her father's death six days later.

The Earl of Arran, as governor, promised her in marriage to Henry VIII's son, Edward, in July 1543, but the agreement was repudiated.

After the defeat of the Scots at Pinkie in 1547 Mary was sent to France, where she remained for thirteen years. In 1558 Mary married the fourteen-year-old Dauphin.

Mary of Guise returned to Scotland in 1551, where she died a few years later.

In August 1561 Mary returned to Scotland, eluding English ships sent to cut her off.

2. Typical guns in use at this time were:

Demi-culverin	9–10	pdr.
Saker	5	pdr.
Minion	4	pdr.
Falcon	2½–3	pdr.
Falconet	1¼–2	pdr.
Robinet	½–1	pdr.

While Sir Richard went off to the flagship, a messenger was sent to Mr. White, telling him about his unexpected visitor. This gentleman immediately rode into Portsmouth, and was at the Camber when the Queen landed. In the limited time available, Portsmouth and the dockyard did their best to follow the King's command. Guards were paraded, a show of flags flown from the ships in the haven, and the High Street was swept. Most of the gentlemen from the surrounding country had been warned, and they formed a gay and colourful escort to Southwick.

After two days at Southwick, the Queen stayed for a short while with Sir Richard Cotton at Warblington, and then went on to Cowdray for a brief sojourn as the guest of the Earl of Arundel. From there she proceeded to Hampton Court, where she was received with the most lavish hospitality by the King.

The following year, His Majesty desired a review of the defences of Portsmouth. Mr. Rogers, a gentlemen of the household well versed in these things, came to assist in the survey, bringing with him Sir Andrew Dudley, a prominent military commander. The two gentlemen, together with Sir Richard, decided to start their survey at the Round Tower. Mr. Rogers had this marked on his map as 'Mr. Rydleyes Tower', after the builder, but was told that Portsmouth people called it the Round Tower. This looked quite formidable and was in a useful position, but had nothing on it in the way of guns. Obviously it should have a saker or two, and possibly some falcons. However, Sir Richard pointed out that even if they did install these guns, there was no one to man them. The whole standing garrison of the castle was not more than a dozen men, and the guns of the town were allowed only one man each.

The sea wall from the Round Tower to the end of the High Street looked strong, as it had more stone than the other walls of the town. Over at Blockhouse, the tower was still made of wood, and looked almost ridiculous as a defence in this era of heavy guns and gunpowder. In the distance, too, they could see Mr. Hasleford's bulwark, over at Haslar. Neither this nor Hasleworth Castle in the further distance, which admittedly had some stone, gave any feeling of confidence for the defence of such an important port.

One gun, a demi-culverin, stood alone on the wall between the Round Tower and the Square Tower. To the eastward of the Square Tower, on the platform, was another gun, and it was from the platform that the main town wall started, with the additional protection of a moat inside its perimeter. There were then no more guns until the Green Bulwark at the end of the seaward wall.

The moat and the defence wall then ran north-east past the four Brewhouses, which had their own gun, a falcon. Presumably this gun would be readily manned, but it was totally inadequate as a defence for the long line of the north-east wall. Just after the four Brewhouses, the moat branched off to the left of the wall in a direct line to the main gate. The wall itself continued as far as the New Mound, three-quarters of a mile from the sea, and this completed the north-east wall. Davy Savour had built the bulwark here, and it appeared that no one had taken much interest in it since that day. It possessed a gun, but this looked as if it had never been fired.

From Savour's bulwark, the wall turned north-west and ran for more than a mile, the main gate and bastillion being in the centre of it. Here were a mixture of past and present defences, with about ten guns of various kinds. One was a demi-culverin ($9\frac{1}{2}$ lbs.), but the rest were falcons, fowlers, sakers and the like. Nevertheless, the defences on this wall were the best the inspectors had so far seen.

At the north-west corner, Mr. Guy's bulwark, there was one small gun, and one more between it and the main gate. From Guy's the defence ran due west to the Dock Bulwark, which abutted the sea. Here was another gun. From here the defence ran back due south, but gradually petered out well before St. Thomas's Street. There was nothing in the way of defence on the northern arm of the Camber.

At the head of the mill pond, outside the town wall, was one small gun. The dockyard, however, had no guns at all, though the yard was enclosed with a mud and wood wall. This completed Portsmouth's defences.

Back at the castle, the three men compared notes, agreeing that this was a sorry state of affairs for one of the premier ports of a country now clearly dependent on her sea power. In due course the survey was sent to the King.

Meanwhile, the King had caught measles and then developed smallpox at the same time. However, he made a good recovery and during his convalescence he read the report on Portsmouth which had been sent to him.

As soon as he was able, His Majesty determined on a 'progress' through southern England. By now it was full summer, and the country was looking at its best. He decided to combine business with pleasure, and began with the latter, taking the reverse route which Mary Guise had followed the previous year through Guildford and Cowdray. From the Earl of Arundel's residence he went to Waltham, and having much enjoyed ten days' hunting in the Forest of Bere, went on to Portsmouth.

After crossing Portsbridge, any traveller entering Portsmouth at this time would follow a rough track through three miles of open cultivated country with an occasional wooden cottage before reaching the hamlet of Kingston.

At Kingston, the track widened and divided into two roads. The one to the left led past St. Mary's Church, and to the manors of Buckland and Froadington, while the main route turned to the right over Kingston Heath. This passed cottages and farmsteads where more frequent rough paths led off to the left across the cultivated land of the town fields, until a sight of the North Gate showed that the journey to Portsmouth was almost over. Here the influence of the country gave way to more ordered conditions. There were strict regulations regarding hedging and ditching and the upkeep of gates. Rights of way were enforced, and people straying off the proper paths could be fined as much as three shillings and fourpence for a first offence, even if they were cutting corners to get to Kingston Parish Church in time for service.

Now the tang of salt air could be smelt, and to the right the tops of the masts of ships in the dockyard cut the skyline. A quarter of a mile further on, the road passed between the town fields on the left and the east and west dock fields on the right. To the west of the dock fields lay the small Portsea common, separating the town from the dock, with the Pond of the Abbess (now, following the dissolution of the monasteries, called the Mill Pond) bringing the common to an abrupt end and running inland almost to the road. At half milestone the traveller could choose between branching left to Southsea Castle, or going straight on to the North Gate, leaving on the right the chapel of Mary Magdalene, where lepers, beggars and destitute pilgrims could find rest outside the defensive wall.

The watchman on the top of the north gate would follow a traveller's approach and, if necessary, order the guard to be mounted. Possibly one gun would be loaded, but he would not wave his flag or ring his bell unless the approaching company was large and unfamiliar.

Once inside the gate, the traveller could look straight down the High Street, with its almost continuous lines of houses, mostly built of wood, but a few with thick party walls, notably the prison. At the end of the street, the view of the sea was obstructed by the Square Tower.

In spite of so much activity in King Henry VIII's reign, the town still had barely a dozen streets worthy of names, of which High Street, Penny Street, St. Nicholas Street, St. Thomas's Street, Lombard Street, Oyster Street, Hogmarket Street and St. Mary's Street were the most important. All of them, except High Street, were narrow, and branch tracks led from them to large areas of common land inside the boundary of the town. Every house had its plot, and most householders their chickens, pigs and a cow.

The church of St. Thomas was still the principal building, dwarfing the Town House, which stood in the centre of the High Street. Away to the north-east the four great brewhouses stood by themselves near the spring. The deserted Domus Dei and the hospital of St. Nicholas occupied the south-eastern corner of the town plan. On the west side, the Round Tower marked the entrance to the harbour, and some way to the north-east of it there stood a chapel around which many sailors had been buried.

The military Governor, representing the Crown, controlled the town of Portsmouth and the island of Portsea, having in the early part of the century superseded the Constable of the Castle at Portchester. His powers were usually resented by the Mayor and his twelve jurators, who exercised their power through the Court Leet.

It was the duty of the Court Leet to ensure that the regulations governing the town were upheld. The Court met twice a year, in June and December, under the title 'Court with view of Frankpledge'. Selected inhabitants served as Jurymen who made 'presentments'. There was no trial, the Jury's presentment itself being the verdict. Punishments were carried out by levying fines or 'pains'—i.e. sentences at the pillory, in the stocks or at the whipping post. The Court was assisted by the Chamberlain and Treasurer, the Sergeant of the Mace, whose cofferer kept the files, and the Town Clerk and the Constables.

There were numerous presentments for failing to keep the town clean. It was every householder's duty to put gravel before the doors into the street, to sweep the gutters clean, amend the pitching, refrain from emptying chamber pots into the street, and have a clean up every Saturday. Sometimes fines which had been imposed by the Court Leet for failure in these duties were ignored, and defaulters were fined double at the next meeting of the Court. But still some of the inhabitants ignored the orders and left the fines unpaid. The streets remained as filthy as ever, and no one seemed to realise the danger of disease from them.

A notable, if humble, inhabitant was the cowherd, or Hayward, who tended the town's cows in the fields outside the walls. He collected them at 6 a.m. outside the gate, and brought them back at six in the evening. Anyone who grazed cows on the common other than under the charge of the cowherd was fined heavily, and there were lesser penalties for being late for the morning collection or evening return to the owners. The cowherd was not considered as important as the Ale Taster or the Clerk of the Market, the latter having to see fair play once a week when the High Street was turned into a market place.

Housed within the walls were about two hundred and fifty permanent dockyard workers, besides fishermen, a variety of tradesmen, the staffs of the royal brewhouses, and all the other folk who go to make up the population of a small town. There was also a shifting population of mariners, but most of these lived in the ships or, if 'paid off', went elsewhere to find more lucrative employment than Portsmouth could offer.

Since the days of Henry VIII, the busy life of the town had gradually slackened because in the dockyard there was no new construction in hand, and the port was now primarily used as the base for laying up the Reserve Fleet. Also fishermen had no longer to provide fish for Christendom to eat on Fridays and Plymouth had become an excellent port for manning ships with experienced deep-sea sailors, now deprived of their previous livelihood.

It was seven years since the Portsbridge had echoed to the sound of a royal escort. On the afternoon of 8th August 1552, King Edward crossed the bridge with his retinue, and was met by Sir Richard Wingfield, who guided them along the route to the halfmile stone, and then across the common to Southsea Castle.

Although it had been considered insufficiently comfortable for Mary Guise, the King stayed the night at the castle. He brought with him the map which Sir Andrew Dudley had carried on his inspection. This marked the castle, which Sir Richard Wingfield told him was locally called Southsea Castle.[1]

On the morning after his arrival the King made his tour of the defences. Edward was discerning in matters of defence, and he found Mr. Rogers' report a most illuminating document. What struck him most was the immense amount of open space inside the defensive wall of the town, and the long lengths of undefended ramparts. He thought most of the guns were badly sited and quite inadequate. Moreover, he noticed that confidence had been placed in the fact that the sea came up to the south-west face, but the King pointed out that at low tide the town was vulnerable from the seaward. He thought that two much more powerful castles should be built at the entrance.

With this, he turned his attention to the Navy. The journey from the North Gate to the dockyard was only a mile, with one hazard, namely, the Mill Pond. The King rode around this at its head, where the stream could be comfortably forded, and a half mile or so brought them to the dockyard gate.

The sight which greeted the King was not as depressing as might have been expected. There were twenty vessels of the active fleet lying at Portsmouth. Eight of these had recently been cruising in the Channel and looked in good repair.

The King took great interest not only in these ships, but also in the new victualling storehouses. William Wynter, the Surveyor of the Navy, had come to the dockyard to wait on the King, and he told him of the improvement, but added that only £2,407 had been spent on victuals at Portsmouth during the last twelve months, whereas Woolwich and Deptford had spent £8,382.

The King spoke to some of the workmen who were ship-breaking. They told him that these ships were the *Grand Mistress*, the *Anne Gallant* and the *Mary of Lubeck*. The men showed him rotting timbers, and explained that the ships were useless. Everyone felt this a sad moment, as these ships had been the cream of the Navy in their day, and had done great service.

William Wynter thought the Regency Council was looking

1. Note on page 53 refers.

E

after the Navy quite well, except that the drain on the royal exchequer was increasing. Previously the Crown had never been put to such heavy and continuous expense, but, as Wynter pointed out, the Fleet was a new instrument of policy. It had done well to date, and the ships looked in good order. Nevertheless, he wondered how long the King could go on paying for his navy himself.

His Majesty left the dockyard pleased but thoughtful. Here was a new problem. Should money be spent on guns around the town and harbour entrance for defence, or would it be better to concentrate on the Navy itself, to drive any enemy away before he reached the port?

After crossing to Gosport, the King rode over to Mr. Hasleford's castle, which he considered was sufficiently strong, but again badly sited for the purposes of defence, especially from the sea-ward.

The King had made his whole tour of inspection in one day and, although he now felt tired, he decided to go on to Titchfield for the night. Perhaps the outstanding memory in his mind after seeing the port for the first time was the excellence of the haven, which deeply impressed him. 'This haven', he wrote, 'is able to bear the greatest ship in Christendom.'

The visit was not forgotten. At the Council of 13th October 1552 the great needs of the country were defined, and the first requirement on the list was 'The fortefying of Portsmouth'. Rather suddenly next year, 1553, the King was taken ill again and died.

Mary Tudor, the first woman to rule England in her own right, never came to Portsmouth. Engrossed in her unswerving passion to restore the Church of Rome to its full authority, she had no time for naval affairs. Her councillors, however, did not neglect maritime affairs altogether, and Portsmouth continued to be recognised as a suitable base for operations in the Channel. Nevertheless, the £7,000 spent at Portsmouth compared unfavourably with the £22,000 spent at Deptford.

The Queen came nearest to Portsea Island when she married King Philip of Spain at Winchester Cathedral, with full Roman Catholic ritual. From that moment the drive to establish the Roman Catholic faith once more in England was pursued with the utmost vigour. No martyrs were burned in Portsmouth, but the rules for attending church, which had not been fully observed in the previous reign, were strictly enforced. No victualler could allow eating or drinking during the times of Matins or Mass. All householders had to see that their wives, children and servants were present during church service times. No carting of any sort was allowed, and all travelling was forbidden on Sundays.

By 1557 the burnings of martyrs such as Latimer and Ridley, and executions, such as that of Lady Jane Grey, were forcing the temper of public opinion against the Queen. Meanwhile, Portsmouth dockyard had its own fire, with the burning of the Queen's storehouses. As one contemporary writer put it: 'A judgment, perhaps, for the burning of so many innocent persons.'

The fire was sufficiently large to call for a special report, and the Mayor and burgesses, having investigated the matter fully, put their signatures to the report, which read as follows:

To all true Christen people to whom These present shall come to be sene or heard, John Younge, for the tyme beinge Mayor of the towne and libertie of Portesmouth, and The Burgesses of the same (whose names are herin underwryten) sende Gretynge in our lord Everlastynge. For as myche as It becometh Every true Christen man to make report and testifie in all suche mattiers as They do know, yf They be thereunto requyred. We Therefore advertyse, That on Corpus Christi daye beinge The xviith daye of June last past before the date hereof Ther did happen a Greet and Terrible Fyer, Begonne within a Stoarehouse of the Kynge and Quenes Majesties in Portesmouth aforsaid, Called The Broome-howse, being a Celloure for beer appoynted for the victuellynge of theire Majesties shipps: Wherin was, at the begynnynge of the said fyer (as by the Oath of Richard Peter and Thomas Dickenson, Clerke of the Provisions, made before us, In that behalfe, It is deposed) Foure skore and seven tonnes of beere of the Kynge and Quenes Majesties. And the Fyer was suche, yet (notwithstondynge all the helpe yt coulde be hadd) There was vtterly perished The said Howse, and fyftye and three tonnes & one hoggshedd of the said beere, with the caske; As vpon the Oath of the said Richard Peter and Thomas Dickenson, It is likewise deposed; And also The Said Fyer did vtterly burne and perishe another stoarhowse (of the Kynge and Quenes Majesties) adioynynge to the said beere celloure (Covered also with broome) Called The Coopers woorkynge howse, In which howse was also vtterly perished (Of the Kynge and Quenes Majesties) (As by the Oath of Thomas Thompson Warden of the Coopers, made, In like wyse before us, It is deposed) One hundredth Tonnes of Emptie Caske, One great hundredth Clapboord, Eyghtene small hundredth, Twentie syxe thowsande Pype and Hoggshedd hoopes, and coopers tooles to the value of viii or ixs. Also Ther perished in the saie broome howse yarde syxtene hundredth foote of Purbicke stone, as by the Oath of Edmunde Kyngesfeeld Free mason (made before us) It is also deposed. And Because This our Testymonyall is requyred by Edwarde Basshe Esquyor, Generall Surveyor of those provisions, We The Said Mayor and Burgesses with our one assente, have done to be put to thiese presente the Seconde daye of the Reignes of our soveraigne Lord and soveraigne Lady Philip and Mary, by the grace of god, Kynge and Quene of England, Spayne, Fraunce, Bothe Cycylle, Jerusalem & Yrlond, Defendours of the faith, Archdukes of Austria, Dukes of Burgundye, Myllayne, and Brabante, Counties of Haspurge, Flaunders, and Tyrroll.

John Yonge, Mayor.	Thomas Goodynowgh.	John Hollowaye.
John Elton.	Henry Sclater.	Thomas Fylder.
Fraunces Bodken.	Fraunces Robins.	Denys Savoye.

One year later, after five years on the throne, the Queen died, and Portsmouth found itself with a growing trade in fitting out privateers, licensed by the Lord Admiral who, together with the Crown, took one-eighth of the prize money. This freedom was already being carried so far that a privateer belonging to the Lord Privy Seal was known to be attacking neutrals, and officers of the Navy did not stop at boarding merchantmen in English ports and carrying off the cargo. At the time these were comparatively small matters, but they set the pattern for an era of privateering on a scale never again equalled in the history of England.

4

Tudor Rose

Man-of-war, 1588

On her accession on November 17th, 1558, Elizabeth I possessed twenty-two effective naval ships of one hundred tons and upwards, and forty-five years later she possessed twenty-nine. She therefore did little more than maintain the strength of the Fleet, but Elizabeth's navy was better administered than that of any other country in the world. In contrast, not only had the French Navy, a serious menace in previous reigns, practically ceased to exist, but the Spaniards, in spite of all their activities on the Spanish Main, still did not possess a separate navy for the protection of their sea communications.

Elizabeth's England was rich in mariners. Her admirals, adventurers and courtiers all served her well at sea. Such names as Howard, Drake, Hawkins, Wynter, Frobisher, Gilbert, Norreys and Cumberland, show how well the country was provided with maritime leaders.

These men favoured the small ships of four to six hundred tons, and hardly used the big ships of one thousand tons. It was this policy which brought much success in 1588. They fought their battles on the Spanish Main, carried out their voyages of discovery, and pursued their profitable trade of piracy in ships which appeared too small to face the oceans almost unknown to mariners of that time, and triumphed because of their superb seamanship and the accuracy of their navigation. Ships were handled skilfully in all conditions and under every possible difficulty. Landmarks were carefully recorded, soundings minutely mapped, and landfalls were accurately made. Nevertheless, to Queen Elizabeth sailors were 'the common lot'. During her reign many who served and fought for their country perished in misery, unheeded except by the officers who had fought with them. Until 1585 the wages for a seaman were the same as in 1546, namely, six shillings and eightpence a month. Sir John Hawkins, Treasurer of the Navy from 1578, raised it to ten shillings a month. There were no special arrangements made on board for the sick or wounded sailor. If he survived, he was labelled and sent to his parish to beg.

Sir Richard Hawkins, his son, estimated that in twenty years, ten thousand sailors died of scurvy. In these years when England relied so much on her sailors, even the custom of providing men with coats and jackets ceased.

It might be wondered why anyone went to sea, and how the sailor existed on his pay. Piracy was greatly to account for the answer. During Elizabeth's reign, piracy took on almost the dignity of a recognised profession. There were four hundred recognised English pirates, some from well-known families, and responsible people traded openly with them. Southampton was a flourishing centre for such trade, with the Mayor at its head and the Lieutenant of Portsmouth working in conjunction with him. The maritime population in Hampshire rose from two hundred and ninety to four hundred and seventy. Piracy lined their pockets.

During this amazing reign only two English men-of-war were captured by Spain, and then only after desperate fighting. With one exception, no dockyard-built ship was lost by stress of weather, while whole Spanish fleets foundered. Many ships became famous, and names such as *Ark Royal*, *Repulse*, *Warspite*, *Lion*, *Vanguard*, *Dreadnought* and *Swiftsure* became household words.

In addition to the privateering, expeditions were undertaken to the Barbary coast. These were not of startling importance, but they had some effect on the life of Portsmouth, in that some of the ships were fitted out there.

At times, during the reign, there were sudden small bursts of naval activity, and the year 1561 was one such period, when the hand of fate led Mary Queen of Scots back to her native land. In this year her husband, King Francis II of France, died, and she sailed for home. Queen Elizabeth hoped to intercept the little squadron bringing the young widowed queen north, but although all routes, including the Channel off Portsmouth, were patrolled, Mary, with her escort of ships, slipped through.

Two years later, all activity, both in the dockyard and the town, was brought to a standstill by a disastrous epidemic, not uncommon in Europe, but which Portsea Island was to experience to the full for the first time. Filth and vermin were at the root of the trouble. Not only did vermin thrive on the appalling state of the streets and open spaces, but in a seaport additional rats found their way ashore, bringing with them germs of whatever disease was raging in the port of their departure from the Continent.

In 1562, the Court Leet jury ordered that no one should suffer hogs to go abroad within the town on a pain of fourpence for the first offence, twelvepence for the second, while for a third, the Hayward was to drive the hogs to the Pound, where they would be sold to the profit of the town. They increased the fines on the butchers, who were always in trouble for throwing offal from the Queen's slaughterhouse down the slipway at the Town Quay. The washing of clothes at the stream by the four brewhouses was also forbidden.

All this was very laudable on paper, but the Chamberlain and Constables had great difficulty in enforcing the laws on a section of the inhabitants or extracting the fines.

It was not altogether surprising when, in the spring of 1563, the maidservant of a well-to-do spinster of Portsmouth was found to have the plague, and died. At first, no great notice was taken of the announcement of the burial posted on the door of St. Thomas's Church, but the Mayor, Mr. Darbie Savell, discussed the matter with the burgesses. They decided that if the plague spread, as well it might with the summer coming on, they would immediately reassure the people by announcing that they would not leave the town. This was a brave act by men who well knew the risks they would be running.

As spring turned to summer, the weekly bill of mortality steadily rose, and the inhabitants, now thoroughly alarmed, came in great numbers to read the lists. The Mayor had by this time issued many orders. Compulsory church was no longer in force, but people gathered together more than ever for prayers, being happier in their minds for having come to Church, rather than having avoided their fellow men and women to keep clear of infection. Everyone turned to God, and there were daily Bible readings by the ministers which were attended by scores who had previously neglected their faith. Unhappily, these dreadful warnings made the hearts of the people sink instead of lifting them up.

Escape to the country was forbidden, and this was easy to control because Portsmouth was on an island, but some took refuge in the ships lying in the harbour.

By mid-April in this year, 1563, there were many houses marked with the red cross, and the majority of these were boarded up and a guard placed outside. Scrawled on the doors were the words: 'The Lord have mercy upon us.' Food was brought by men specially appointed by the authorities for this duty. The beerhouses opened only for very short periods, and those shops which did not shut by the order of the Mayor were visited in ones and twos by a people fearful of coming into contact with their neighbours.

Much bravery was shown during this dark time. Apothecaries and nurses in most cases stuck to their posts. Burials were carried out quickly and at night, and no bodies were brought through the streets by day to terrify the inhabitants. Small numbers of individuals took advantage of the situation to line their pockets, and set themselves up as doctors and nurses without having any experience at all, profiting by the sorrow of relatives and the terror of the afflicted. Astrologers and fortune-tellers were greatly in demand, and handed out charms at high prices to the despairing population.

By August, all trade was at a standstill, and the unemployed wandered the streets by day and thieved at night. No one else dared to go out after dark, except the burial teams trundling their carts through the streets and calling the terrible cry: 'Bring out your dead.'

Somehow the authorities managed to keep the supply of provisions going, chiefly from the Queen's storehouses, whose keepers, not being permanent residents, petitioned the Lord Chancellor to allow them to leave the town for their native homes in other parts of the country.

At long last the tragic summer passed. Over one third of the population had died. As the winter came in and the plague subsided, life slowly returned to normal, except that almost every family had lost one or more of its number. On the other hand, there was a total absence of beggars.

Once again shipping began to move, and for the first time since early March, the music of the wandering minstrels lifted the hearts of the townspeople.

In 1566 new hope came unexpectedly like a fresh breeze, blowing away some of the memories of the trials of 1563. This hope was centred in the Queen's 'Great Lotterie'. From this enterprise it was hoped that enough money would be raised 'to increase the defences and amenities of the best havens in the land'. Portsmouth was specially mentioned as deserving better fortifications.

A lottery was nothing new to the world of the sixteenth century. The distribution of war booty had been made this way from the earliest times. Moreover, medieval Europe used lotteries for all manner of schemes, notable centres being Ghent, Utrecht and Bruges.

Queen Elizabeth's 'Great Lotterie' was run on the lines similar to those employed at Bruges, and her Lottery Bill was issued in August 1567. It was described as:

A very rich Lotterie General, without blanks, containing a great number of good prizes, as well of ready money as of plate, and certain sorts of merchandise, having been valued and priced by the commandment of the Queen's Most Excellent Majesty, by men expert and skilful; and the same Lotterie is erected by Her Majety's order to the intent that such a commodity as may chance to arise thereof, after the charges borne, may be converted towards the reparations of the havens and the strength of the Realm.

The number of lots were four hundred thousand, and each lot cost ten shillings. This latter sum was undoubtedly arranged from experience in Europe, but it was to prove the stumbling block. Certainly the prizes were attractive. The first prize was three thousand pounds in ready money, seven hundred pounds in plate gilt, and the rest in good tapestries and goods of linen cloth.

Regulations for the entry to towns where tickets were on sale were relaxed, and certain adventurers were given freedom to pass in and out of these cities. The nearest city to Portsmouth where tickets could be bought was Southampton.

At first the tickets went quite well. People often sent in their requests for lots with posies attached, while one young woman stated her hope in these terms: 'I am a poor maiden and fain would marry, and lack of goods is the cause that I tarry.'

Unhappily, this state of affairs did not last. After a year, during which time messages had been sent to all mayors to encourage people to take tickets, and the Queen had despatched many personal notes to men and women of influence, she had to accept the fact that the scheme was failing. It was a great blow to her personal pride.

The draw was a most protracted business. St. Paul's Churchyard, London, was selected, and the proceedings took sixteen weeks. By the end, everyone, from the Queen downwards, was heartily tired of the whole thing. In Portsmouth it was realised that any hope of the defences being improved from this source had long vanished.

Yet some further effort had been made when in 1560 a certain Richard Popynjay was appointed Surveyor of Portsmouth. He held the appointment until 1587, and did what he could year by year. Popynjay was also a landowner of some substance. During his term of office he acquired houses in the High Street between the Hogmarket and St. Thomas's Street, and a house and garden in St. Thomas's Street. Besides these possessions he owned nine acres in the common field and an orchard and garden in Buckland.

Popynjay's main improvement was to substitute stone for mud and wood, and he began with the Platform. He found he had a major task. Besides the weakened Quay Gate and Platform, the arch over the Landport Gate had fallen down, none of the town gates would shut, and the Round Tower was so decayed that the guns had been removed. The work went ahead very slowly, and as late as 1585 no salute was fired on Coronation Day, as the Platform was still unsafe for guns. Eventually improvements were made, and the military garrison strengthened so that the position of the Military Governor gained in importance, too, and it was decided that the rotting Domus Dei should be restored and a part of it converted as a residence of the Governor. Thus, the Domus Dei began a new and exciting life, not this time as a hospital, but as the cornerstone of the defended town of Portsmouth, though it retained something of its old character in that the kitchens were so built that the poor could be fed from them in times of depression and difficulty.

Meanwhile, the port was in use by the Navy in a small way. English privateers had become so outrageously piratical that it became necessary to restrain their activities by royal proclamation, if wars were to be averted. At Portsmouth, Sir William Woodhouse was commissioned to take charge in the Channel. He fitted out a small but fast squadron consisting of the *Lion, Hart, Swallow* and *Hare*, and made frequent cruises south of the Isle of Wight. It became almost routine to see this workmanlike squadron sail for operations, and return a week or so later for provisions. Eventually, even this modest activity soon died away, and the years went by without Portsmouth taking part in any further maritime enterprise.

On 27th July 1585 the people of Portsmouth witnessed the return of part of the first expedition to America, organised by Sir Walter Raleigh with the object of founding a colony. The expedition, under Sir Richard Grenville, had gone out the year before. It was commanded by Sir Richard Grenville himself, and in it were Ralph Lane, one of the Queen's equerries, appointed to take charge of the colony, and Thomas Harriot, a leading scientist and mathematician.

After nearly a year in the New World, they had been called on by Drake, who initially intended only to bring news of their progress to the Queen. In the event, because of the hostility of the natives and the loneliness of their life, the small band of settlers decided to accept Drake's offer of a passage home. On reaching England, Drake naturally put in to Plymouth, but Lane and Harriot came on to Portsmouth.

This in itself was an event of much interest, but the colonists had something more in store for Portsmouth. Greetings having been exchanged with the Governor, Sir Henry Radclyfe, and the Mayor, Mr. Thomas Thorney, they drew from their pockets some leaves of a plant, and having pushed them into small bowls, to which they had attached long wooden stems, proceeded to light the leaves and apparently breathe smoke from their mouths. The sight of these men walking down the High Street with smoke billowing from them astonished everyone, not least Mr. Thorney, who, as Member of Parliament for Portsmouth, with two-shillings-a-day travelling expenses, would be taking this sensational story to his friends in Westminster.

By now the crossing of the Atlantic was no novelty, and English seamen had made their presence felt so strongly on the Spanish Main that King Philip could stand aside no longer. Plans for the invasion of these islands, so long discussed and often urged in Spanish circles, were completed, and preparations were begun for the sailing of their great armada.

Everyone in England, and more especially those living along the south coast, realised that the hour had come when English seamen must face their greatest test, and preparations were feverishly put in hand. Lord Howard of Effingham, Lord Admiral of England, sent instructions to every port along the south coast, and Portsmouth began to awake from its long period of semi-activity. However, there was little that the dockyard could do at such short notice. Three ships, the *Nonpareil*, the *Hope* and the *Advice*, were fitted out, and this proved to be Portsmouth's total contribution to the fleet. In other respects the port was not ready, and indeed fell short of the expectations of the Lord Admiral who, writing to Lord Burghley on 8th April 1588, complained of the shortage of victuals in the port. He wrote:

King Harry, Her Majesty's father, never made a lesser supply of food than six weeks; there was ever provisions at Portsmouth and his baking and brewing there; so as, for the service then, it was ever at hand upon any necessity.

Time was not on the side of the dockyard, and throughout that fateful summer Portsmouth was found lacking in many departments of naval administration.

News of the sailing of the Spanish Armada was brought to Portsmouth by Captain Gilbert Lee, commanding the *Rat of Wight*, who entered the harbour on the 5th July. Immediately the local warning beacons were got ready, and the defences, such as they were, manned by the scanty garrison, augmented with large numbers of volunteers. Merchant ships in the harbour were hurriedly prepared, and a variety of stalwarts took a few to sea to join in the fighting as best they could. Robert Carey, afterwards Earl of Monmouth, was one who succeeded in getting to sea from Portsmouth. Sir Horatio Palavicino was another.

The English High Command confidently expected there might be a landing in the Isle of Wight, and that a Spanish army would be put ashore in force at Portsmouth. The Spanish Duke of Medina Sidonia, however, was intent on joining General Parma near Calais, so when the Armada came in sight off the Isle of Wight on the morning of 25th July, and the troops in the island anxiously watched for the great fleet to turn towards the shore, they found all their fears quickly dispelled. Instead, they had a grandstand view of the Spaniards being chased by the British Fleet from Plymouth.

Few had witnessed a naval battle before, and none had seen a fight like this. Firing went on all day. The English ships, seemingly dwarfed by the Spanish galleons, fired at long range and picked off stragglers. So much ammunition was used that it became obvious that many of the ships must run out of powder and shot. Unhappily Portsmouth, in its state of unreadiness, was unable to replenish these ships to the full extent of their requirements. In mitigation it must be said that no action had been fought like this before. To fire all day at long range was quite unprecedented.

By noon it was clear that the Spanish could not then land at Portsmouth, even if that had been their earlier intention, as the Armada was running before the wind past the Isle of Wight. Troops on the Island broke their camp, and by evening the sound of the firing could no longer be heard at Southsea Castle.

Portsmouth men and women slept well that night. When in due course news was received that the Armada had been dispersed off Calais, and the danger of invasion averted, the Mayor and burgesses showed their gratitude to the Lord Admiral by declaring him a freeman of the town.

That Portsmouth should have contributed so little to such an important event as the defeat of the Armada gained them nothing in the challenge for supremacy against Plymouth and the great building ports on the Thames for a greater share in the maritime affairs of the country.

During Elizabeth's long reign, many towns and hamlets were visited by the Queen on her progresses. These places were mostly in the south of England. Progresses were a feature of the time when Monarchs continually rode through the country visiting their castles and estates. In the passage of years the journeying had been reduced to one or two months a year, confined to the precincts of London, the Home Counties and an occasional venture slightly further afield. In Queen

Elizabeth's reign they were made both for the purpose of a holiday, and also as an instrument of her policy to win the hearts of her people.

It was not until 1591 that the Queen decided to include Portsmouth in one of her progresses. She left London in early August, and as she travelled no more than ten or twelve miles a day, made numerous stops before arriving on Portsea Island. She had been at Chichester, staying with Lord Lumley, from the 20th to the 22nd August and, after putting up for one night at Stanstead, where the noble Lord had another suitable residence, the Queen came on the same day to Portsmouth.

Queen Elizabeth was met at the Portsbridge by the Earl of Sussex, Governor of the island, and Lieutenant of Southsea Castle. The Earl had been Lord Chamberlain from 1572 to 1583, so he was well known to Her Majesty. Thomas Eyston, Mayor, together with his burgesses, the constables, the councillors and the aldermen, met Her Majesty at the Landport Gate, and carried out all the traditional ceremonies. John Rider, chaplain to the Earl of Sussex, acted as orator.

Thereafter, for five days the Queen was entertained as best possible within the limits of the meagre resources of the town. Already Southampton had written to the Lords of Council, asking to be excused the burden of building a ship, which was to cost only £500, probably with a view to having some money in hand for the Queen's visit. Portsmouth was even poorer, and there is no doubt that the Earl of Sussex found he had to meet the majority of the costs.

Nevertheless, at Portsmouth it was not necessary to stage tremendously expensive pageantry. There was business to combine with pleasure. The fortifications had to be inspected, the ships reviewed, and, of course, days could be given over to the excellent hunting a few miles distant in the Forest of Bere.

There is no record of where Her Majesty stayed in Portsmouth, but by this date considerable improvements must have been made to the Domus Dei, and the Governor's residence may well have been completed.

Before leaving, the Queen ordered the defences to be improved, and increased the size of the garrison. She directed that a permanent watch was to be kept from the top of the church tower, and arranged for various signals to give the alarm. There was also to be a continuous watch at the town gates.

Nine years after her visit Queen Elizabeth remembered
Portsmouth by granting its first Charter of Incorporation.
Often a charter was a confirmation by the Sovereign of the
privileges previously granted, and was known as an 'Inspexi-
mus'. It would begin: 'We have inspected the Charter of . . .'
and then recite the full text, confirming the various clauses.
Queen Elizabeth I's charter of 1600 was of a different nature,
and recognised what was in fact an existing state of affairs,
acknowledging for the first time the governing body as a
corporate entity under the title of the Mayor and burgesses of
the borough of Portsmouth. It declared that the Mayor was to
be chosen each year 'from the senior and principal better and
more honest burgesses'. Queen Elizabeth also declared that
the Mayor and three of the senior burgesses should serve each
year as Justices of the Peace.

From this time the Sessions of the Justices overlapped the
Court Leet, until the latter ceased to exist.

By now the long reign of Queen Elizabeth was beginning to
draw to an end. In some ways it was remarkable that she had
survived unscathed to the close of the century, as plots continued throughout her life, the origin of some being traced to
landings at Portsmouth, where a check on immigrants was
none too strict, and the watch at night was lazy. Indeed, the
coming and going of Catholic priests through Portsmouth,
particularly at night, disturbed the authorities at Westminster,
but Portsmouth never bothered to stir itself unduly in such
matters. Foreign spies came and went without trouble, and the
French Ambassador was able to write to his government that he
had full knowledge of the defences of Portsmouth and the
situation in the dockyard. Writing from Antwerp, John
Middleton, Envoy at The Hague, told Cecil:

They say here that they know the very secret bowels of England;
of the removing of captains from the Isle of Wight and Portsmouth,
with the names of the new; that Portsmouth is nothing strong and
that a man may gallop his horse up the ditch.

Indeed, though orders were given that no foreign ships were
to be allowed to enter the harbour, it was common knowledge
that the French came and went as much as they liked.

At this time Portsmouth was notable for the constant
sailings and homecomings of the Earl of Cumberland. For

years this great sailor and adventurer used Portsmouth as his base. All was achieved without fuss. He fitted out, went his way, and returned with a regularity which eventually surprised no one.

Occasionally there was an event of unusual importance. The return of Martin Frobisher's fleet to Plymouth and Portsmouth in 1592 set the town talking, and there was some excitement at the main gates when merchants from London tried to enter against the regulations, as there was plague in the capital, while Portsmouth for the time was free of it.

Portsmouth ended the century by honouring one of her sons, Sir Charles Blount. His body was laid in the church of St. Thomas by his cousin, Lord Mountjoy, who was Governor in 1593–4.

'Hereunder', the inscription reads, 'resteth the body of Sir Charles Blount, one of Her Majesty's band of Pensioners, third son of Sir Michael Blount, Knight, lineally descended from Walter, first Lord Mountjoy.'

After describing his military career and how he was knighted for valour, the inscription goes on:

'But on his return home upon the sea he departed this life in his prime and flourishing years about the age of 32.'

Blount was obviously a worthy son of Portsmouth, but it would have been more representative of the port if, at the end of this great maritime age, a great seaman could also have been honoured.

However, the port could claim one mariner who was notorious, if not famous. In the very year that the Queen died, 1603, so the story was told in later years, a seaman of Portsmouth named Ward, hearing that a gentleman of Petersfield had much valuable property in a vessel in the harbour, induced a number of his companions to board and capture the ship under cover of darkness. When they found that the owner, fearing for its safety, had removed the treasure to a safe place, Ward decided to sail away in the ship. He became one of the most successful pirates in the Mediterranean, finally settling in Tunis, where he built himself a marble palace.

5

Civil War

Immigrant ship

In spite of Queen Elizabeth's parsimony in maritime affairs, there is no doubt that in 1603 the Navy of England was supreme in northern European waters, and feared on the Spanish Main.

The reign of James I ushered in a very lean period in the fortunes of the island of Portsea. One of the King's first actions was to conclude peace with Spain and put an end to privateering. For the mariners of Portsmouth, and the shipwrights, sailmakers and riggers in the dockyard, this was nothing short of a major disaster.

Though King James himself had the best intentions for his navy, and allocated to it more money than his predecessors, he was served by dishonest and incompetent administrators, and the rot, starting near the top, seeped down to the lower orders. Corruption soon set in. Many naval storekeepers sold their goods, made false entries in their books, and neglected the ships. There were large numbers of admirals on full pay without any commands, ships were manned with fictitious ship's companies, and pay passed into the pockets of senior officers. Money was squandered in the firing of endless salutes. As much

F

as one hundred pounds was sometimes shot away in saluting the health of a senior officer. The travelling expenses of the Navy Board and their juniors were fantastic. The Surveyor of the Navy charged nineteen pounds for a journey from London to Chatham and return.

As the years passed, with admirals of the north, south, east and west commanding nothing, and two vice-admirals and three rear-admirals commanding seven ships, corruption led to indiscipline, and finally to such inefficiency that many of the royal ships were utterly unfit to put to sea.

In 1618 Lord Howard of Effingham, who had commanded the Fleet at the time of the Armada, and had been created the Earl of Nottingham, retired. He had done nothing to correct the corruption and decline in the Fleet.

The man who took over the post of Lord Admiral was the court favourite, Charles Villiers, Duke of Buckingham, who assumed the title of Lord High Admiral, the word 'high' being written into the patent for the first time. He at once began to try to pull things together, but unhappily the corruption in high circles was too deeply rooted; moreover, in his position as the confidant of the King, Buckingham busied himself far more with matters of State policy than with the Navy.

One of these State matters directly affected Portsmouth. King James I, largely through the influence of Gondomar, the Spanish Ambassador, decided to try and arrange a marriage between his son Charles and the Spanish Infanta. Accordingly, in 1623, Charles, accompanied by Buckingham, left secretly for France. After innumerable adventures the Prince and the favourite arrived in Madrid. Charles failed in his suit, however, so he and Buckingham had to come home. The King was determined that the return journey should not be a repetition of the hazards outward overland, and the Earl of Rutland was told to form a squadron at Portsmouth and go to Cadiz to bring the travellers home.

At the very moment when the Earl of Rutland had been appointed to bring Prince Charles home, Sir Henry Mainwaring, Governor of Dover Castle, was dismissed from his post for boisterous conduct. He had not changed his ways from those of his early days in the Navy. Seldom did he spend a night in the castle; rather, he preferred Canterbury, where he found plenty of strong drink and complaisant ladies ready to keep him company.

On leaving the castle at Dover, he sent a request to London to be given a sea command—this would break the blow. Buckingham gave him the *Prince Royal*. The return to sea completely reformed Sir Henry, and in shorter time than anyone could have imagined he had the squadron in fine fettle. He wrote and told the Earl of Rutland this, saying that he had got things in strict order. He had put his coxswain in the bilboes for being drunk, and a man who stole a jerkin was, by his command, ducked at the yardarm and then towed ashore at the stern of a boat and dismissed.

King James, with his court, went to Beaulieu for the latter part of August. From there he sent a stream of messages to the squadron, which was anchored in Stokes Bay, waiting for a favourable wind to get away.

After three or four days at Beaulieu, the Fleet still being wind-bound at Stokes Bay, the King paid it a surprise visit. The Earl of Rutland was not on board his flagship, the *Prince Royal*, which disappointed the King, but Secretary Conway was instructed to send a note to the Earl that His Majesty was pleased with the state of the ships, and with his reception on board. Sir Henry Mainwaring had indeed done well.

During the visit it was explained to King James that part of the delay was the want of mariners, so he gave orders for two hundred to be impressed from along the coast, if necessary as far as Plymouth. Whatever the result of the impressment, the Earl set sail from Stokes Bay 'with a bare wind' on the 24th August. But in the event the wind died away altogether, and the squadron put in to Portsmouth. The King, having decided to lengthen his progress a day or two, came round to Portsmouth from Beaulieu, and was taken to the *Prince Royal* and dined with the Earl.

There had been no time for detailed preparation when King James made his surprise visit to the squadron. But there is no doubt that Captain Mainwaring and others had brought their ships and men to a good standard and this time, there having been previous warning that the King would come to the flagship, things were done better still. The Navy Board, too, in spite of the prevalent neglect and corruption, were gradually making improvements based on King Henry VIII's organisation. Indeed, in this very year the 'slop stores' were introduced, and as soon as a seaman's clothes wore out, he was issued with his 'slops'. The majority of these were made up in the fashion of the seaman of the last two hundred years. It was a shapeless garment made of a very rough coarsely woven material, belted at the waist and reaching to the knee.

A few men were bold enough to begin a different fashion. They made their material into short coats and breeches, tight fitting at the knee. Both the old diehards and the progressives made 'thrumbed caps' for their heads. These were shaggy-looking things, made by passing hundreds of short lengths of twine or wool through canvas. Having shaped these objects into something resembling an inverted tumbler, the loose ends of the twine were cut off.

If the admiral or captain possessed his own livery the colours were sometimes introduced into the men's clothes, and on occasion into the cap. The 'purser' would issue the extra material with the 'slops'. Some uniformity in dress on the lower deck was therefore achieved, and with the prospect of a Royal visit, the ships' company of the *Prince Royal* were no doubt issued with 'slops' and appeared well dressed, moderately uniformed and clean.

The seamen, however, were still very much outclassed by their officers in this respect. The 'gentlemen' each brought his own wardrobe for the trip, which was a cross between the Elizabethan style and that of the Cavalier. They wore elaborate doublets, billowing breeches called 'galligaskins', coloured hose and shoes, some of the latter having the new heels. There being no naval uniform, it was a case of every man for himself, but they were guided by two things. Firstly it was considered proper to wear as much red as possible when on military operations, and secondly, each officer took steps to wear, in some appropriate manner, the colours of the livery of his admiral. These splashes of colour, worn against a background of highly embroidered materials, and with swords donned, made a fitting setting for the reception of the Monarch.

The arrival of King James at the town of Portsmouth was very different from that of any previous monarch. His court had none of the splendour of Elizabeth's, and gone, too, were the grand progresses. His were more in the nature of quiet and shielded hunting trips.

James crossed the Portsbridge in his carriage, passed through Portsmouth to the Camber, and was rowed silently to the *Prince Royal*. Few, if any, of the ordinary inhabitants of the town knew that their King was among them, and those who did were not allowed to come near his route. The return journey was no different, and so an event of the greatest historical interest to Portsmouth, the presence of the first King of England and Scotland, passed off without so much as a gun being fired or an address of welcome.

The squadron which eventually sailed consisted of ten ships, three of which were flagships. On the 5th October 1623 the squadron returned from Cadiz, bringing Prince Charles and the Duke of Buckingham. They had had a spanking westerly wind in their favour, and, having separated a skirmish between Hollanders and Dunkirkers off the Scilly Isles, anchored in St. Helen's Roads at about 9 a.m. The royal traveller and his favourite were brought to Portsmouth in a longboat, and landed at the Sally Port at about 3 p.m.

There was no ceremony or delay at Portsmouth. The bulk of the people were at St. Thomas's Church, and most of the others were spending their Sunday afternoon in their houses, sheltered from the high October wind which had blown so favourably for the return of the Prince. Mr. Owen Jenens, the Mayor, and Sir John Oglander, Lieutenant Governor of Portsmouth, greeted the Prince and the Duke, and within an hour the royal party had left by coach with a small escort for Portsbridge and Guildford.

There had, however, been time to mention the maritime affairs of Portsmouth to the Duke. These were at a very low ebb. Apart from the general corruption which was still much in evidence, unprecedented gales had caused anxiety over the dock, and the Navy Board had ordered it to be filled in, thus bringing to an end the first dry dock ever built in England. There is little doubt that the dock could have been saved if the Navy Board had been so determined but some of them, in particular Mr. William Burrell, had vested interests in Chatham, and were working against any revival of the yard at Portsmouth. Buckingham listened with care to this story of decline and, happily for Portsmouth, did not forget it.

Meanwhile, riders had set out at full speed with the news of the Prince's safe arrival. Everywhere along his route there was unconcealed rejoicing, not only because the heir to the throne had returned in safety, but because nothing had been given away to Catholic Spain. Portsmouth later erected a bust of the Prince on the walls of the Square Tower, which bore the inscription:

King Charles the First, after his travels through all France and Spain, and having passed through many dangers by sea and land, arrived here on the 5th day of October 1623. There was the greatest applause of joy for his safety throughout the kingdom that was ever known or heard of.

The great age of colonisation in the New World was now getting under way. In Portsmouth the colonial enterprises had little effect at first, but in time they were to change the fortunes of the town. As the new century developed, it became clear that the country which possessed a strong navy would hold its colonies. For the next two hundred years, therefore, the men of Portsmouth and the dockyard prospered, since by their work they were supplying the ships needed for the protection of the colonies and the overseas trade with the New World.

James I died in 1625, and among those who mourned him was Captain John Mason. Mason had been a personal friend of James, who had given him a number of important posts, all of which he filled with much ability and loyalty to the Crown. First, he successfully reclaimed the Hebrides, where a violent and rebellious people were defying all allegiance to the King and Church. Later, the King sent him to Newfoundland, when Guy of Bristol gave up the governorship. Mason organised a most prosperous fishing industry and by his own hand mapped the whole Island. He returned to England in 1624, and with his wife and family took up his abode in the High Street at Portsmouth.

Mason's experience in Newfoundland inspired him to join with others in acquiring territory in the New World. From James he obtained a patent of all land between the Nahumheik and Merrimak Rivers in the new colony. He sent out representatives to claim his patent, and joined the Council of New England, going up to London from time to time to attend the Council meetings in Fenchurch Street. His own territory he named New Hampshire.

The reign of King Charles I began with a disastrous venture in Europe. His belligerent Parliament demanded a renewal of hostilities against Spain and war was immediately declared. The King placed Buckingham in charge, and Parliament voted about one tenth of the money necessary. A fleet of three squadrons under Viscount Wimbledon escorted about ninety transports, carrying some six thousand men, for an attack on Cadiz, sailing from Plymouth.

Although Portsmouth's turn was to come, the port was lucky not to have mounted the first combined operation of the new reign. It was doomed from the start. At Plymouth, prior to sailing, disease raged among the soldiers and sailors, men deserted right and left, recruits arrived already stricken with disease, and provisions and clothing were desperately wanting. Then, when the ships got to sea, it was found that many of them leaked, and that the gear was unserviceable. Cordage was rotten, beer casks leaked and the beer came up in the ships' pumps. To crown it all, the sailing date, originally planned for midsummer, had to be put off until October.

The expedition had failed before it began, and on the fleet's return to various west coast ports, mayors refused permission for men to land for fear of contagion. The *Anne Royal*, with one hundred and thirty dead and one hundred and sixty sick, had less than fifteen men in a watch, and there were many ships like her.

John Mason had unwillingly gone on the expedition from Plymouth and when he returned to his house in Portsmouth High Street, he had much to think about. The victualling had been totally inadequate. The contractors had sent on board what provisions they pleased, without any accounting of amounts or costs. Money, although so short, was squandered. Only half the meat ordered was ever sent, the dried fish was rotten, and the clothing was of exceptionally bad quality.

Not all the ships returned to west coast ports. Some came to Portsmouth, where they lay with their dying ships' companies on board because there was no money with which to discharge them. When the stage was reached at which the officers were not much better off than the men, some captains pledged their own credit to help, and pathetic letters were written to Buckingham and the commissioners, all in the same vein. 'Eight or ten die here every day', one captain wrote. Another said: 'Every hammock is infected and loathsome.' All these protestations were ignored in Whitehall.

John Mason could see for himself in Portsmouth distress almost unheard of even in the times of galley slaves, while a few miles away were the manors of Hampshire, beautifully built, and paid for by rich merchants with money to spare. Those who lived on that plane perhaps never really knew what suffering went on in the ships which made their homes secure.

Human suffering through lack of trade was great, and men were unruly and violent. When a Dutch ship was driven ashore by Dunkirkers opposite Lumps Farm, the men of Portsmouth murdered the crew and divided the cargo. The citizens of Portsea Island had already petitioned the King to alleviate their poverty by ordering all sailings for the colonies to be made from Portsmouth, and all imports of tobacco to be unloaded at the Camber. But King Charles, engrossed with affairs at Whitehall, ignored their pleas.

The dockyard at Portsmouth was totally inactive so far as ship construction was concerned. It was really a collection of storehouses. The King's principal shipyards were still those on the banks of the Thames south of Greenwich, where they could draw their materials from the great City of London.

The experiments with the new swift-sailing whelps[1] had given Portsmouth some hope, but no orders came, and prestige was further given to the Thames yards with the laying of the keel of the great ship the *Sovereign of the Seas*.

A new situation now arose across the Channel. Charles quarrelled with his brother-in-law King Louis XIII of France, and Cardinal Richelieu, having made peace with Spain, steered his country against England. War between England and France was declared in 1627. An expedition to France was mounted, and once again the leadership was entrusted to Buckingham. This time, the Duke planned to relieve the Huguenots at La Rochelle. Ships were got ready and were ordered to assemble at Portsmouth. This assembly lacked much which was needed to satisfy the Fleet and the mariners, but in the transports conditions were at least tolerable for the sailors. Buckingham looked for someone who would see that the soldiers were embarked on time, and decided that a local man could best deal with the problem of billeting. His choice happily fell on John Mason. This able administrator billeted over six thousand soldiers on Portsea and in the neighbourhood with little fuss, in spite of private residents resenting the imposition. He managed to get enough money to pay the residents and the innkeepers promptly. He arranged for the soldiers' clothing to be correctly distributed in the transports, and he saw to it that every man should be on board the correct ship at the correct time.

1. Whelps: Small fleet auxiliary vessels, the first one designed to attend on H.M.S. *Lion*.

Thus, this expedition sailed with better chances than the Cadiz operation, but Buckingham, who sailed with them and commanded the landing on the Isle de Rhe, failed again in his task, and returned to England for reinforcements. To the surprise of the sailors, they were paid on arrival in port. Nevertheless, there were murmurings against the Duke from all sides.

Since Portsmouth had been chosen to mount the expedition the commissioners became concerned with the condition of its defences and amenities. Very early in the year it was decided to draft some twenty artificers to Portsmouth, firstly to repair the munition storehouse, then to redecorate the Governor's house at the Domus Dei, and later to help fit out some of the ships for the expedition. Leaders of the expedition were aghast to see the appalling state of the fortifications, particularly as they hourly expected an invasion, this time by the French. When, in April 1627, Southsea Castle was burnt out, urgent messages were sent from London to ensure the safety of the King's ships. However, Matthew Brooke, a senior storekeeper in the dockyard, wrote to Buckingham to say that the fire was an accident, there being no one in the castle at the time. Indeed, the castle had been neglected for so long that its burning did not in any way affect the strength of Portsmouth's defences.

By this time, 1627, Buckingham had become interested in improving Portsmouth and, remembering what he had been told when he landed with the King after their travels in Spain, asked for an immediate estimate for the building of a new dock. It was as well for Portsmouth that Buckingham, whatever his faults, was an enthusiast. He ignored a letter from Sir George Blundell, who had come to Portsmouth with the soldiers, in which he described the port as 'a poor, beggarly place, where there is neither money, logding nor meat, and no man will lend a penny or give a soldier a meal'. He turned a deaf ear to Sir William Burrell, the Commissioner, who, having vested interests in Chatham, tried to quash the project for a dock. Burrell pointed out that recent storms at Portsmouth had done untold damage, and that the proposed site for the dock was totally unsuitable, but the Duke remembered that it was Burrell who insisted that the old dock should be filled in. Moreover, he had received a letter from Captain Richard Giffard, who was testing some new ships built at Chatham, in which he reported that the ships built by Mr. Burrell were not well found, and, indeed, one or two were not safe to put to sea. Burrell was undoubtedly feathering his own nest. Buckingham ordered the building of the dock to be put in hand.

The fear of invasion by Spain was never far from people's minds. On 30th May 1627, at Hampton Court, an urgent message from Portsmouth, reached the King and Buckingham. Seventy ships had been sighted off the Isle of Wight, and eye-witnesses judged them to be Spanish.

A second message, a few hours later, spoke of great ships, double-decked, and a third which arrived the following morning amplified the scare. In remarkably quick time riders alerted the whole of the south coast of England. Buckingham galloped all the way to Dover, and joined the active fleet lying in the Downs. The wind being in the east, Admiral Pennington soon brought the ships to Bembridge, only to find that the 'Spaniards' were Hamburghers and Hollanders laden with salt, awaiting a change in the wind. Buckingham was rowed ashore to the Camber in a long boat, and, borrowing the best horse, set out for Whitehall.

Early in 1628 Buckingham persuaded the King to let him try again to relieve the Huguenots at La Rochelle. It was not so easy this time to assemble a fleet manned by contented sailors and transports full of enthusiastic soldiers. The job was begun in a sullen mood by all, especially the rank and file, and when payment of the sailors was delayed by lack of ready money, they complained and worked slowly. Once again time was important, so the Duke decided to come to Portsmouth himself to speed things up, and arranged with Captain John Mason to stay at the Captain's house in the High Street. He brought with him the Duchess and a moderate staff of menservants, lady's maids and grooms. King Charles, wishing to be near his favourite, arrived at Southwick Priory. The King was accompanied by the whole retinue which he insisted on in his new rules for the court.

Buckingham's unpopularity had steadily increased since his first failure to relieve the Huguenots, and there was little doubt in the minds of those close to him that his life was in danger. Some time before coming to Portsmouth he had been given a 'supernatural' warning, but, though Buckingham was impressed, he took no practical notice. He may have been foolhardy, but he was also a brave man.

On the 6th June 1628 King Charles I had written to him:

I command you to send my army together to Portsmouth, to the end that I may send them speedily to Rochelle. I shall send after you directions how and where to billet them until the time when ye will be able to ship them; for the doing whereof this shall be your sufficient warrant, it being the command of

Your loving, faithful, constant friend,

Charles R.

The Petition of Right had just become law, and by it 'no man is forced to take soldiers, but inns, and they be paid for them'. This problem again fell on the shoulders of John Mason, who managed well, and was ready by early August with the soldiers all billeted near Portsmouth, their clothes for the campaign on board the respective transports, and their pay moderately up to date. Not so the mariners, however, and when, on the 17th August, Buckingham, having had a quick look round to see the state of the Fleet, decided to take coach to Southwick to see the King, about three hundred men appeared in the High Street opposite Mason's house, demanding their pay. One man loudly offered to pull the Duke out of his coach, but Buckingham was too quick for him. He leaped out of the coach, grasped the man, and hurried him into the house. Going out again, he addressed the men, who seemed moderately appeased. The Duke then drove off, but as soon as he was out of sight, the men threatened to pull down Mason's house unless the prisoner was released, so Mason let him go.

Five days later, the man was again arrested and brought ashore for trial. Having been condemned to death, he was on his way to the prison, which was at the southern end of the High Street, when a crowd of mariners tried to rescue him, but the Duke quickly called on some army officers who were riding with him, and drove the men at the point of the sword out of the town by the Point Gate. In doing so, they killed two and wounded a number of others.

Buckingham had enough trouble on his hands without the addition of the incentive which this man's presence in prison presented to the mariners, so the unfortunate sailor was taken immediately to the gibbet on the common and hanged; not, however, before the Duchess had pleaded with her husband, who, in fact, was not prone to hanging mutineers, but was certain that he must in this case maintain discipline. One of the difficulties was that in Portsmouth there were a number of

Frenchmen and some professional agitators inciting the mob against the expedition. Their task was to make the ignorant and simple sailors refuse to sail. So far, they had partly succeeded, as the majority of the men in the Fleet were by now totally misinformed as to the purpose of the expedition, and were rapidly becoming the dupes of these sedition-mongers.

That Buckingham's life was now seriously in danger was obvious, and it seemed equally obvious that he had most to fear from the sailors. In the event, he met his death at the hands of a disgruntled army lieutenant named John Felton, from Greenwich, the greater part of whose grudge was that he had been unjustly treated as regards promotion.

Felton, having decided to kill Buckingham, bought a dagger for tenpence, and made his way to Portsmouth, partly by horse and partly on foot. He arrived on the morning of 23rd August 1628. The Duke was having breakfast with Monsieur de Soures and Sir Thomas Fryer in the hall of John Mason's house. Monsieur de Soures, a Huguenot, was well acquainted with La Rochelle, and had advised on the planning of the first expedition. There was a good deal of coming and going, so the presence of a fairly well-dressed stranger aroused no notice. Both the Duke and Sir Thomas were keenly interested in the breakfast conversation and they, too, took no notice of a young man who walked in unannounced.

Breakfast over, the Duke moved to a passage, and Felton, waiting there, thrust the dagger into his heart. Buckingham staggered back to the hall, at the same time trying to pull out the dagger, but within a minute he collapsed and died. Hearing a cry, the Duchess came out of her bedroom and, seeing the Duke prostrate in the hall below, collapsed into the arms of her companion, the Countess of Anglesey.

For a time everything was confusion. Some people thought a Frenchman must have done the deed, others a sailor, and as they ran about looking for the culprit, Felton sat in the kitchen until, when the hubbub had died down, he calmly gave himself up. His reasons for his action he had pinned in his hat, as he had expected to be killed instantly.

Sir Thomas Fryer despatched a rider to Southwick with the news of the tragedy. His Majesty was in the private chapel at prayers. Against all precedent, a gentleman usher interrupted the King to tell him the news. King Charles received the message in silence, continued his prayers, and when he had finished, rose and went to his private apartments, where he remained without receiving anyone except his personal servants for two days.

Dudley Carleton, a member of the court, wrote the same day to Queen Henrietta: 'Madam. I am to trouble Your Grace with a most lamentable relation . . .'

But the country did not mourn. Buckingham's body was taken to London, where its progress was greeted by the people with unrestrained cheering. Felton was tried in London and hanged at Tyburn. Later his body was brought to Portsmouth and hung in chains from the gibbet where so recently the sailor had died.

Not long after, the Fleet and transports sailed, under the command of the Earl of Lindsey, who had been appointed by the King in place of Buckingham. Lindsey was a fine man, both sailor and soldier, intelligent and brave. Unhappily for him, on arrival at La Rochelle it was found that Richelieu had ordered a mole to be constructed across the harbour mouth. This precluded all hope of a successful attack and, while Lindsey was searching for a way round his difficulties, the Huguenots suddenly surrendered, so the expedition returned home.

John Mason continued on his steady course of serving his country whenever asked, and promoting his colonisation in the New World. When peace came in 1629, he took out a patent for lands bordering the Iroquois Lakes, and two years later joined with others in a patent for territory embracing part of the valley of the Piscataqua River.

By 1634 Mason's personal fortune had prospered considerably, and it was not surprising that he was appointed Captain of Southsea Castle and Inspector of Lights and Castles on the south coast. By now he had assumed the title of Vice-Admiral of New England, and had seen quite large numbers of settlers start out from Portsmouth for the New World and New Hampshire.

No doubt John Mason would have risen to a position of considerably greater importance if he had not died suddenly. His friendship with members of the court, particularly in the reign of King James I, and his respected position in the Council of New England, demanded something more than a burial in a small provincial seaport, so he was interred in Westminster Abbey.

As exploration and colonisation proceeded, a struggle developed between the maritime powers for trade with both the old and the new worlds. Charles I, realising that the safety of England's sea communications depended on her having a strong navy, planned to repair and rebuild the Fleet, which had been so neglected during his father's reign. To do this he needed money, and in 1634 he levied his ship-money tax on the ports. This was understood by those who lived by the sea, but when, a year later, the tax was extended to inland districts, some people refused to pay.

Charles and his Parliament were diametrically opposed to each other from the beginning of his reign. Between 1629 and 1640 the King carried on the government of the country fairly successfully without a Parliament, but he was eventually obliged to summon one on account of his financial difficulties. But by this time relations were naturally still more embittered, and the almost inevitable outcome was civil war. On the 10th March 1642 Charles sent the Queen out of the country and left his capital for York.

The first half of the year was taken up with preparations for war, and on 22nd August the King raised his standard at Nottingham. He was encouraged in this decision by the fact that Colonel Lord Goring, the Governor of Portsmouth, had declared for him on the 2nd of this month. The results of this declaration were very far from what the King might have hoped, for Goring was far from being an asset. It has been written of him that:

From first to last, devious uncertain and unprincipled, he shed disgrace upon the nobleness of his name, and upon the honourable profession of a soldier. This was the man that whom, on account of his private vices of drunkenness, cruelty and rapacity, and of his political timidity and treachery, scarcely anyone was more unworthy to be trusted with any important matters for counsel or execution.

Such criticism was well founded. Born in 1608, the son of the Earl of Norwich, Goring was one of a band of brilliant, prodigal courtiers. He had received ten thousand pounds from his wife and, having run through that sum, he obtained a further eight thousand pounds from other sources. When this was gone, he proceeded abroad to redeem his extravagance.

Through his friend Lord Wentworth he was given a senior position in the Dutch Army, during which service he was wounded in the ankle. Returning to England, he was made Governor of Portsmouth on 8th January 1638, and much enjoyed himself in riotous living with his friend Mr. Weston, Governor of the Isle of Wight, and brother of the Earl of Portland.

Goring was first and foremost a soldier, and as such he was determined to command the horse, whether of King or Parliament. Pursuing this policy, he had been a traitor to the King in 1641, when he betrayed the Army Plot to Parliament, while at the same time treating with King Charles. Parliament, feeling sure of him, gave him some thousands of pounds to improve the fortifications of Portsmouth and, concurrently, Queen Henrietta Maria handed him three thousand pounds and some valuable jewels to help him win over the garrison to the Crown.

Goring continued his double dealing during the early summer after the rupture between Charles and Parliament. While Parliament was moving troops into Hampshire, Goring mounted guns facing the land, and Colonel Norton of Southwick warned Parliament that he was not to be trusted. Goring countered this by going to London and making a brilliant speech in Parliament which so completely deceived the Members that they apologised for giving him the trouble of coming to Town, and promised him he would be appointed Lieutenant General of the Horse of the Parliamentary New Army. At the same time Goring informed the King that he would soon be in a position openly to declare for the Crown.

Parliament ordered Goring to London to receive his commission as Lieutenant General, whereupon he wrote what was described as 'a jolly letter', in which he said that he had received the command of the garrison of Portsmouth from the King, and could not absent himself from it without the King's leave. Hearing of this King Charles, presuming that Goring had laid in stores for a siege, decided on a premature move to begin hostilities, and sent the Marquis of Hertford and Lord Seymour to raise troops in the west.

When Goring finally and openly declared for the King, there were in Portsmouth three hundred soldiers, one hundred townsmen able to bear arms, and fifty officers, together with their servants. It was estimated that about a hundred men on

Portsea Island outside the town could fight. The total number of horses was not more than fifty. Goring mustered his forces on the bowling green. Any who showed Parliamentary inclinations were immediately disarmed. To strengthen his case, he showed that he had received nine thousand pounds from the Governor of the Isle of Wight to finance the defence. He sent twenty horsemen to Portsbridge to reinforce the half-dozen or so men stationed there. They took with them a couple of guns, and were covered from seaward by the pinnace *Henrietta Maria*. Goring ignored the dockyard, because its importance had been so reduced without the dry dock. Nearly all building was being done on the Thames. The number of shipwrights had fallen to under one hundred, and they were only on repair work.

During the next few days most of the Corporation took the oath for the King, but a large proportion of the meagre defence force contrived to escape. Goring had also told all women and children who feared a siege to quit the town, and many of them did so, not so much in fear of a siege as of the soldiers of the garrison, who were a base, undisciplined lot.

Dissatisfied with their pay and conditions under royal rule, the major part of the Fleet went over to the Parliamentary side. For the first time for years the men were now getting their pay promptly, the victuals had been greatly improved and clothing issued, whereas the King's service was associated with starvation and beggary, with putrid victuals and delayed wages.

On the 8th August five naval ships appeared off Portsmouth. These, which were the squadron commanded by the Earl of Warwick in the name of Parliament, severed all connections between Portsmouth and the Isle of Wight. This was a small but effective indication of the importance of sea power in the conflict now developing and, in fact, control of the Navy was one of Parliament's most important assets, specifically since it made it almost impossible for the King to get help from abroad.

On land, Colonel Norton raised a force of musketeers at Southwick, who effectively cut communications on the landward side.

On the 10th August Parliamentary forces under the command of Sir William Waller appeared at Portsdown, so Goring, realising he was late with his preparations for a siege, plundered

Portsea Island. One thousand cattle and over one thousand sheep were driven into the town. All bread and cheese was taken, and such bacon as could be found.

Communications with the outer world from Portsmouth had now become difficult. Nevertheless, some of the women and children who had stayed behind, but now wanted to get out of the town, found boats from the Earl of Warwick's squadron ready to ferry them over to Hayling Island. Much amateur intelligence work went on. Three women were arrested in a boat on its way to Stokes Bay, as they were thought to be men in disguise. This followed the arrest of a rustic on the Chichester road with a letter sewn into his boots, and the searching of a woman carrying a baby which turned out to be a doll with messages concealed in its head.

On the 12th August the Parliamentary forces made a sally against Portsbridge. This was not a large affair; twenty horsemen rode down the hill and charged the bridge, to find only eight troopers still there. Seven fled for their lives and one was made prisoner.

This opened up the way for the Parliamentary forces to cross to Portsea Island, and the honour of doing so first fell to Colonel Norton's men who, thus encouraged, advanced to the town wall and began a skirmish when they tried to burn the mill close by the Town Mount. They were driven off.

That night, the 15th August, long boats from the Earl of Warwick's naval squadron 'cut out' the *Henrietta Maria*, which had sought shelter under the guns of Portsmouth after the fall of Portsbridge. Her half-dozen guns were landed at Southampton, brought round by road, and mounted against the town. This so incensed Goring that he sent Lord Wentworth with sixty men to get them back, which they did very successfully.

By the 17th of the month there were two hundred and forty Parliamentary troopers on Portsea, supported by five hundred infantry. Even this number did not prevent the odd Royalist supporter getting into the town and one of these, a servant of Lord Wentworth, stated that the King was at Oxford with twelve thousand men, foot and horse. While this gave the garrison courage it was, in fact, entirely untrue, and some of the more discerning soldiers continued to desert.

The next day, the noise of many pick-axes could be heard on the Gosport side. This was a sure sign that a battery was being

G

mounted to support the two already on that side. Goring opened fire, which was returned, and much casual firing went on all day and into the night. To get a better idea of the effect of the night bombardment, Goring's own gunner went up to the parapet, taking with him a lantern. He was immediately shot.

Rather than let this affair develop into a real pitched battle, both Goring and Sir William Waller decided it would be best to talk things out at a 'parley'. Unfortunately, neither side recognised the bugle call, and Goring's men fired on the trumpeter. Fortunately this missed him, but the incident was sufficient to put an end to negotiations for the time being.

It took three more days to erect the new battery at Gosport, and its completion was celebrated by a bombardment of the tower of St. Thomas's Church, which was being used as a look-out station. One shot broke a bell, another fell into the church, and a third crashed through the bed of the miller in the water-mill nearby, his life being saved by the fact that he had got up unexpectedly early that morning because of the noise of the guns.

Following these exchanges, there was a short pause, until a drunken Parliamentary soldier advanced against the town single-handed, carrying a lantern in his hand. All the cannon on the north ramparts opened fire, but all missed, so the man continued his advance until he fell to musket shot. This incident seemed to touch the hearts of both commanders and, after much bugling on both sides, a parley was arranged. Goring said if he was not relieved by a certain date, he would be willing to hand over to Sir William Waller. For his part, Sir William demanded an immediate surrender. Goring flatly refused, saying he would hold out to the last.

Another lull followed, until Colonel Norton suggested to Sir William Waller that the attack should be shifted to Southsea Castle, and a decision was made to try and take it on the night of Saturday, 3rd September.

The castle was quite a formidable obstacle. It was surrounded by a wall twelve feet thick and about thirty feet high. There was a moat twelve feet deep and fifteen feet across. Besides the small arms fire power of the garrison, there were fourteen guns, all twelve-pounders. But if the castle were taken it would be a great blow to the hopes of Portsmouth, besides providing good accommodation for Sir William Waller and his officers.

Naturally neither the Governor of the castle, whose name was Chaloner, nor Lord Goring, knew of these plans, and in any case they had other interests. Although Chaloner was strongly suspected of being a Roman Catholic and not altogether seeing eye to eye with Goring on this matter, the two men had one thing very much in common, namely the enjoyment of an evening spent in a drinking orgy. It was therefore more than unfortunate that at midnight on Saturday 3rd September, Chaloner staggered across the common to his castle in a drunken state, and on arrival sank into a deep sleep which he hoped would carry him through until well into the late morning.

The besiegers—four hundred infantry and eighty musketeers —left their billets at 1 a.m. on the Sunday morning, carrying two dozen scaling ladders, and singing hymns. The Portsmouth garrison subjected them to random fire, but no one was hurt. At 2 a.m. the stormers halted two bow-shots from the castle, while a diversion was staged purporting to make the garrison of Portsmouth think there was to be a major attack on the town from the Gosport side. As soon as the diversion had begun, the storming party advanced to the beach in front of the castle and then got on the seaward side, the tide being very low at that time.

This was a well-thought-out manœuvre. As soon as the scaling ladders were in place, the musketeers entered the castle almost unopposed, and reached the drawbridge on the landward side. Not only were they surprised at their easy success; they had never realised that the garrison had been depleted by desertions to no more than twelve men.

Immediately a parley was sounded, but Chaloner, on learning what was happening in his castle, requested the attackers to come back in the morning, when he would be in better health to discuss the situation. However, guns were fired to signify the capture of the castle, and Goring in Portsmouth, now thoroughly roused, replied with a heavy bombardment which was utterly ineffectual.

The captors left eighty men in the castle and moved towards Portsmouth, where a mutiny had broken out among the garrison. By morning the Mayor and some of the officers had fled the town, and all but a few soldiers had laid down their arms. Goring, having seen some more batteries going up at Gosport, realised the opposition was too strong and sounded a parley. This he obtained by making it clear to the attackers that if they did not treat with him, he would blow up the magazines and everybody with them. Indeed, this threat enabled him to arrange his own passage to Holland, after he had disposed of his estates. In addition, Cavalier knights were to leave the town unmolested. All the garrison who wished to leave were to do so with free passes to anywhere except the Parliamentary lines, and these passes would cover a journey of up to twenty days. Goring then promised to leave the magazines untouched and that an amnesty should be granted to all except deserters from the Parliamentary forces.

When Sir William Waller inspected the town, he found far more provisions than he had expected, and it was clear that, with proper attention to military affairs, the town could have held out for weeks. Before leaving, Goring mounted the ramparts on the seaward side and threw the key of the town into the sea. It remained for the Earl of Warwick and his five ships to enter harbour, having fired scarcely a shot in anger.

The presence of Warwick's ships gave a true sense of power to the town. There was a new atmosphere of smartness and discipline about them which could be detected just by looking at the squadron as the ships entered the harbour and let go their anchors in the inlet between the town and the dockyard.

The Civil War developed slowly, with both sides gathering their forces. Lady Norton, a staunch Puritan, gave her son Colonel Norton practical as well as moral support. Defying all precedent, she organised a company of thirty maids, and with this force could be seen daily, digging additional defences at Portsbridge.

The attention Parliament devoted to the Navy and its activities was motivated by fear of the King's receiving foreign reinforcements; but the great revival could not have taken place had not the majority of the non-combatant servants at the Admiralty remained at their posts and served Parliament. Parliament set to with these officials to put right much that was wrong, apart from the better treatment of the sailors. There were, for example, hardly four hundred good trees in East Bere, from which forest Portsmouth now obtained much of the wood for building and refitting. Accordingly, timber was seized on the estates of Royalists, and very soon the dockyard was alive with activity.

No more fighting took place at Portsmouth, but three years later, in January 1645, Colonel Goring reappeared with a small force, intending to lay siege to Portsea Island from the landward side. However, he found the place far too well fortified and strongly manned to warrant operations against it; thanks, at least in part, to the energy of Lady Norton and her maids. Colonel Norton was made Governor later the same year.

In the period 1646 to 1648, between the end of the first Civil War and the beginning of the second, the Navy kept a close watch on the Channel, and maintained most of the old traditions. Once a fleet of fifteen Swedish ships, passing down the Channel, refused to lower their topsails to Captain Owen of the *Henrietta Maria*. He immediately attacked them and kept up a running fight until Captain Batten came up with reinforcements, whereupon the Swedes were overpowered and brought into Portsmouth. Their cargoes were sold, and the officers and crew shared one-third of the prize money, which totalled one hundred thousand pounds.

Meanwhile the King, having escaped from Hampton Court, was now close to Portsmouth in Carisbrooke Castle. His presence there and his eventual second escape in 1648 did not affect the town or the dockyard. When Charles lost the second Civil War a year later, and paid the extreme penalty of death in doing so, the people of Portsmouth heard of his execution without interrupting their daily work or showing any great feeling in the matter.

The future of the town and dockyard under the Commonwealth soon became clear. One of the first acts of the Council of State was to appoint Portsmouth's first Dockyard Commissioner. A certain Colonel William Willoughby was chosen, and directed on the 13th March 1649 to hurry to Portsmouth and get a fleet to sea to stop the marauding of pirates and rebels who were roaming the Channel.

Portsmouth's first Commissioner was born in the year of the Armada, the son of Christopher Willoughby, of Chiddingstone in Kent. In the year of Buckingham's death he was a purveyor of timber, and eight years later he had turned over to salvage, operating in the Thames. In 1643 he was captain of one of the Trained Bands, and a staunch supporter of Parliament. When in 1648 the second Civil War broke out, he was one of a committee appointed for two years to raise militia. He combined this duty with serving at times on the full Council of

War, and assisted in the arrangements to equip the Parliamentary Fleet.

When Willoughby was appointed to Portsmouth dockyard, Commissioners were also sent to the Thames yards. The appointment of dockyard commissioners marks an important stage in the rather complicated evolution of naval administration.

In the days of King John, William de Wrotham's title had been 'Keeper of the King's Ships', and, as this title implies, he had dealt with all that was necessary to equip the Fleet, while the King himself commanded at sea. By 1300, the title 'Admiral' had displaced that of 'Keeper', and was held by one of the great Officers of State. This officer did not necessarily command at sea as well, but if he did he was known as 'Captain and Admiral' while actually afloat.

In time the post of 'Admiral' increased in importance, and the holder became known as 'Admiral of England'. This continued until the time of Henry VIII, who decided that those holding the title of 'Admiral of England', and now sometimes styling themselves 'Lord Admiral' or 'High Admiral', were delegating too much work, whilst collecting a large salary. Nor were these gentlemen going to sea. He therefore ordered that the 'Lord Admiral' or 'High Admiral of England' should in future command at sea as well.

Having established this, Henry came to the conclusion that there must be someone ashore to carry on naval administration in the absence of the Lord Admiral. This man was called the 'Lieutenant of the Admiralty', or sometimes the 'Vice-Admiral of England'. In practice it was found that the Navy of the day had grown so large that the Lieutenant of the Admiralty could not manage by himself, and by the time Queen Elizabeth came to the throne a committee had been formed under this officer, the whole being known as the 'Principal Officers of the Navy'. This committee was soon to be known as the 'Navy Board'. There were four members: the Treasurer, the Comptroller, the Surveyor and the Clerk of the Ships, later called the Clerk of the Acts.

By 1627 the title of Lord Admiral of England had been enlarged to Lord High Admiral, the first holder who had these words written into his letters patent being the ill-fated Duke of Buckingham. During his particular term of office he both commanded at sea and, true to his character, took complete charge of the Navy Board.

When Buckingham was murdered, King Charles I decided there would be no single successor, and appointed a committee to execute the office of Lord High Admiral. From this decision evolved two separate bodies, a superior or directive body, the Commissioners of the Admiralty, representing the Lord High Admiral, and the Navy Board. Lastly, after the execution of King Charles I, Parliament renamed the Navy Board and called the members the Navy Commissioners. There were the two bodies, the Commissioners of the Admiralty and the Navy Commissioners, and William Willoughby was responsible to the latter.

Willoughby did a difficult job extremely well, never sparing himself. Constant streams of instructions flowed from the Navy Commissioners, and these he carried out to the letter and with great urgency. He also had his personal problems, and soon after his appointment pointed out to the authorities that he had nowhere to live. The Admiralty Commissioners told the Navy Commissioners to report on Willoughby's petition and the best way to accommodate him. Either a house should be built in Portsmouth on State land, or a salary be allowed for a house, and land for a garden plot. As a result, he was given a little close called Chapel Field, within the walls of Portsmouth, which was in the hands of Mr. Holt, the Navy Victualler, who was willing to move elsewhere.

Besides the ships for which he was directly responsible, Willoughby found that other ships escorting convoys in the Channel called in at Portsmouth for stores and victuals. Contractors, too, came to him with all manner of proposals, notably one John Smith, who wished to serve in all iron work 'above a tenpenny nail'. But Willoughby, a good commissioner, not only kept the iron work in the yard, but often handled other contracts himself, and was soon buying great masts of 166 hands and over from Percival Gilbert, a Hampshire merchant.

The commissioner's own notes paint a frightening picture of all he undertook. He records that he took on the task of Commissioner for Peace in the county of Hampshire, on the instructions of the Navy Commissioners, as they thought these powers would help him in his work. He notes that he put Captain Bawden in safe custody and committed him for trial, and placed other captured pirates in the county gaol. He chartered the *Patience* to carry treasure from Chester to Dublin, ordered new masts for the *Happy Entrance*, and ordered the *Leopard*'s rudder to be repaired at the next low tide. On top of all this work, ship construction was resumed in the yard. In 1650 the first *Portsmouth* was launched. She was four hundred and twenty-two tons, and ninety-nine feet long, and was built on the new slip which Willoughby had constructed in 1649, the first ship to be built in Portsmouth since the building of the *Jennet* of two hundred tons in 1539. Indeed, no ship of any real note or size had been built in the dockyard since the *Mary Rose* and the *Peter Pomegranate* in 1509.

No man, however robust, could stand this pace. Early in 1651, after only two years in office, Willoughby died, and was succeeded by Captain Robert Moulton.

On broader policy, the Commonwealth Council devoted large sums to the Navy by confiscating property from Royalists and by living on capital. For this they had good reason. Prince Rupert, the dashing Royalist cavalry leader, having failed on land, went to sea and took the few remaining Royalist ships to Kinsale in Ireland, whence he eluded the Commonwealth ships sent to destroy him. Moreover, war clouds were gathering, as it was clear that the Dutch would have to be challenged for supremacy on the high seas. To bolster the country's finance foreign trade was essential, and English merchantmen would have to be protected. Thus began the first Mediterranean Fleet and squadrons for the West Indies and North American waters.

During the Commonwealth the English fleets outnumbered those of all the combined European fleets, and never before in England had the combatant forces been better supported by the administration. Such a policy had far-reaching effects on Portsmouth. At last the days of being only an embarkation port and sometimes merely a repair yard or re-storing depot, came to an end.

Portsmouth's first two commissioners were destined to be short-lived in office. When Captain Robert Moulton accepted the position, he had the example of his predecessor, who exhausted himself in the space of two years. Moulton survived even less time, and died within twelve months. Portsmouth honoured these two dedicated men by erecting commemorative monuments in St. Thomas's Church.

Moulton was succeeded by Colonel Francis Willoughby, son of William. There was even more urgency about the work

Lord Howe receiving the sword from King George III (accompanied by Queen Charlotte) on board H.M.S. *Queen Charlotte* on his return to Portsmouth after the Battle of the Glorious First of June, 1794.

View of Portsmouth from Portsdown, 1723

Lord Nelson leaving the George Hotel to join H.M.S. *Victory*,
Saturday, 14th September 1805.

now, for war with the Dutch was not only plainly inevitable, but imminent.

War broke out in 1652. The Fleet was commanded by three generals at sea: Blake, Popham and Deane. During the year there were hard-fought battles with the Dutch under Tromp and De Ruyter, culminating on 30th November, when Tromp hoisted a broom to the masthead to signify that he had swept the English from the sea.

Portsmouth, together with the Thames dockyards, had been speedily stepping up its shipbuilding and expanding its store-houses, so that in February of the following year, 1653, when Blake re-challenged Tromp and De Ruyter off Portland, he now had a well-equipped fleet, and in engaging the enemy off the Dorset coast under a westerly wind, he knew he had an efficient dockyard under his lee. By the time the combatants, running before the wind, had sighted the Isle of Wight, Blake had captured seventeen men-of-war, fifty to sixty merchant-men, and taken fifteen hundred prisoners.

At this point Blake himself was seriously wounded, and also being short of stores and ammunition, came into Portsmouth with his damaged ships, his prizes and his prisoners. This set a major problem to the Mayor and burgesses. The sick and wounded on both sides were accommodated in private houses and beer halls. Over fifty surgeons were sent from London and the southern counties, and both trained and untrained nurses did their best in very difficult circumstances.

'The filthy nastiness of this place, unpaved, undrained and enduring an epidemic of smallpox,' wrote one surgeon, 'showed that Portsmouth had prepared for mending ships and replacing stores, but not for the human aftermath.'

Among those who came to Portsmouth to nurse the wounded was 'Parliament Kate', the Florence Nightingale of her day.

Blake himself remained some months before he could travel to his home in Somerset for convalescence. He stayed at the Governor's House in the Domus Dei, where he was joined for a few weeks by General Monk. Colonel Whetham was Governor of Portsmouth at the time, and he and Monk struck up a friendship. When Monk left to govern Scotland, he took Whetham with him, an association which had its repercussions in Portsmouth later on.

Portsmouth dockyard was now growing rapidly. Already orders had been given that one-third of the Navy was to be stationed there, and Willoughby found it necessary to have thirteen watchmen in the yard, which was only three less than Woolwich, although Chatham had thirty-two.

Two vital requirements were missing from the yard; a rope walk and a dry dock. Willoughby decided to tackle the easier of the two problems first, and set about organising a rope walk. He told the Navy Commissioners that he could now build twenty per cent more cheaply than elsewhere, and desired five and a half acres of land adjoining the dockyard to be purchased. He would use part of this for erecting a rope walk. He also wanted the whole dockyard surrounded by a brick wall, seventy-three perches in length. To both the first two petitions the commissioners agreed.

Though for some years past Portsmouth had had rope-makers plying their trade outside the dockyard, and inside it there were at least three ropers for mending cables and the tackle of ships, a proper yard for storing rope in the dockyard itself, and a rope walk, were now essential. Since 1645 James Barnes had leased a portion of land running from Wimbledon Mount to Four Houses Pond on the east side of the town, where he had a rope walk, and many communities in Hampshire had their own rope walks, but Willoughby was convinced that the Navy should no longer rely on these sources. Hitherto lack of manpower had been one of the stumbling blocks against erecting a rope walk in the yard, but Blake's victory off Portland had provided the county with plenty of prisoners.

Willoughby built two rope walks, three storeys high.[1] They were one thousand and ninety-five feet long and fifty-four feet broad, and ran alongside each other. Close at hand he built a house in which to keep the prisoners, and provided a bridge from the house to the rope walk. The bridge was necessary

1. Rope walk: The hemp from which the rope was made came from Russia, Italy or the New World. First it was hackled by combing it straight over a board studded with sharp steel teeth. A bunch or 'head' of this hackled hemp was then placed round the waist of a spinner, who attached a few fibres to a hook on the spinning-wheel. As the hook was revolved by means of a large wheel turned by hand, he walked backwards from the wheel, feeding the fibre from the supply round his waist. This formed a 'yarn'. The same process was then carried out with yarns, thus forming a 'strand', and finally a further repetition with strands completed 'laying a rope'.

The rope walk was so called because of the long walk the spinner and rope-makers made, going backwards all the time.

because it was laid down that no prisoner was to be allowed in the dockyard.

Throughout 1653 the war at sea went in favour of England, and Willoughby urged his men on to greater efforts. Shipbuilding was now the order of the day, and to meet all the requirements Willoughby constantly toured the yard, visiting every storehouse and loft. By now he had upper and lower storehouses, upper and lower hemp houses, a block loft, a ropemaker's house, an office, a nail loft, tar house, canvas room, hammock room, kettle room, iron loft, oil house, sail loft and a boatmaker's house. In addition, he had constructed permanent residences for the senior officials, such as the Master Attendant. But he still lacked what was perhaps the most important facility of all, namely, a dry dock, and began to petition the Navy Commissioners on this subject. Nevertheless he had to wait. Monk and Deane having won a victory at the Texel in 1654, in which Tromp lost his life, English supremacy at sea was acknowledged by the Dutch and the war came to an end. By now the Navy was costing the nation one million pounds a year, and the commissioners hesitated to go ahead with the dock, so it was another two years before the project, so often recommended in the reign of King Charles I, was approved.

On 18th August 1656 the Admiralty Commissioners finally gave the order to the Navy Commissioners for making a dry dock at Portsmouth to hold third- and fourth-rate ships. The cost was not to exceed three thousand two hundred pounds, the magistrates and inhabitants of Portsmouth having offered five hundred pounds towards defraying this. It was stipulated, however, that the order was not to be carried out until the five hundred pounds from the town had been produced.

From this date until the 8th March 1658, when it was completed, the construction of the dock underwent varying fortunes. The principal actors on the stage were Colonel Francis Willoughby, the Navy Commissioners, Captain Thorowgood, the Master Attendant, John Tippetts, the Master Shipwright, Nicholas Pierson, the Contractor, and his partner Benjamin Brewer. The Navy Commissioners and the dockyard officers let Pierson get on with the job without interference until 2nd May 1657, when they realised things were not going as well as they had expected. For one thing, all the shipwrights had been on strike for six weeks and Brewer was pressing to take charge himself, as he felt he could do better than Pierson, but Tippetts had no great opinion of Brewer, and wrote to the Navy Commissioners that 'they promise much and perform little'. Pierson tried to speed things up by paying extra money from his own purse, but there was another setback when Brewer was suddenly taken ill and died. Pierson suggested his foreman, Miles, should take Brewer's place and this was agreed, but now bad weather stepped in and held up the work, particularly on the foundations, about which Tippetts had no personal experience and was very worried. At long last Thorowgood was able to forecast that a ship could be docked in February 1658, but the job was not finally finished until March. Thus Portsmouth dry dock came into being, but not without labour troubles and a completion date months after the original timing.

Meanwhile, much else had happened in the wider sphere of things. England had gone to war with Spain in 1655, Blake had destroyed the Spanish treasure fleet at Santa Cruz, but had died as he was entering Plymouth with his captures and treasure. Most important of all, Cromwell had died, and had been succeeded by his son. To Willoughby this seemed a moment for stocktaking.

After all the shipbuilding, Cromwell had left 157 vessels, one-third of which were based on Portsmouth. Willoughby found he had in the yard 62 anchors, 498 masts, 70 cables, 508 loads of timber, $63\frac{1}{2}$ tons of hemp, 10,600 yards of made-up canvas and 7,650 yards on reels, 99 barrels of tar and pitch, and 2,020 hammocks. Under his conscientious eye the Fleet would not want. Little wonder that he needed the extra five and a half acres of land, and a wall to enclose the whole yard, besides the vigilance of thirteen permanent watchmen.

After the army under Generals Fleetwood and Lambert had taken control from Richard Cromwell and formed the Committee of Safety, the country was dangerously near being governed by the military. Some Members of the old Rump Parliament under Ashley-Cooper began to work for a return to Parliamentary rule. In this Portsmouth played a prominent part, for Ashley-Cooper regarded it as a suitable base for setting up Parliament. He felt that Colonel Whetham, the Governor and Member for Portsmouth, would support him. It was agreed that Whetham would hold the town on behalf of a Parliament as soon as it could be formed.

Ashley-Cooper's principal confederates, Sir Arthur Haselrig, Colonel Valentine Walton and Colonel Herbert Morley, arrived in Portsmouth on 3rd December 1659, and put up at the 'Red Lion', opposite St. Thomas's Church. With Whetham's help they cashiered all the army officers in the garrison whom they felt they could not trust, and then secured the loyalty of the ships in the harbour. With this success, Whetham proposed to Ashley-Cooper that a Parliament could be called at Portsmouth.

It would have been difficult for them to do this but for the help of the Vicar of St. Thomas's Church, Benjamin Burgess, and his curate, who had done splendid work among the sailors.

During Christmas and New Year 1659–60 a force numbering upwards of three thousand men, of which about one-third were cavalry, was formed in the town. Many of these men had defected from army troops sent to Gosport. Meanwhile, in London, Ashley-Cooper had found further support from dissatisfied soldiers and had occupied the Tower, so the Portsmouth contingent marched to London and billeted themselves in the Borough of Westminster and around Covent Garden.

However, by this time General Monk, Governor of Scotland, had seen that a speedy settlement must be made in the affairs of the country, and marched south with his army, arriving in London on February 11th, 1660. He took complete control, and a new Parliament was called which voted for the return of the Monarchy. Monk had been in communication with Charles II, who agreed to return and assume the Crown.

When Parliament met, Portsmouth's part in bringing about this momentous development was fully recognised with votes of thanks, particularly to Benjamin Burgess and his curate.

6

Pepys and the Shipbuilders

The Ipswich

On 25th May 1660 King Charles II landed at Dover, and England once again became a monarchy.

Portsmouth did not have long to wait before the first royal visit of the new reign. Early in the first week of January 1661 the Governor, Colonel Richard Norton, had notice from Hampton Court of the impending departure of the Queen Mother, Henrietta Maria, and the King's sister, Henrietta (Minette), for France. The Queen had crossed from France, accompanied by her daughter, in a vain attempt to prevent James, Duke of York, from marrying Anne Hyde, and now, her mission having failed, she was about to return to Paris from Portsmouth. Orders were given that the *London* should convey her across the Channel.

As soon as the news arrived, Colonel Norton and the Mayor, Richard Lardner, set both soldiers and civilians to work sweeping the streets. This was hardly a congenial task for January. But fortunately the weather was mild and their efforts were well rewarded when a rider, who had been sent forward when the Royal party reached Portsbridge, informed the Governor that the King himself had decided to view the departure.

All Portsmouth turned out to greet the King who, with his mother and sister, was received by the Governor, the Mayor, aldermen and burgesses at the Landport Gate. To the onlookers the retinue seemed very small, but at that time few of the nobility could spare the money to accompany their sovereign on every journey.

His Majesty rode ahead of the carriage carrying the ladies and, having accepted the keys of the town from the Governor, led the riders and carriages down the High Street. Turning left at the bottom, the procession arrived at the Governor's house in the Domus Dei.

This was on 6th January. Three days later the ladies boarded the *London*, and the King bade them goodbye. Slowly the *London* tacked her way out to Spithead, where an escort of frigates was waiting. Those watching from the shore began to drift back to their homes and businesses.

It was at this point in the apparently satisfactory culmination of the royal visit that the unexpected happened. Princess Henrietta had complained of feeling ill during the previous night, so the Queen Mother was anxious whether her daughter could stand the sea crossing. When the *London* reached St. Helens Roads, she asked the captain to anchor, as the Princess was undoubtedly worse.

The surgeon was called, and pronounced measles. What was to be done? The Queen Mother thought the best thing to do would be to go back to Portsmouth and accordingly the pilot, who was still on board, was summoned to take the ship back.

The tide was now running fast at the end of the ebb and the wind was light. To bring a first rate back to Portsmouth would be a difficult task. Foot by foot the heavy rope anchor cable was wound in by the capstan, sixty men heaving on the bars while the ship's fiddler rendered encouragement, and meanwhile sails were unfurled.

After an hour's hard work the anchor was aweigh, sails were set, and the pilot ordered the helm to be put over, but the *London* did not respond. Quickly boats were lowered to haul her bows round, but by now it was too late and the ship ran straight on to the Horse Sands, where she stuck fast, a position which could have proved dangerous. Happily, no one in Portsmouth realised what had happened until after the ship came off with the flood tide, and the court did not get the news until the 11th January, so there was no alarm ashore. After this anticlimax the Queen Mother decided to remain on board the ship until the Princess felt well enough to continue the voyage, which they did after spending a few days quietly moored in Portsmouth harbour.

That King Charles should have come to Portsmouth to see his mother and sister safely on their way was understandable in itself, but the King was also interested in his navy, and welcomed opportunitites to see his ships and dockyards, and test the efficiency of the administration. Already he had made a change in the latter by following his father's action in appointing a single Lord High Admiral, and abolishing the Commission of the Admiralty. The man he chose for this very important position was his brother, James, Duke of York.

His Royal Highness took the appointment seriously and went about his duties with a strong hand. He determined not only to fulfil his role of Lord High Admiral with complete authority over matters of strategy and planning, but he meant also to control, with a strong hand, the subordinate Navy Commissioners.

Of the four posts which made up this body—Treasurer, Comptroller, Surveyor, and Clerk of the Ships—the Duke considered he needed a particularly good man for Clerk of the Ships, and his mind turned to Mr. Pepys, secretary to Admiral Sir Edward Montagu. Pepys had accompanied the Admiral when the squadron went to The Hague to bring back the King, and the Duke, who had returned with his brother, had been struck by the efficiency and loyalty of the Admiral's secretary, and had gone so far on the voyage as to call Mr. Pepys by his name. Montagu did not stand in Pepys's way, and by the time when the *London* ran aground on the Horse Sands, Pepys had been appointed Clerk of the Acts. He carefully noted the incident of the measles, and the pilot's error, in his diary.

It was in his capacity as Clerk of the Acts, therefore, although suffering from a bad head on the morning after drinking the King's health on the night of the Coronation, Pepys 'had some thoughts to order his business so as to go to Portsmouth'. It was the 26th April 1661. Pepys decided to take his wife, and after picking up his great friend Mr. Creed, who had married Elizabeth Pickering, niece of Sir Edward Montagu, and a Mr. Hater, and their respective wives, he set out for Portsmouth.

They were in Petersfield by the 1st May, where Pepys secured the room used by King Charles when he came down to see his mother and sister sail for France. He was pleased about using the same room as the King, and then, on arrival at Portsmouth, added to his pleasure by putting up at the 'Red Lion' where, he noted, Haselrig and others had held council against the Army. Unfortunately the pleasure of this was partly damped because the lodgings at the 'Red Lion' were not, in his opinion, well kept.

Pepys was delighted when several officers of the dockyard took the trouble to call on him. He stood them drinks and they all got merry. The next day he and Mr. Creed walked the circumference of the town on the walls, returning to the 'Red Lion' in time to receive the official calls of all the principal officers of the yard. The little Clerk of the Acts was very flattered by the respect which each one paid to him. They then all walked to the yard, where Willoughby showed Pepys the dock and his storehouses. The Clerk of the Acts was much impressed, and invited the whole party to lunch at the 'Red Lion' where, he records, he gave them a very good meal.

After the meal, Pepys went back to the yard, this time by water, and there he supervised a sale of old stock and provisions. This done, the party was joined by their wives, and all went on board the *Montagu*, which Pepys thought a fine ship, and was greatly pleased at her being named after his late master. The whole party ended the day by returning to the town by boat and then walking up the High Street to see the house where Buckingham was murdered.

Next day, 3rd May, the official visit was over, but the Clerk of the Acts waited for a short while, walking up and down the town with Mr. Creed, because it was rumoured that there was a chance of his being made a freeman. The Mayor, however, had refused to allow this, so the party left for Petersfield. This time Pepys secured the room where the Queen Mother had slept on her way to join the *London*, and this touch of history again gave him pleasure.

Unlike most of the visitors to the town during the last three hundred years, he thought Portsmouth 'a very pleasant and strong place'. This condition was notably different from that of the previous century, because the Grand Jury of the Justices had sat twice a year since Queen Elizabeth had appointed them

H

in her charter of 1600. Not only the passage of time, but the authority of the Justices, greater than that of the Court Leet, had made Portsmouth 'a pleasant place'. During the sixty-two years of the century so far, the Justices had dealt with all manner of offences in this town, ranging from uncleanliness to the selling of beer without licences, failure to attend the court, and so on. No detail had been overlooked. In 1630 the Grand Jury had even turned its attention to parking offences, ordering that no one was 'to suffer their carts to stand in the street unless it be about their necessary business to the prejudice of the passing and repassing of Her Majesty's subjects through the streets'. A 'pain' of one shilling was imposed for the first offence of this nature.

The Justices concerned themselves with the safety of the young, and ordered the Chamberlain[1] 'to make a stone wall about the four house well to prevent children drowning'. The danger from fire also exercised their minds, particularly with gunpowder stored in the Square Tower. In 1656 the Grand Jury 'presented' John Lewyne for 'having his oven with a low chimney and laying a faggot pile and truss of hay adjoining it, to the danger of setting the Square Tower on fire'. Ordinary chimney fires were subject to fines of three-and-fourpence by day and six-and-eightpence by night.

As ever, some of the inhabitants rebelled against the law. In 1656 Mr. Nicholas Pierson and Mr. Ridge, who were selling wood under measurement, abused the members of the jury when they were checking up. Mr. Pierson said, 'You will be accounted for fools when you have all done,' and Mr. Ridge said, 'He valued them no more than the dirt on his shoe.' Both were fined twenty shillings. Two years later James Plover was 'presented' for annoying the churchyard with chamber pots, and later, on the subject of the church, and its services, John Fuzans, who owned 'The Man in the Moon', was 'presented' for having a fiddler playing on his instrument and other roistering and drinking on the Lord's Day. The information was given to the jury by the schoolmaster, Mr. Craxley. Seditious conventicles were greatly frowned on, and heavy fines imposed.

Almost a year passed before the Clerk of the Acts again came to Portsmouth. This time he was in a hurry because his late master, who had been created Lord Sandwich for his part

1. Town Treasurer.

in the Restoration, had sent him an advance message from sea that Charles II's future queen, Catherine of Braganza, would shortly be landing at Portsmouth.

Pepys never liked to miss a good show, and first of all he hurried to Whitehall to check the news. On the way in his coach he heard the bells ringing, but in Whitehall there was no news at all. However, he was determined to get to Portsmouth, and this time decided that no wives should accompany the party. Mrs. Pepys did not take kindly to this, but he persuaded her to stay behind. He then picked up Admiral Sir William Pennington and Sir George Carteret, Vice-Chamberlain to the King and Member for Portsmouth, together with their servants, Pepys bringing his own Will Hewer, his faithful clerk and personal attendant. All possible haste was made, so the party did not rest at Petersfield.

Unfortunately they met with some delay on the last stage of the journey. Pepys got hold of a countryman to guide them to Havant, to avoid going through the Forest of Bere, but the fellow lost his way. Nevertheless, they were in Portsmouth on the 23rd April, where Pepys put up at Wiard's, the Chyrurgeon's (surgeon's).

After breakfast on the 24th April, Pepys went to the Pay House, but, there being nothing prepared for him to see, he joined up with the others and all went to hear a lecture in St. Thomas's Church. Here they met the Duke of Ormond, Lord High Steward, and the Duke of Manchester, the Lord Chamberlain, together with a good many other people from London, all of them waiting for the arrival of the future queen. While remarking on this collection of important people from the capital, Pepys expressed his surprise that so few had made the journey. As it happened, those who had arrived were rather kicking their heels, as there was no news at all of the Queen. She was, in fact, in the middle of the Bay of Biscay, a very, very seasick lady.

On the 27th April Pepys joined a crowd of high-ranking people at the Domus Dei, where they saw the rooms which had been prepared for the arrival of the Queen. He thought them beautifully furnished, but heard that the whole place had only just escaped catching fire the night before. After looking over the royal apartments, Pepys attended a service in the chapel of the Domus Dei. He found it difficult, though, to keep away from his first love, the Navy and the dockyard, so as soon as the church service was over, he ordered a coach and went to the yard, where he boarded the *Swallow*. The ship was actually in the dry dock, but he found that in spite of this there was to be an evening service on board, so he remained for it. It was conducted by a naval chaplain, whose sermon, he thought, was 'full of nonsense and bad Latin'.

On returning to his lodgings, he saw people running to the sea front, and quickly joined them. It appeared that a ship had come in from Portugal and was securing in the Camber. Everyone thought there would be news of the Queen, but the excitement was short-lived. It was only a merchantman which had taken a cargo of horses to Portugal, and on the return voyage had put in to Portsmouth for provisions before going up Channel to London. The master knew nothing of the Queen.

Pepys did not allow this anticlimax to dampen his interest, so he called on the Mayor, Mr. Timbrell, who in fact was the anchor smith. Mr. Timbrell showed Pepys the present which the town was to give to the Queen. It was a salt cellar of silver with four eagles and four greyhounds bearing a tray on top. This he much admired, including the special case which had been made for it.

Two more days were spent waiting for news, but none came. Pepys might have been minded to go back to London that day, 30th April, but, after his midday meal, Mr. Stephenson, one of the burgesses of the town, called to inform him that the Mayor would like to make him a burgess. Pepys put on his best clothes, 'lined with silk', and arrived at the Town House, where he took the oath and shook hands with everyone. He then invited the whole assembly to join him in a drink at a nearby tavern. Later, he noted that becoming a burgess cost him 'one piece of gold to the Town Clerk, ten shillings to the Bayliffes, and the drinks in all came to five shillings'.

On the 1st May he felt he could not wait in Portsmouth any longer, and returned to London. Had he remained, he would have had to wait another fourteen days before the great event, which he would so dearly have liked to witness, took place on the shore at Portsmouth.

During the following week Portsmouth filled up appreciably. Among the new arrivals were the Duke of York and many members of the court. The majority were lodged at the Governor's house, the old Domus Dei. The arrival of the Duke was particularly important to Portsmouth, since His Royal Highness was governor of the town. He held this office from 1661 to 1673, an arrangement with a motive which was not generally known at the time. The fact was that the Duke was determined to remain loyal to his Roman Catholic faith, and, realising that this might be an embarrassment to him, and could cause civil strife, felt it wise to have under his jurisdiction a south coast port through which he could, if necessary, obtain help from France, or alternatively flee to the Continent. During this time there was always a resident lieutenant governor, and in 1662 this post was held by Sir William Berkeley.

Almost the last arrival of importance was the Bishop of London, who was to marry the King and Queen. (Long before her arrival in England, Catherine of Braganza had been referred to as 'Queen', although she was not yet married to King Charles, or crowned.)

Meanwhile Lord Sandwich, in his flagship the *Royal Charles*, an eighty-gun ship built by the Commonwealth and named the *Naseby*, but re-christened after the Restoration, had sailed from Lisbon with the Queen on board, escorted by a fleet of fourteen ships. The actual date of departure was Monday, 15th April 1662, and on that date the Admiral wrote in his diary:

By 6 o'clock in the morning we weighed anchor, the wind at N.W., and got out of the river to sea; as I passed by the Castles the Queen commanded me to loose the Standard, which was done. As soon as we were out at sea the Queen and all the ladies were seasick.

Lord Sandwich was glad to be on his way at last. Four weeks of negotiation over the marriage portion, mingled with elaborate festivities, dinners and conferences with the King and Queen of Portugal, together with their ministers, had exercised to the full the Admiral's diplomacy and charm, but had been difficult at times and given him many moments of anxiety.

Rough seas now added to the delay. Already the ladies were incapacitated, and there was worse to come as the Bay of Biscay behaved traditionally. Lord Sandwich logs on the 19th April:

Wind at N.N.E. fresh gale. Having tacked to and again the last 24 hours, at noon we were where we reckoned last noon.

Fast frigates were sent to England to tell of the delay. Then, on the 6th May, Lord Sandwich 'turned up within 2 leagues of St. Michael's Mount at 7 o'clock at night and there we came to anchor'. Colonel St. Albans came on board and brought a present of fresh provisions for the Queen.

His Royal Highness, the Duke of York, had not waited all this time in Portsmouth. Wearing full dress and attended by members of the court, he had boarded his special barge and joined his yacht *Anne* at Spithead, whence, escorted by four frigates, he had sailed to the west to meet Lord Sandwich. Among those who accompanied him in the *Anne* were the Duke of Ormond, Lord High Steward, the Earl of Suffolk, the Earl of Chesterfield, and other courtiers.

On Sunday, 10th May, in calm weather, the topmasts of the *Royal Charles* and Lord Sandwich's fleet were sighted, and in the afternoon the meeting took place in Torbay. Salutes were fired and then the Duke placed his yacht on the quarter of the *Royal Charles* and the whole fleet proceeded up Channel.

Next morning, His Royal Highness boarded the *Royal Charles* and met the Queen for the first time. Contact having been made, the Duke of Ormond went ahead in a faster ship, so as to be at Portsmouth to greet the Queen on landing. His Royal Highness meanwhile continued to sail his yacht on the quarter of the *Royal Charles*, and visited the Queen each day.

On the night of Tuesday, 13th May, Lord Sandwich brought his fleet to anchor in St. Helens Roads off the Isle of Wight. It had been a long and tedious voyage, and although the young queen was still suffering from days of seasickness, at least all were safe and sound at their destination. The Navy had done its part well in difficult circumstances. Next day, the 14th, the Fleet again weighed anchor, and in majestic order came to anchor at Spithead at two o'clock in the afternoon.

Now came the great moment. Decks had been scrubbed, clean flags hoisted, sails perfectly furled on their yards, and boats' crews dressed in their best. Shortly before four o'clock a barge from the Duke of York's yacht called alongside the *Royal Charles*. Her Majesty, accompanied by Lord Sandwich and senior officers, was rowed to the yacht, which was already under way, and were taken on board. Immediately, the guns of the Fleet fired a royal salute. It was a lovely spring afternoon, with the sun shining and a light breeze perfect for the yacht. Helped by the last of the flood tide, the master brought his ship to anchor just off the Town Gate.[1]

The scene ashore was brilliant. Everywhere flags were flying, and on the foreshore under the battlements of the Round Tower, Platform and Square Tower, there were drawn up companies of soldiers in bright uniforms, while on the special landing-stage the Duke of Ormond, the Duke of Manchester, lords and ladies, the Mayor and burgesses, and representatives of the dockyard awaited their queen.

All was quiet as the royal barge crossed the short distance from the yacht to the Sally Port, but as the bows touched land another royal salute sounded, this time from the ramparts. Catherine, escorted by His Royal Highness and Lord Sandwich, stepped ashore. She was dressed in English clothes, as a compliment to her new country. Accompanying the Queen were two elderly ladies of the highest rank, six noble young ladies, maids of honour, and six chaplains. In a second boat were four bakers, a perfumer and a barber. But this was by no means the whole suite, which consisted of over one hundred persons.

Catherine listened with dignity to the address of welcome, and then passed through the Point Gate and entered a gilded State coach. The Duke of York and Lord Sandwich took their places ahead and walked in front of the coach as the Queen made her first journey in her new country. She had not far to drive, which was just as well, because she was still very weak from so many days of seasickness, and in a few paces she was entering the gate of the Governor's house. Catherine was received by the Countess of Suffolk, principal Lady of the Bedchamber, and her maids of honour, and taken immediately to the specially prepared Royal apartments and put to bed. From her bed, Catherine sent a message to the King at Whitehall.

That evening the bells of Portsmouth rang out a welcome, and bonfires were lit in celebration. Similar bell-ringing and lighting of bonfires went on in London and other large cities. As for the King, if Pepys who loved a scandal is to be believed, he supped that night with Lady Castlemaine, who was expecting his child. But Charles' failure to meet his bride may well have been because he had much to do. Parliament had to be

---

1. This description probably means the Point Gate—a gateway in the battlements to the east of the Platform and Square Tower.

prorogued, Orders in Council signed, and much else seen to
before the King could devote all his time to his wedding and
the festivities which would follow at Hampton Court.

In Portsmouth, Officers of State and local officials alike were
worried by the absence of the King, but on the third day after
her arrival, Catherine, while still resting from the strain of the
voyage, showed symptoms of a sore throat and fever. This
made the King's absence easier to bear.

Charles left Whitehall in great haste on the 19th May,
accompanied by Prince Rupert and a very large court. They
arrived at Kingston-on-Thames at ten o'clock, where they
changed horses. At this point the King entered Lord Chesterfield's coach and, together with troops of the Duke of York's
bodyguard and the Life Guards, galloped to Guidford, where
they arrived at midnight. Next morning, after a short night's
rest, the whole party set off again at a great pace, and arrived
at Portsmouth at two o'clock.

The King went straight to his apartments in the Governor's
house, where he changed out of his travelling clothes into his
formal attire. Then, accompanied by the Portuguese Ambassador, and Prince Rupert, he entered Catherine's chamber.
The bride, a little, solemn, dark-eyed creature noted for her
lovely hands, received them from her bed. It was immediately
arranged that the marriage should be put off for twenty-four
hours, until the Queen felt better. This suited the King, who
was very tired. Next morning, at eight o'clock, he wrote to
Lord Clarendon:

It was happy for the honour of the nation that I was not put to
the consummation of the marriage last night, for I was so sleepy,
having slept but two hours in my journey. . . .

That day, Wednesday, 21st May, the weather was again
perfect, and in the morning, to please Catherine, she and
Charles were married first in a secret ceremony in her bedroom with Roman Catholic rites. They then moved to the
Great Chamber, where the official Protestant ceremony took
place. It was necessary to use the Great Chamber, since the
Governor's Chapel was much too small to accommodate all
the nobles, courtiers, clergy and retainers who had to be
present.

It was about noon when the King and Queen came into the

Presence Chamber, and sat on two thrones specially made for the occasion. They were accompanied by the Bishop of London, the Marquis de Sande, and Sir Richard Fanshawe, the ambassadors to the two courts. A rail separated them from the rest of the company. The contract, formerly made with the Portuguese Ambassador, was then read in English by Sir John Nicholas, and in Portuguese by the Portuguese secretary, de Saire. After this, the King took the Queen by the hand, and, both standing, said the words of matrimony appointed in the Book of Common Prayer. Lord Sandwich then records:

The Queen also declaring her consent, the Bishop of London stood forth and made the declaration of matrimony and did pronounce them man and wife in the Name of the Father, the Son, and the Holy Ghost.

Following this, the Queen removed the ribbons which she was wearing, and instructed that they were to be cut into little pieces so that everyone present might have a memento of the occasion.

Although the date was most certainly 21st May 1662, the marriage register was wrongly recorded with the date as 22nd May. It reads:

Our most Gracious Sovereign Lord, King Charles II, by the Grace of God, King of Great Brittaine France and Ireland, Defender of the Faith, etc. and the most illustrious Princess Donna Catarina, Infanta of Portugal, daughter of the deceased Don Juan the fourth, and sister to the present Don Alphonso, King of Portugal, were married at Portsmouth, on the two and twentieth day of May, in the year of our Lord God, 1662, being in the fourteenth year of His Ma'sties reign; by the Reverend Father in God Gilbert, Lord Bishop of London, Dean of the Chapel Royal, in the presence of several of the Nobility of His Majesty's dominions and of Portugal. Anno 1662.

The King and Queen spent the first days of their honeymoon in Portsmouth, lingering there while carriages and carts were organised to convey Queen Catherine's train of young ladies. The Portuguese had also landed a number of very pious monks, each of whom had brought some of his relations, and no provision had been made for these extra people, either at Portsmouth or at Hampton Court. Eventually, however, on the 27th May, the whole cortège, with their escorts and baggage, trundled down the High Street and out of the Landport Gate to make their way along the Portsmouth road to London.

As the sentries on the walls abutting the gate watched the last of the carts and the rear mounted escorts fade into the distance towards Portsbridge, Portsmouth seemed suddenly to have lost half its population. It had been a week of glamour and excitement unequalled in any other seaport except London. Now, with the departure of the King and his bride, the town, and more especially the dockyard, once again settled down to its real task, that of building and equipping the major portion of the Fleet.

For some time Francis Willoughby had been thinking of returning to the family home in Massachusetts, and he intended, when the new régime at Whitehall had settled down, say in a year's time, to ask for a relief. Accordingly, late in 1662, the Navy Commissioners began looking round for a new commissioner for Portsmouth Dockyard. Their choice fell on Colonel Thomas Middleton.

When Middleton took over in 1664, he found himself almost immediately involved in fitting out ships for the second Dutch War, but his worries were far less than those of his predecessors, as they had done a first rate job, and the yard was well stocked with stores and provisions, and worked efficiently. He was lucky in having as master shipwright John Tippetts, whose knowledge and ability compared well with the famous Pett Brothers of Woolwich and Deptford.

At first the war went well. It had begun through our seizure of New Amsterdam, which Portsmouth people were pleased to hear had been renamed New York, after their governor. The first battle with the Dutch, off Lowestoft, showed that the English Fleet was a fair match for them. Middleton, therefore, was able to turn his attention to more domestic matters. Of these, two particularly worried him, and he wrote to Pepys about them both. The first concerned a fire in the dockyard:

23rd March 1665.

Sir,

I question not but you will heare from severall the sad news that happened in the King's yard this nyght, and with all the mercy which God hath bestowed on us that the mischief was noe greater.

Mr. St. John Steventon's wife being in her tyme a deboosh drunken woman, such a one as I can believe she hath not left behind her, rose from her husband in the night, or rather towards day, goeth down stayers, lyteth a candle, and withall being exceedinge drunke sat in a large wicker chayre which was set on fyre, wheare she was burnt to ashes. The house excaped, which had it taken fyre, would have burnt ships in docke, storehouse and whatnot. The mantelletre of the chimney took fyre, but day being at hand, people stirringe, was quenched. It happened at lowe water, and noe water in the yard considerable to put out fyre if it should happen, which hoope will be considered of.

Pepys took the most sensible action and wrote back telling Middleton to buy a fire engine for twenty pounds. Encouraged by this, Middleton waited a suitable period and put in his second letter, which he wrote in August of the same year.

Sir,

For my part to you as frinde I declayn I intend not to make Portsmouth my habytation if I can avoid it. TIS TREW if the King command me to live underwater if it weare possible I must and would do it, I shall not live heare for the rent of Hampsheare. To tell yow of the strayght I have been put to sence my comynge to Portsmouth for my accommodation would be to small purposes but that I have a boddy that can indure any things I hadd been dead. Wheare I now am wee are forced to packe nyne people in a roome to sleepe in, not above 16 foot one way and 12 foot the other. Wee are 26 in famyly, in the Mayoures house, nyne of which are small children. What comfort can a man have in such a condition soe being together.

Once again Pepys did the sensible thing. He authorised Middleton to build a house for the Commissioner in the dockyard, and by 1666 this was completed. It stood close to the rope house.

Meanwhile Middleton had by no means neglected his other duties. He foresaw that the Dutch might attack Portsmouth, and told Edward Silvester, the Gosport blacksmith, to make 'one Substantiall chaine to replace the one made in 1522 for blocking the entrance to the harbour'. In the light of subsequent events on the Thames, this was a most timely measure.

Others, too, were keeping an eye on Portsmouth and her ships, not the least of them the King himself. A fortnight before Mr. Steventon's wife had been burnt, the King had again come to Portsmouth. His suite found the place 'cold and unwholesome', but there was business to do 'to give all necessary orders for the advantage of the great Enterprise now in hand'.

His Majesty visited the *Catherine*, the *Charles*, the *James*, the *Triumph*, the *Resolution*, the *Royal Prince* and the *Royal Oak*. He went twice to the *Royal Oak*, and ended up in the *Henry*, where he had dinner with Sir George Askew, her commander. Wherever the Sovereign went he was warmly greeted, and he greatly raised the morale of the Fleet. He was sincerely delighted with all he saw, and particularly with the *Royal Oak*. This ship had been built at Portsmouth by Tippetts, whom he ordered to build another exactly the same, because he thought the design and workmanship could not be improved upon.

Among other high-ranking people who were to be seen in Portsmouth at these times was Lord Sandwich, by now a beloved figure commanding the respect and devotion of all whom he met.

Although the King's retinue had thought Portsmouth 'an unwholesome place', it had been free of any major epidemic for some years. But when news reached the town that plague had broken out in London, the inhabitants offered special prayers that they might be spared a second visitation. It was therefore with some alarm that, in the summer of that year, 1665, they heard that the King and his court were coming to Portsmouth. They feared that some member of the court would surely bring the infection.

When he came, King Charles, as a measure of his concern, gave orders for pest houses to be built, so that any infection could be quickly isolated. He also ordered some wooden houses to be converted to stone, to reduce the danger of fire. This forethought impressed the people of Portsmouth, and they felt less disturbed about the future.

It was perhaps typical of Pepys's courage that he found no excuse to leave plague-ridden London by visiting Portsmouth, as he might easily have done. He remained at his post in the capital throughout the epidemic of the plague.

Portsmouth was not to be spared however. When the *Essex* came up harbour, with some men aboard her suffering from this dread disease of the plague, the situation was realised too late to stop the sailors landing, and in no time the worst happened. Quickly the pest houses were brought into use, but it was not long before fifteen people were dying every day.

This looked like another shattering blow for the town, but miraculously the epidemic ceased almost as abruptly as it had begun.

During these anxious days the war had still to be fought. Middleton's fears of a Dutch attack on the town were not unheeded, and in 1665 an expert in defences was called in to make a plan to improve those at Portsmouth. This man was Sir Bernard de Gomme. Curiously enough, he was of Dutch extraction, and had specialised in town fortifications, having erected a number in Flanders. Some of his work was entirely new in ideas, and these he brought to Portsmouth. Unlike Popynjay in Queen Elizabeth's time, he had a better labour force recruited from the Dutch prisoners of war, so that he completed his work within fifteen years. In this time he fully compassed the town with defence walls, dug a properly constructed moat, and at the Landport Gate built a defensive ravelin[1] with two bridges, making assault on the town from the landward side extremely difficult. The corner bastions were also strengthened, and all the strategic gun emplacements were made to last and take the weight of the guns. The Platform looked like a broadside of a first rate man-of-war.

Not only did de Gomme's work make Portsmouth a properly defended town for the first time in its history; he also included the dockyard, the Portsbridge and Gosport in his plan. The King came to see the work when it was half completed, and was greatly impressed. De Gomme did not have an entirely free hand, for a commission was formed to supervise the work and see that it was carried out in reasonable time. Sir William Berkeley, the Governor, headed the commission, and was assisted by Sir Philip Honeywood as his deputy, with five others under them. To complete the work two forts were built, Fort Charles on the Gosport side on the mainland, and Fort James on one of the islands slightly up harbour.

Just when the work on the fortifications was beginning, Middleton moved to the Admiralty. His successor was an obvious choice, namely, Mr. John Tippetts. Now Portsmouth had as her Dockyard Commissioner one of the great master shipwrights of the century. But Tippetts was a worried man, because the war was going badly, and his fears seemed justified

---

1. An outwork in fortifications consisting of two faces which formed a salient angle constructed beyond the main ditch. From it flanking fire could be directed at attackers trying to cross the ditch.

when, in 1667, the Dutch Admiral, de Ruyter, appeared off the Isle of Wight with a fleet. De Gomme's defences were still only half completed, and Portsmouth had no fleet of sufficient size to challenge the enemy. There was nothing to stop de Ruyter coming up to Spithead and perhaps even attacking Portsmouth itself, except the sandbanks, knowledge of which was fortunately scanty to the Dutch. To the great relief of all, de Ruyter sailed away. Not long afterwards news came that de Ruyter had been up the Thames, and even as far as Chatham. Among the ships burnt was the *Royal James*, while the *Royal Charles*, the very ship which had brought Queen Catherine to England, had been captured in the entrance to Chatham and taken to Holland.

Fortunately for England, a peace was concluded on account of the increasing Dutch preoccupation with the land war in the Low Countries, and they were glad to end the fighting on the high seas.

In Whitehall, the fury of Parliament with the misconduct of the war led to changes at the top, and the new Ministry, the 'Cabal', negotiated the Triple Alliance between England, Holland and Sweden against France. Pepys was delighted, but little did he know that King Charles was at that very moment negotiating the Secret Treaty of Dover. In this treaty the King, who was desperately short of funds, promised his cousin, King Louis XIV, that in return for a large annual payment he would join the French in an attack on Holland, declare himself a Roman Catholic, and re-establish the Roman Catholic Church in England. He obtained the help of Minette, his sister, who had married King Louis' brother, to arrange the signing of the treaty.

Meanwhile at Portsmouth, Tippetts, who had the same sort of clear-headedness as Pepys himself, used the intervening years to fill the slips of the dockyard with ships under construction. The biggest ship, destined to be a flagship, was the new *Royal James*, to replace the one burnt by de Ruyter at Chatham.

In the summer of 1671 the King, always with his heart in naval affairs, and still smarting under the disgrace of the Thames raid, came again to Portsmouth to inspect the dockyard. He had with him the Duke of York and Prince Rupert, together with a large number of high-ranking nobles. After the inspection, the King took leave of the Governor, Sir Philip Honeywood, and Mr. Tippetts, and went over to the Isle of

Wight, where he and his entourage were dined by the island's governor, Sir Robert Holmes. They then embarked in the royal yacht and, escorted by the frigates *Foresight*, *Diamond*, *Swallow*, *Assurance* and *Greenwich*, sailed down the Channel to Plymouth to inspect the port and naval ships there. 'This way of travelling is new for Kings', as the Earl of Arlington remarked in a letter, adding, 'I hope God will bless him for it.'

The following year, 1672, Anthony Deane, master shipwright, took over Portsmouth from Tippetts. Never can there have been a period when the dockyard was better served with commissioners of the highest ability. When Deane took over, Tippetts had begun to build a replacement for the second royal ship, the *Royal Charles*, and Deane put everything into the completion of this ship.

This period of respite from war was ended this year by King Louis, who attacked Holland on land. King Charles, who was by now following a foreign policy of his own, contrary to that of his Ministers but true to the Secret Treaty of Dover, also declared war on Holland.

Foreign affairs were sufficiently puzzling at this time even to Ministers in Whitehall, and few people in Portsmouth could understand them at all. They had thought they were allied to the Dutch, but now they were at war against them again, and allied to the French. This fact was clearly brought home by the sudden arrival at St. Helens of a very strong French squadron of thirty-two ships of the line and eight fire-ships under their famous admiral, the Comte d'Estrées, Vice-Admiral of France. With him was Admiral Duquesne, a firebrand known to every sailor.

Colonel George Legge, who had just relieved Sir Philip Honeywood as lieutenant governor, sent a messenger to Hampton Court at breakneck speed. The King did not delay. Gathering all the great officers of his household, he rode to Portsmouth in considerable haste.

The 4th May 1672 was long remembered in the town. The King arrived between two and three o'clock in the afternoon, and immediately the Vice-Admiral of France, attended by several high-ranking officers, came ashore. They were greeted by the royal party in the Governor's House, where the Comte d'Estrées kissed hands. After a short discussion, the French took their leave and entered their boats at the Camber. Most people thought they would return to their ships, and they looked as though they were going to do so, but instead the boats suddenly turned and went up harbour to the dockyard. Nothing had been said about this at the meeting, so there was a dash to the yard in the King's barge, which fortunately was in the Camber at the time. The rest of the afternoon was spent touring the yard with the Frenchmen, who were duly impressed by all they saw, as were the royal party, particularly with the new *Royal Charles*, still on the slips. Meanwhile some lesser local officials had contrived to visit the French ships and, when they landed, were able to tell the King a good deal about them.

Next morning the King sailed out towards the French fleet, which had moved to Spithead. On anchoring they had saluted the town, and now they fired twenty-one guns for the King. The fortress of Portsmouth replied on both occasions. King Charles then visited the *St. Philip*, the *Terrible* and the *Superbe*, spending three hours in all with the Frenchmen.

That evening, they all dined at the Governor's House and then walked on the Platform, from which vantage point they saw, rather to their surprise, the English Fleet coming over the horizon. The Fleet had come from the Nore with a good north-easterly breeze behind them, and had made a first-class passage. Ahead of the Fleet was a frigate, from which Captain Killigrew landed and informed the King and the French admiral that the Duke of York wanted to rendezvous next morning. D'Estrées agreed with this if the wind was fair.

Although the wind blew hard during the night, by morning it was only fresh. The King was up early and, boarding his yacht the *Cleveland*, sailed out to view the meeting of the two fleets. This spectacular conjunction took most of the day. There were salutes, an exchange of visits of the Admirals, and the manœuvring into position. By nightfall the combined fleet —sixty-five English men-of-war with twenty-two fire-ships, and the thirty-two French men-of-war with eight fire-ships— had taken up their appointed stations and were over the horizon on their way up Channel through the Straits of Dover and into the North Sea in search of the Dutch. The King and his court, exhausted by the events of the last forty-eight hours, returned to Hampton Court in easy stages.

There were twenty-three thousand five hundred and thirty officers and men in the English Fleet, and of these many came from Portsmouth and Hampshire. Anxiety now filled the hearts of the inhabitants for their husbands, brothers and sweethearts, for fights with the Dutch were grim affairs, and no one quite trusted the French.

One man was particularly in the minds of all, namely, Lord Sandwich. Respected and well known in Portsmouth, the Second-in-Command would never spare himself in battle, and people had a curious feeling that they might not see this great and beloved figure again, walking with dignity down the High Street. On board the *Royal James*, Sandwich himself experienced a premonition that he, too, would not see Portsmouth again. Anthony Deane's thoughts were more for the ships; at least the *Royal James* could stand a hammering, and so could any of the ships built by him and Tippetts. The other royal ship, the *Royal Charles*, was still fitting out, and he regretted that he had not been able to complete her in time.

The Battle of Solebay was fought on the 28th May 1672 off Southwold on the Suffolk coast. News took some time to travel, but early in June the story came through. Sandwich had been killed; the *Royal James* burnt to the water-line; the Duke of York had changed his ship four times, but was safe. The Dutch, having had enough, had retired to Holland, and the English Fleet to the Thames.

Everyone wondered what part the French had played in the battle. It was weeks before it was fully realised that D'Estrées, for reasons which have been argued over ever since, went off on a different tack from the Duke of York and Sandwich, leaving the English to take the weight of the Dutch Fleet's attack.

No wonder the losses were so great. Rumour had it that neither side would continue the war and Portsmouth men, who were tired of fighting the Dutch, could not have been more thankful when the rumour proved to be a fact. While mourning the loss of so many brave men, the death of Sandwich was felt deepest of all, and Portsmouth knew the country had suffered a loss which would be difficult to replace.

It had taken three first rates and four fire-ships to subdue the *Royal James*, so Anthony Deane decided there was no need to alter the construction plans of the *Royal Charles* and he would lay the keel of the next *Royal James* as soon as possible.

The Secret Treaty of Dover and the subsequent indecisive Battle of Solebay spelt the beginning of the end of the Stuarts. Parliament brought in the Test Act, thereby depriving the Duke of York of his position of Lord High Admiral and

I

Governor of Portsmouth. The internal struggle between Protestants and Roman Catholics entered its last phase.

With the end of hostilities, the King decided to honour Portsmouth in a way which was peculiar and certainly unexpected. In 1673 he created Louise de Querouailles[1] Duchess of Portsmouth, and added for good measure the titles of Baroness Petersfield and Countess of Fareham. This lovely little Bretonne had waited on Minette, the King's sister, and the Queen had offered to make her a Maid of Honour. She was King Charles' only link with his beloved sister in France and her friendship with the King was much encouraged by the French Ambassador, who saw in it possibilities far greater than the personal contact with the King's sister. King Charles gave her apartments in Whitehall, paid her card debts, and set every tongue wagging.

In 1675 the new *Royal James* was ready to be launched. This ship would join the *Royal Charles*, which had left the slips two years earlier. The King wanted to be there for the launching and, once again deciding to go by sea, set off in a squadron from the Thames. Unfortunately the prevailing south-west winds blew steadily up the Channel, and the ships had to tack laboriously against it.

At Portsmouth both Tippetts and Deane, the *Royal James*'s designer and builder, waited anxiously. The new Commissioner, Sir John Kempthorne, a son of Portsmouth with a splendid war record, consulted with them as to what they should do. Tides would not wait, and after letting two spring high waters go by, they decided they must launch the *Royal James* without the King. They did so, and two days later the royal squadron arrived at Spithead.

The King, being perfectly familiar with the ways of the sea and ships, was delighted to hear of the decision to launch, and that all had gone well. He inspected the *Royal James* from truck to keel and, as ever with the work of Deane and Tippetts, was extremely pleased. When the party returned to the Governor's House, the King knighted both the master shipwrights, which was a fitting reward for their skill and services to their country.

1. Louise Renne de Penancort Keroualle was born in 1649, and died unmarried in 1734. Her name has been written, Keronal, Keroch, Queroual, and in English is normally written Querouailles. (*The Complete Peerage*, page 607).

In 1683 the Duchess of Portsmouth decided she ought to see her town. As the King was going to Southampton, whence he would make a trip in his yacht, arrangements were made for Madame de Querouailles to meet him at Portsmouth. In due course the King embarked at Southampton and sailed round to Portsmouth. He had with him the Duke of York, Prince Rupert and the Duke of Sutherland. After meeting at the Governor's House, the Duchess and the King visited the Round Tower, then inspected the new tower on St. Thomas's Church, designed as a look-out station and some of the bastions and, walking along the ramparts, looked at Blockhouse Point from the Platform. Then it began to rain, and the Duchess, who had wanted to see 'her castle', refused to go there in the rain, so the visit ended in some disappointment all round. The Governor, the Earl of Gainsborough, gave them dinner, after which King Charles returned to his yacht. They were all due at Newmarket shortly, so could not wait for better weather, but at least Portsmouth had been honoured by another royal visit, and the Duchess had seen the town after which she was named.

With the King's death in 1685, both he and his mistress passed out of the life of Portsmouth.

King James II's unpopularity, caused largely by his determination to bring England back to Roman Catholicism, and a foreign policy which resulted in his being regarded as the tool of King Louis XIV, may have led him to keep Portsmouth in mind as a possible 'bolt-hole' to the Continent, or as a port at which French soldiers could land in an emergency. Consequently he was very willing to grace the town with his presence at the opening of a new gate, which was erected at the bridge leading from Broad Street on to the point of land forming the Camber.

This gate, which gave added strength to the defensive north wall of the town, also acted as a safety valve for sailors and soldiers who were in the habit of expressing their opinions in the strongest terms, particularly when in their cups. What they said within the town walls might well bring offenders before the Justices, but what was said outside the gate was accepted to a great extent to be without the law. So 'Point', as the area just outside the gate was called, soon became notorious for roistering, drinking and loose living. There were, for example, thirty-nine beer houses in this small area alone.

Even within the walls of the town, the Justices were tolerant of what sailors and soldiers said and did, where their religious views were concerned, and generally bound over offenders to keep the peace, unless the conflict of opinion led to a fight. There were hotheads in both the Protestant and Roman Catholic camps. George Wassal, a gunner of H.M.S. *Harwich*, only received a caution for drinking the Pope's health, and several men were simply bound over for burning an effigy of the Pope. Others who toasted Monmouth were similarly treated, and Anne Wood, who expressed the view that the Duke 'was no more a bastard than she was', a remark which started a brawl, did not have to pay any penalty.

It was in the autumn of 1687 when the King came to Portsmouth for the opening of the gate on his way to Southampton, Salisbury and Bath, the Queen having gone direct to Bath. The Governor lined the streets with three thousand soldiers. Though the people of Portsmouth had known the King well as Duke of York, Lord High Admiral and Governor, he was not a personality who aroused much popular enthusiasm. An expert in ceremonial, James could be stiff and constrained on certain occasions, and this was one of them. He had a particular dislike of drinking, and care had been taken to see that no one offended.

Not until he had inspected the fortifications did the King move to the gate where, in a short ceremony, he declared it open.

Next morning, His Majesty announced that he wished to 'Touch for the King's Evil'.[1] Normally this ceremony required the presence of the Clerk of the Closet, generally a bishop, and the Chamberlain, but so long as the Keeper of the Closet, who kept the register and drew the 'Touch' coins of gold and silver from the exchequer, was present, it could be performed with the attendance of lesser persons.

King James sat on a specially prepared chair in the Presence Room of the Domus Dei. To the accompaniment of prayers, the sick were brought by their doctors. They knelt before the King, who laid his hands on them. They were led aside, and then returned for more prayers to be said. Each person was presented with a gold or silver coin, which had a hole in it and was hung round the sick person's neck. At the end of the

1. This 'Evil' was scrofula. The glands of the neck became swollen and inflamed. Various eye diseases were also included in the 'Evil'.

ceremony the King washed his hands. He touched one hundred and fifty-one people, and it was noted that he had reverted to most of the Roman Catholic prayers instituted by King Henry VII.

Next year, 1688, the King again came to Portsmouth, this time bringing with him the Intendant Général of the French Navy, d'Usson de Bonrepaus. Later, Bonrepaus made a report to King Louis of France in which he said:

It appears to me that the King of England is very ill-informed of the subject of the management and details of work in naval arsenals. He was very much astonished at what we saw of the forging of arms and flukes of anchors. I gave him my estimate of what a certain anchor weighed, he had it weighed at once, and I was only six pounds out. Then he asked me several questions about cables and pieces of wood which we saw laying about. He told me laughing that I must have sat up all night weighing anchors, counting the ply of cables and measuring up wood. But if the King is ignorant about such things he is by no means ignorant about navigation. He often talks to me and enjoys talking, and I have an infinity of things to learn from him.

This time the King sought Portsmouth's friendship by presenting some excellent plate to the church of St. Thomas, but the pleasure of his gift was soon offset by his next action.

It was now that King James's fanatical desire to bring England under Roman Catholic domination led him to courses which made his downfall inevitable. Some of these affected Portsmouth very closely; and, conversely, some events in the town had major repercussions in the mind of the King and strongly influenced his actions.

For his purposes, King James decided he must call a Parliament, but to call a free one would be to gather together a majority opposed to his schemes; therefore he must use every device open to him to pick a Parliament which would support him. To do this it was necessary to instruct the Lord Lieutenants of the counties to retain in public employment only those who would be disposed to support his policy.

Among those who refused to carry out the King's instructions was the Earl of Gainsborough, Governor of Portsmouth. The Earl was also the Lord Lieutenant of Hampshire and Ranger of the New Forest. Only a few months before he took his stand against the King, he had paid five thousand pounds for the three positions which he held, but James dismissed him from all three, and he lost his money into the bargain.

Gainsborough was not alone in his action. All over the country others took their stand against the King's plans, many declaring that they would put life and property in jeopardy for the King, but that the Protestant religion was dearer to them than both these things. People thought that this failure by the King to obtain his wishes would make him think again, but they were mistaken. Far from conciliating his opponents, he persisted in his unpopular courses, and, in particular, he antagonised Portsmouth and the whole county of Hampshire by appointing his natural son, James Fitz James, as the new Governor of the town, and adding the positions of Lord Lieutenant of the County and Ranger of the New Forest.

Portsmouth's new Governor, who was still in his early twenties, had been created Duke of Berwick and loaded with other honours, including that of Colonel of the Blues. Confident of his position, he rode to the county boundary, where he expected to be met, as was customary, by a large gathering of knights, squires and gentry, including some very special representatives from Portsmouth; but not one single person of note went to greet him. It was the same when he rode into Portsmouth. Only a handful elected to serve in the administration of the town while its governor was a Papist.

On the morning of Sunday, 10th June 1688, the Queen gave birth to a son, and Portsmouth burgesses, realising that the succession was apparently assured, in spite of rumours that the child was believed to be supposititious, sent a most loyal address to His Majesty, proclaiming their loyalty to him and to the new-born Prince of Wales. The birth naturally encouraged the King in his plans, and he felt reasonably confident while the Army was loyal to him. Once again, however, it was in Portsmouth that the first major step in a great national event took place, because it was there that the Army first began to show its hand.

The King had thought it wise to place a contingent of Irish troops in the town, and the Governor ordered that these men should be enlisted in the Eighth Regiment of the Line, of which he was colonel-in-chief, and which was stationed in Portsmouth. On hearing this order, John Beaumont, the lieutenant-colonel of the regiment, protested in person to the Duke. Apart from the fact that the men were Papists, it was accepted in England at that time that the Irish were foreigners, and that they were barbarous and savage. Colonel Beaumont was supported by five captains in the regiment who all declared that, if more men were needed, they never had any difficulty in enlisting sufficient numbers of their own countrymen.

All six officers offered to lay down their commissions. The Governor asked for instructions from Windsor, and the King, who was furious as well as secretly anxious at this turn of events, sent a troop of horse to arrest the 'six Portsmouth Captains'. A court martial followed in London, and all six were cashiered. But the conduct of the six captains was applauded throughout the whole country, and the King knew then, for the first time, that he could not count on his army in time of personal trouble.

Portsmouth was to play one more part in the great drama now unfolding. Already Admiral Herbert, dressed as a seaman, was on his way with a letter to William of Orange and his wife Mary, the elder daughter of King James II and his first wife, Anne Hyde, offering her the throne of England.

King James, by now fully aware of the feeling against him, decided to send the little Prince of Wales to France. The child was brought to Portsmouth under special escort, and Lord Dartmouth, commanding the fleet assembled there, was ordered to see that Sir Robert Strickland, captain of one of the yachts, took the Prince to France. Dartmouth found himself in a very difficult position. He was absolutely loyal to the King. During his career he had held high office in the Navy, the Army and at court and in Whitehall. Previously, as Colonel Legge, he had been Governor of Portsmouth, a capacity in which he styled himself 'Warden and captain of the town and isle of Portsmouth'. With all this experience behind him, he realised that, apart from the matter of legality, if the baby prince was embarked, there was a possibility that his orders would not be carried out, and that the Prince might be taken to Holland instead, or transferred to a Dutch ship.

He discussed the position with the Governor, and between them they decided to send the baby back to London. Dartmouth's letter to the King was 'courteous, submissive, but decided in manner'. In it, he told the King it would be 'treason to your Majesty and the known laws of the Kingdom' to take the heir to the throne out of the country 'without the consent of the nation'.

The little prince arrived back in London on the 8th December, and two days later the Queen and the baby left Gravesend secretly in another yacht for France. The Prince of Orange was already at Hungerford, and by Christmas King James himself had fled the country.

William of Orange and his wife Mary were proclaimed king and queen on the 13th February 1689.

It might have been supposed by the inhabitants of Portsmouth that the new régime would bring an era of peace, but their new king, who was allied with Spain and the German princes in the League of Augsburg, was already at war with France. There was no great opposition to this, as it was clear that Louis would try to replace James II on the throne, but it meant war once again, and Admiral Herbert sailed for Bantry Bay to cut the French communications with Ireland. Herbert had an inferior force to the French, who came out of Bantry Bay to fight, and after some mild firing, Herbert withdrew. Both sides claimed victory, and Herbert came in to Portsmouth.

Whether it was a victory or not, King William acclaimed his naval forces, and came to Portsmouth to do this in person.

William III's entry to the town was much more personal and friendly than James's had been when he had opened the gate at Point. His Majesty stayed the night at Colonel Norton's house at Southwick. From there he drove by coach, and was delighted to find lined up outside the Landport Gate a hundred horsemen of the principal inhabitants, who acclaimed him as he passed through their ranks. At the Landport Gate, the Governor, now Colonel John Gibson, handed over the keys of the town. His Majesty was then received by the Mayor, Mr. Nicholas Hedger, and Corporation, the Recorder reading a speech of welcome.

The Mayor then preceded the royal coach on foot, carrying the mace, and the whole company passed down the High Street, lined with soldiers of the garrison, as far as the Sally Port. Here Admiral Herbert awaited the King, and took him in his barge to his flagship, the *Elizabeth*, where a banquet was held. Afterwards, on the quarter-deck, the King conferred an earldom on the Admiral, and knighted Captain John Ashby, of the *Defiance*, and Captain Cloudesley Shovell, of the *Edgar*. Having done this, William ordered ten shillings to be given to every man in the Fleet.

Nothing could have made a better impression. The officers and men all acclaimed their new sovereign, and pledged their lives to his cause. Nevertheless, the naval war did not go well for the time being, for Herbert, now Lord Torrington, was defeated at Beachy Head, and King Louis might well have brought King James back, if the war on land in Ireland had not gone against him.

In Portsmouth, as in all the naval yards, every effort was made to replace the ships lost in the battle and, as events turned out, they had fifteen months in which to do it, for not until the spring of 1692 did Louis XIV try again to replace James II on the throne of England.

James joined the French fleet and transports then collecting in Normandy ports, ready to embark the soldiers encamped on the Cherbourg peninsula. There was to be another 1066. In England for a moment it was uncertain whether the entire English Fleet would be loyal to King William, who at that time was in Flanders, so the Queen wrote a note to Admiral Russell questioning the position. The Admiral took immediate steps and, visiting every ship in the Fleet, called for absolute loyalty.

Among those who heard this call to duty was a young admiral by the name of Rooke, who was second-in-command of the Blue under Sir John Ashby. How the French were defeated at Barfleur, and then had their ships and transports burned by Rooke at La Hogue is another story, but it led to William coming again to Portsmouth.

It was ten o'clock on a cold winter's night when the King arrived in February 1693. Late though it was, the Mayor and representatives of the Corporation, together with the Military Governor and high-ranking soldiers, received His Majesty at the Town Gate. And, to the delight of the royal party, Portsmouth had put on a show. All the houses in the town were displaying illuminations. There were torches, lamps and candles everywhere, making the High Street in particular look like a picture from a fairy tale as the lights flickered and twinkled in the still, frosty night. At the same time the ships at Spithead fired a royal salute, which was taken up by other ships in the harbour.

After sleeping at the Governor's house in the Domus Dei, the King inspected the fortifications and the dockyard, whence he was taken in a yacht to Spithead. Here he boarded Admiral Rooke's flagship, the *Eagle*, and knighted the Admiral. Early in the afternoon he landed at the Camber and took coach at once to the Portsbridge, where he was met by the Earl of Scarborough, at whose residence, some ten miles inland, he was to spend the night before enjoying a good day's hunting in the woods at Petworth.

Admiral Russell's victory at La Hogue virtually ended the naval war, although hostilities on land went on for another five years, until both sides decided they wanted peace, which came in 1697.

For many years Portsmouth had been turning more and more to sailors and soldiers to represent the town in Parliament. With the growth of the dockyard, and with the main fleet using the harbour almost continually, the Services aspect of affairs, and particularly the naval side, needed strong representation at Westminster. Among those who had already served in Parliament for Portsmouth were Admiral Sir John Kempthorne, Colonel George Legge (later Lord Dartmouth) Admiral Russell and Colonel John Gibson. The town now turned to Admiral Sir George Rooke, who gladly accepted the representation, and was immediately made a freeman.

In the year that Rooke took his seat in Parliament, 1698, Portsmouth dockyard and harbour were full of ships, some new, others refitted, and all in first-class order and manned by well-trained crews.

William III was busy in the diplomatic field. Never entirely popular throughout England, and a lone figure after the death of the Queen in 1694, he worked hard for his country, and deserved better recognition of his efforts.

One of the rulers he wished to flatter was the young Tsar of Russia, whose sympathies were anti-French. William invited the Tsar to England, and decided that a day with the Fleet would be both memorable and impressive. Portsmouth was the obvious place for this entertainment, and on the evening of 20th March 1698 the young tsar arrived at the Governor's House with a large retinue. He immediately inspected the ships in the harbour, under the benevolent wing of Vice-Admiral Mitchell. Naturally he was taken on board the *Royal William*, a first rate of a hundred guns, and then walked round the *Association*, of ninety-six guns.

Later in the day the whole fleet sailed as far as the Solent, the Tsar being entertained on board Admiral Mitchell's flagship the *Humber*. That evening the captains of the Fleet gave a banquet in honour of the Tsar. It remained for a suitable wind to grace the visit so that manœuvres could be carried out. Quite rightly, Admiral Mitchell waited two days until conditions were just right, and in the meantime the Tsar visited a number of ships of all sizes.

The manœuvres consisted of a mock battle. Never before had such a thing been staged. It called for all the skill of seamanship and gunnery that a well-trained Fleet could display, and the Fleet did it all admirably.

As the two lines of ships approached each other, firing their broadsides into the air, the young tsar was beside himself with excitement. He had never seen anything like this before, nor for that matter had anyone else. It was all most spectacular and impressive. Finally, in perfect formation, the Fleet returned to Portsmouth and, as the Tsar was rowed ashore, every ship fired a salute of twenty-one guns and gave three cheers. When he heard the story from the Tsar, King William was delighted, and the young ruler told him that in all sincerity he would rather be an admiral in England than a tsar in Russia. Nevertheless, he became Peter the Great of Russia.

While comparative peace reigned for England in international affairs, a local war blew up in Portsmouth. Captain Sir William Gifford, the Dockyard Commissioner, needed a much larger labour force if he was to keep the Fleet repaired and maintain a lively building programme. The regulations, enforced by the Military Governor, Colonel Gibson, were that no one was to live outside the defences of either the town of the dockyard. He threatened to open fire on anyone building a house on the common abutting the yard, and said he would blast their houses to bits.

Even Admiral Sir George Rooke could not solve the impasse, either locally or in Westminster. However, it so happened that early in 1702 Prince George of Denmark visited both the town and the dockyard. The problem was explained to him and, when he got back to London, the wheels of State began to move on his recommendation, and Gibson was overruled. Immediately houses began to spring up, and the secondary town of Portsea, next to and outside the dockyard, was founded.

King William III died that same year. The fifteen years which ended the seventeenth century had been memorable enough, but for Portsmouth they were perhaps of greater importance than almost any other short period.

The issue for the coming century was clear. England was now a Protestant country, with the Channel dividing her from hostile Roman Catholic France. On her southern seaboard stood Portsmouth, now the undisputed premier naval port in the realm, which De Gomme's defences made secure. As for the dockyard, with houses now to be built outside the fortress, there was nothing to stop the growth of the labour force necessary for expansion.

Thus Portsmouth was able to enter the new century in the sure belief that the town and dockyard, and the Navy which they served, would hold the key to England's supremacy on the high seas in the years to come.

7

Pour Encourager les Autres

The Royal Charles

The eighteenth century saw the creation of the British Empire, and during the year 1704, when Admiral Sir George Rooke sailed from Portsmouth to capture Gibraltar, until 1805 when Admiral Lord Nelson also embarked from these shores to bring British sea power to a peak at the Battle of Trafalgar, in the United Kingdom the fortified garrison of Portsmouth, with its royal dockyard and naval arsenal, played a major part, the principal enemy now being France and not Holland.

The century saw many wars, large and small, beginning with the Spanish Succession, followed by the Austrian Succession, the Seven Years War, the American War of Independence, and culminating in the Napoleonic Wars. When the Navy was neglected generally we were unsuccessful—and indeed the loss of the American colonies was sealed at the indecisive Battle of Ushant—but when the Government supported the Navy the outcome was nearly always successful. Throughout the century, naval thinking was always governed by the fear of invasion. This was very real, and sometimes the apparent need to hold overwhelming naval forces in the Channel and Western Approaches unnecessarily depleted our fleets in the New World, or on the coasts of India and in the Far East.

Successive Commissioners of the Dockyard strove to meet the nation's needs in ships and repairs, at times with adequate backing from London, and at other times struggling to meet all the calls made on the dockyard without adequate means of doing so.

During this century most of the great seamen of the era came to Portsmouth. Such famous sailors as Rooke, Rodney, Anson, Howe, Jervis, Hood and Nelson could have been seen walking in the High Street before embarking for the wars, or again on their return from action against the enemy. Members of the Royal Family also came to Portsmouth from time to time to visit the Fleet, and in some cases to join ships as young officers in the Navy.

Occasionally an age produces a storm of such magnitude that it remains in the minds of the people to be told and re-told for generations. The storm which destroyed King John's dock in the thirteenth century must have been one such event, but the storm of 1703 surpassed them all. It was even greater in violence than the tempest which Henry Teonge wrote about so vividly when ships at anchor, riding under bare poles, lost their masts.

For a fortnight preceding the night of November 26th, 1703, the winds had been higher than normal, including those expected at the equinox. Defoe records that some people detected strange vapours in the atmosphere which, in their opinion, 'raised the nitro-sulphurous or other heterogeneous matter in the sky and exploded', giving the impression of severe lightning. But it was the wind which was so terrifying. People mistook the noise for thunder, but again Defoe finds that the roar was undoubtedly the sound of the rushing wind as it mounted to a crescendo.

During the fourteen days immediately preceding the 26th there had been constant danger from tiles being blown down and chimney-stacks falling. People kept indoors as much as they could and although apprehensive of the night generally slept well enough. It was about 10 p.m. on this terrible night when most people had gone to bed that they noticed the storm was increasing. The noise was so great that many got up. Some looked out to see what was happening, but soon returned indoors as tiles and bricks were being hurled horizontally across the streets. Most realised that their very houses might come down, but it appeared to be safer to remain in them than to go outside except, as Defoe remarked, into the fields, but the night was so terrifying few took this course. More than one household noticed that the mercury in the barometer had suddenly fallen lower than in living memory. One man thought a servant had broken the glass, as the mercury practically disappeared.

On the morning of the 25th the sky had darkened and the wind and rain increased throughout the day until at 10 p.m. the very earth shook. Some thought it was an earthquake and there were many such reports throughout southern England, although this was not in fact correct. The apparent movement was caused solely by the wind. Between 10 p.m. and midnight the sky appeared to be filled with meteors and vaporous fires and in places not far from Portsmouth waterspouts appeared. One parson solemnly walked after one for some miles watching it pick up trees and houses as it traversed the country. Apparently the only hazard not encountered was fire and it was thought the drenching rain was the reason for this.

From Plymouth to the Thames every harbour was attacked by this act of God. In Portsmouth the scenes were devastating and the suffering tragic. Frightened women gave birth prematurely, and midwives who went to their aid were either struck by tiles or bricks or even driven back by the sheer violence of the wind. Many did not attempt to go out when beseeched to come to women in need of aid. Meanwhile, gangs of hardened robbers took the opportunity to break into unguarded houses and make off with the loot.

The devastation went on from midnight until 3 a.m. on the 26th, when at last the fury seemed to abate and Portsmouth people went to bed to await the morning and count the cost. They were still dazed and shaken when, two days later with the new moon, the spring tides rose eight feet higher than usual, depositing ships and debris high up on the beaches and even as far as the fields. Streets were flooded, foundations of houses collapsed and shingle, feet high, filled every low-lying passage and alley in the town. Finally, on December 2nd at long last the wind began to die down and the town set about clearing up the debris.

At sea the damage was appalling. Part of a large fleet was lying at Spithead and it took superb seamanship to ride out such weather, but the majority of the big ships succeeded, only the *Newcastle*, a fourth rate, being totally lost when she drove ashore at Chichester. Captain William Carter, a carpenter and twenty-three were saved. The greatest losses were suffered by the ships attending on so large a fleet. Dozens were driven out to sea and never heard of again, while others were lost with all hands along the coast of the mainland. From the decks of the battleships many of these smaller ships were seen to be in distress, but nothing could be done. One moment a gun would be fired, the signal for severe distress, and men could be seen in the rigging, clinging on for dear life, and the next the whole ship would have vanished in the sea and foam. Sir Clowdesley Shovell with the other half of the main fleet rode out the storm in the Downs and very similar experiences were met there. It speaks wonders for the seamanship of the Navy that none of the really big ships foundered. Ships which broke adrift in the Downs were wrecked mostly on the Goodwin Sands. At Portsmouth the greatest scene of wreckage was on the shores of Stokes Bay where, amongst many of the smaller ships, one carrying soldiers was driven from Cowes and foundered with the loss of all hands. As people examined the wreckage they read such names as *Resolution, Eagle* and *Advice,* once smart ships of the Fleet and unhappily carrying many a Portsmouth man.

It was a sad Christmas for Portsmouth with so many families depleted, and not only sailors, but wives and children too, apart from the material losses on land of livestock drowned, houses demolished and crops utterly ruined. As one inhabitant said, 'Not since the French raised the town in Edward's day was such devastation seen'. News from other parts gradually trickled through and sailors in Portsmouth were given a final shock when they heard that the Eddystone lighthouse had collapsed and there were no survivors from the crew, including the designer himself.

The dockyard, which set about refitting the damaged ships, was going through another period of expansion. More slips and graving docks were being built and land was being reclaimed from the sea. The harbour front was being further developed so that more ships could lie alongside. A masthouse had been built near the main gate and mast and timber pounds arranged close by. A chapel had just been completed. These improvements and the general work of the yard were the subject of voluminous correspondence between the commissioners and the Navy Board, covering every aspect of naval warfare and the administration of the most important naval base. These letters give a picture of great endeavour to meet the requirements of the Fleet.

When various members of the Royal Family and foreign royalty made passages in H.M. ships, these occasions were the subject of the most detailed instructions, particularly if the passenger was a lady, and in 1708, when the Queen of Portugal returned to Lisbon in the *Royal Anne*, the fitting out of her cabin with all the curtains, carpets and bedclothes, together with a special gangway, which had to be carpeted and have specially constructed steps, all formed the subject of much thought and care.

In 1710 the commissioner suggested that the palisades surrounding the dockyard were not sufficient protection for it and that a wall could be built for the sum of £1,061 10s. He was told by the Navy Board to do it straight away, but not to spend a penny more.

Not only were the commissioners busy in replying to the correspondence from the Board, but they were constantly giving orders for the administration of the dockyard. Sir William Gifford decided to tighten up the security, and appointed inspectors selected from the dockyard officers. They were to have a roster and look around at nights. When Thomas Horton, a shipwright, endeavoured to embezzle two iron bars and was found out the Commissioner sent him to sea as punishment. When Elizabeth Swan and Susannah Mould broke open a storehouse and took some oakum the Commissioner had them publicly whipped at the dockyard gate. There were a considerable number of cases of watchmen being drunk, but they were generally discharged. Wood chips from the shipyards were kept for the poor of Portsmouth, but the dockyardmen pilfered some of these. When the regulations were tightened, the shipwrights chipped good wood, but the building of the dockyard walls in place of the palisades made it more difficult for the sacks to be chucked into the street. There was extra work to do at each quarter, when the sale of old stores 'by candle' took place. The candle was an inch long, and bidding went on until the candle went out, and the man making the last bid got the lot.

Beer was sold in the yard, and regulations for this caused a

K

lot of trouble. The greatest nuisance was caused by the keeping of hogs inside the dockyard itself. Most people with residences kept them and they were always getting out and finding their way into private houses and gardens. Commissioners generally let it run on, until the hogs got into their own gardens, and then they took very strong action.

During their term of office, however, most commissioners had greater problems than these to contend with. It was the fate of Captain Sir Isaac Townsend, during his second term as commissioner, to have to report to the Board in February 1721 that the third *Victory*, having the weed burned off the bottom, caught fire and was completely destroyed.

Another factor which caused periodical trouble was that in 1733 Captain Richard Hughes (senior) found himself saddled with a naval academy in the dockyard.

From first to last this establishment had a bad name and deserved it. It began with good intent in 1733. Founded by an Order in Council, the Admiralty planned to enter its own nominees into the Navy as an alternative to the usual channel of captain's servants. Naval officers rebelled against this undermining of their privileges. There was accommodation for forty young gentlemen aged between thirteen and sixteen. They learnt 'French, Drawing, Fencing and the use of the Firelock'. The young students sometimes caused trouble. Like all young people, from time to time they became disorderly. They over-painted ships' figureheads with the wrong colours and the young gentlemen used a great many 'disrespectful words', for which some were discharged, and they were always complaining about their meals, probably with justification.

How different has been the story of Portsmouth Grammar School, the money for which was provided from private funds in 1732. The building was not completed until 1750, but from that time the school has taken a prominent and most successful place in the life of the town and the city.

On the purely naval side, ships came and went so often that when, in 1740, Commodore Anson in the *Centurion*, with five other ships, called to take on board crew and soldiers to augment his depleted ships' companies, the event was hardly noticed. Anson left to operate against the Spaniards in western South American waters with his ships partly manned by seamen who had long since been invalided, and a sprinkling of decrepit Chelsea pensioners. He returned to Portsmouth in

June 1744 with vast treasure, having circumnavigated the globe, but his was the only ship of the squadron to complete the voyage. This time Portsmouth turned out in great numbers to watch the unloading, and cast enquiring eyes at those who had survived the terrible privations and losses. Unknown to them, they were seeing a galaxy of men who rose to the top of their profession, among whom were Saunders, Saumarez, Keppel and Hyde-Parker—men whom Portsmouth learned to know well in later years.

The town turned out again in force in 1747 when Hawke arrived at Spithead with prizes following the Battle of Finisterre on October 14th during the War of the Austrian Succession, and on December 28th the same year they voted him into Parliament. Hawke joined Admiral Isaac Townsend, thus presenting an all naval representation in the Councils of State. These events gave copy for the *Portsmouth and Gosport Gazette*, founded during the year.

As for Portsmouth itself, it was now two towns, one inside the fortifications, and the other, rapidly expanding, and housing the majority of the dockyard labour force, was beginning to sprawl unprotected across Portsea Island. They had certain features, all bad ones, in common. Streets were extremely narrow, unlighted and uncleansed. There was no proper sanitation and no water supply except from wells. Public houses abounded. There were one hundred and fifty-five inns, brandy shops, coffee-houses, and forty of these were clustered on Point. The one real improvement was the new Town Hall, replacing the one built by Carpenter in Tudor times. All the same, like its predecessor, it stood in the middle of the High Street, successfully hampering the traffic which, when the Fleet was being manned, thronged the streets, sometimes bringing all movement to a standstill. This situation was at its worst at the time of the annual Free Mart Fair.

Gradually through the years the important mercantile side of the fair had declined, and in its place there had sprung up amusements and menageries, together with all manner of monstrosities. Not only birds and beasts both rare and deformed were exhibited, but humans as well, and behind the scenes there crept in booths of ill fame, while vagabonds and pickpockets increased in numbers each year. Although the standards in some entertainments improved, Miss Saunders' troop of horses being described as 'matchless', and the Theatre which hired some of the best actors and actresses giving excellent plays of the times, the fair fell from grace to the extent that the inhabitants of Portsmouth began to dread the time when the fortnight came round.

So much for the lighter side of the Portsmouth scene. But in 1753 John Wesley records in his journal: 'I preached at half an hour after six in an open part of the Common. The congregation was large and well behaved; not one scoffer did I see.' Later, after his second visit, he wrote: 'I admired not so much the immense number of people as the uncommon decency of behaviour which ran through the whole congregation.'

By the middle of the century the world scene was set for the great struggles for the possession of colonial empires. Five Powers were concerned. Portugal and Holland soon dropped out of the race, but France and Spain fought together against Britain. From India to America the struggle steadily mounted and in 1756, with the opening of the Seven Years War, the action became almost world-wide. First fruits went to France when, without a declaration of war, she landed a force on the island of Minorca.

Few people living in Portsmouth had ever heard of Minorca until Admiral Byng went to its relief, and fought an indecisive action with the French, under Admiral de la Galissonniere, within sight of the island. The French admiral returned to Toulon, and Byng withdrew to Gibraltar, leaving the sea communications between Minorca and France open to the enemy, and shortly afterwards the British garrison there surrendered.

The loss of Minorca shocked the country and Newcastle, the Prime Minister, who should have taken action much earlier, and Lord Anson, the First Lord of the Admiralty, whose dispositions retained unnecessarily large numbers of ships in home waters for protection against invasion, at the expense of the Mediterranean, were really the responsible persons. They decided that there must be a scapegoat, and the obvious person was Admiral Byng. Unhappily for Byng, he had given sufficient grounds for the full blame to be shifted. He had lacked judgment in the action and his withdrawal to Gibraltar, which he feared might be in danger, sealed the fate of Minorca.

The drama began for Portsmouth with the arrival of the

Antelope bringing Byng home. Orders had been sent by the Admiralty to Admiral Osborn, the Commander-in-Chief, Portsmouth, to arrest Byng. Osborn was at once in a most difficult position, as his elder brother was married to Sarah, Byng's sister. The *Antelope* reached Spithead on July 26th, and Osborn went out to her in his barge. There, with all the tact that he could muster, the Commander-in-Chief carried out his distasteful duty. Byng, for his part, was utterly astounded.

Orders followed saying that Byng was to be taken to Greenwich to await court martial. On the 9th August the Marshal of the High Court of Admiralty with fifty dragoons set off for the Royal Hospital for Disabled Seamen at Greenwich, where, on arrival, the prisoner was placed behind bars.

This court martial was not to be a straightforward affair. Men with immense power and influence were against the Admiral, in order to shield themselves, headed by Newcastle and Anson.

On December 3rd Admiral Smith, commanding the Fleet in the Downs, was appointed President of the Court. Orders were given by the Admiralty to begin the trial on Monday, the 27th December, which threw into confusion all the Christmas arrangements of numerous senior naval officers and interested civilians alike. The *St. George* was ordered to be fitted out for the trial. Byng left Greenwich on December 21st, again under escort, and two days later arrived at the house of Edward Hutchins, the Boatswain of the Dockyard, whose residence was near the Pitch House Jetty, where the stench from the pitch and the sea mud at low tide pervaded every corner of the building.

On the morning of the 27th December Portsmouth was crowded with the curious, who saw the Union flag hoisted at the mizzen peak in the *St. George*, and heard a single gun fired at 8.30 a.m., signifying that a court martial was to be held. All admirals and captains in the port repaired on board the *St. George*, the latter bringing with them their commissions. It took all day to constitute the Board, which finally was agreed with four admirals and nine captains. Amongst these was Captain Augustus Keppel, of whom much will be heard later.

The next day, Tuesday the 28th, Byng was brought from Hutchins' house and escorted to the *St. George* by boats manned by armed marines. In the boat in which Byng travelled men sat on the thwarts with their muskets ready. Byng had been captain of the *St. George,* and this was a very different scene from the last time when he mounted the gangway and was received with all the honours accorded to an officer of his rank and position. As soon as the court was assembled, Byng found that he was to be tried under Article Twelve, and the first charge was that during the battle he did 'withdraw or keep back and did not do his utmost to take, seize and destroy the ships of the French King'.

Byng had feared that he might find he was being accused of cowardice, and was relieved on hearing the wording of the principal charge, although he well knew that failure to carry out Article Twelve invoked the extreme penalty of the death sentence.

The trial lasted seventeen days until January 19th and its detail does not concern Portsmouth, but it was not until January 27th that the court pronounced themselves ready to announce their findings and sentence. Byng was in good spirits and had been dealing with a lot of his personal affairs with his cousin, Mr. Branston. Just before he was called into the court, an officer had a quick word with Branston, who turned ashen white and half staggered into Byng's cabin. Byng guessed the significance of his cousin's confusion. Completely composed, he said, 'Well, I understand. If nothing but my blood will satisfy, let them take it.' As soon as the sentence had been read, the President, Admiral Smith, read a passage which was to be laid before the Board of Admiralty, asking them to intercede with His Majesty to extend his clemency to the prisoner. When later this was presented the King was completely adamant and would neither listen to pleas nor, in some cases, receive high personages who wished to intercede.

The execution was fixed for the 28th February, and on being told this Byng appeared to be little concerned. At the Admiralty, one of the Board, Admiral Forbes, refused to sign the warrant. At Portsmouth, Admiral Osborn could not face being the Commander-in-Chief during this period and took leave. Admiral Smith, the next senior officer, stated clearly that it would not be appropriate for him to take over command of the port, so the Admiralty sent one of their own number, Boscawen, temporarily to take up the appointment of Commander-in-Chief, Portsmouth. Boscawen on arrival ordered that the *Monarch* should be prepared to receive Byng, and that the execution was to take place on the forecastle. Byng immediately said that although there had been no precedent of a British admiral being shot, he felt that his rank deserved better treatment, and asked that the quarter-deck should be the place of execution. This was granted.

Twenty-four hours before the time of execution scenes in the House of Commons and last-minute action by Captain Augustus Harvey, Captain Keppel and, to some extent through the writings of Horace Walpole, moved the Board of Admiralty to delay execution for fourteen days. As these came to their fateful end Byng never lost his cheerfulness, while his friends could hardly contain their distress. Indeed, he gave a dinner party on board the *Monarch* the night before the fatal day, and kept all his guests in great humour, until many broke down with the strain of the situation. Byng slept well on the night of Sunday, March 13th, and when he was called at six o'clock next morning with a cup of tea he remarked to the steward: 'The court martial has acquitted me of everything criminal or ignominious', and this seemed to be the kernel of what mattered to him most. Byng took great trouble in going through the procedure, and decided that he would not have a handkerchief tied across his eyes, but was persuaded that it would be very difficult for the marine firing squad unless he did this, and he bowed to their wishes. He said, however, that he would give the signal, and he would hold a white handkerchief in his right hand and when he was ready he would drop it. The morning of Monday, March 14th, was wild and grey. The crests of the waves were turning into spray and the rain lashed down on Portsmouth and the dreary scene. Boats going to the *Monarch* had great difficulty in getting alongside, not the least the one bringing the coffin. The Officer of the Watch noted at 7 a.m.: 'Mr. Byng's coffin was brought on board.' Meanwhile, in spite of the weather, every mast and yard of all the ships in the harbour was filling up with spectators and by mid-morning, when the rain ceased, thousands were still climbing to points of vantage. A moment before twelve Byng walked out on to the quarter-deck and, saying a few cheerful words to Branston and Brough, knelt on the cushion. He had some difficulty in tying the handkerchief across his eyes, but managed it eventually. Meanwhile, Captain Murray had to shout his orders against the wind for his marines to hear. At the order of 'Present', the Admiral took his white handkerchief and held it in his right hand. For a few moments everything was still. Those watching could hardly contain themselves, and then the handkerchief dropped. In a second the volley was fired and Mr. Byng fell down dead. Mr. John Paynter, the master of the *Monarch*, wrote in the ship's log: 'At twelve Mr. Byng was shot dead by six marines and put into his coffin.' Ashore, Admiral Boscawen wrote a note to the Admiralty, in which he said that having ordered all the captains and officers of H.M. ships in the harbour to attend the execution of Admiral Byng, he respectfully wished to report that the orders of the Board of Admiralty had been duly carried out. Byng's body was taken to the family vault, where there is a tablet on which is written:

To the perpetual disgrace of public justice the Honourable John Byng, Admiral of the Blue, fell a martyr to political persecution on March 14th in the year 1757, when bravery and loyalty were insufficient securities for the life and honour of a naval officer.

'Roistering on Point', George Rowlandson

The 1795–1837 Guildhall: looking towards the Square Tower

Above left The Quay Gate.

This gate led from the fortified town to the Camber. Before it was built in 1734 the exit from the town at this point was through an open arch.

Above right Unicorn Gate.

This gate pierced the fortifications at the end of North Street, Portsea. It was erected in 1778–9, taken down in 1873, and re-erected as an entrance to the Dockyard at the end of Unicorn Road.

Left Lion Gate.

This gate pierced the fortifications at the western end of Queen Street. It was built in 1777, removed in 1871, and re-erected as an entrance to the Naval Barracks, but was finally moved to the Signal Tower in the Dockyard.

Right The Landport Gate.

The Landport or Town Gate was erected in 1760 at the north-east end of Warblington Street, and was the main entrance to the town. It is the only one of the old gates standing in its original position.

View from the saluting platform, Portsmouth, *circa* 1836

8

The *Royal George*

The Royal George

The dockyard in which Byng had stayed awaiting his trial had been further improved and enlarged in the first half of the century both on the north side and the land immediately inside the main gate, providing more slipways, a second basin and better storage for masts and wood. There was also a spate of house building for dockyard officers, much of this being completed as early as 1717. The successive commissioners were always busy.

Hundreds of orders such as for strangers coming into the dockyard, national holidays, and plans for improving the state of roads in Portsea, all came under the Commissioner's pen, but these were straightforward matters compared with the day when the dockyard was presented with a statue of King William III, which nobody really wanted, and nobody could think where to place it.

Individuals came to the Commissioner with their troubles. In 1745 a warrant officer aged ninety-one said that after sixty-one years' service he would very much like to be relieved of his post in the *Royal William*, and this was granted.

The Commissioner was very concerned with his labour

force, and from time to time was short of skilled men. As the century went on, more men were always required. For example, on the 17th January 1728 there were one thousand and eighty men employed in the yard, of all trades and grades, from shipwrights to oakum boys, pitch heaters and lime burners, whereas in 1770 the force had been doubled to two thousand one hundred and fifty-five.

Generally speaking, the correspondence from the Board to the Commissioner and vice versa, and the Commissioner's orders for the yard, were in straightforward language, but on occasion there were some extremely flowery letters, generally from people not immediately connected with the Navy. Godolphin, the Lord High Treasurer, for instance, wrote: 'My very loving Friends the Principal Officers and Commissioners of Her Majesty's Navy, now and for the time being', and went on to tell them it had been agreed to cut furze in the New Forest for breaming ships, as directed by the Regarders and Keepers. The Board themselves could also be very considerate on some occasions. When John White, in 1737, submitted to the Commissioner, who sent the correspondence on to the Navy Board, that his uncle had left him a plantation in Virginia in his will, and he found it difficult to administer this from the dockyard, the Board said that he was to be given indefinite leave to go to America and get his plantation put in order. Meanwhile, a vacancy was to be kept for him in the yard against his return.

By 1759 the Seven Years War was going better. Admiral Saunders had sailed from Portsmouth with General Wolfe and Quebec was captured. But November 20th of that year was a sad day in Portsmouth after the return of the *Royal William*. At 7 a.m., while lying at Spithead, the ship fired two signal guns, and the body of General Wolfe was lowered into a twelve-oared barge and, towed by two other twelve-oared barges, moved slowly in shore. Minute-guns were fired at Spithead until the body was landed at Point, when it was transferred into a travelling hearse (sent from London) and attended by a mourning coach. Soldiers from the garrison lined the route to the Landport gate, everywhere colours were at 'half flag staff', St. Thomas's rang a muffled peal and a company of soldiers preceded the cortège with arms reversed. Thousands of silent, weeping people filled the streets to pay their tribute to the national hero.

While military exploits steadily added to the far-flung colonial possessions, much had yet to be learned by the Government at home how best to rule these vast and numerous territories overseas. Misjudgment of this task led the American colonists to seek their independence, and war broke out in 1775.

One aspect of this major event in world history directly affected Portsmouth. An indecisive battle was fought at sea in 1779 which sealed the loss of the colonies, the aftermath of which battle was enacted in Portsmouth. But before that, the action of an individual also had its repercussions in the port, although in a very much smaller way.

'Jack the Painter', otherwise James Hill, alias James Hinde or James Aitken, was born in Edinburgh. He trained as a painter and possessed, in the words of the Annual Register of 1777, 'an extraordinary spirit of rambling with a strong propensity to vice'. He wandered the countryside committing highway robberies, burglaries and rapes. Eventually, fear of arrest made him take ship to America, and while there he listened to endless talk of the injustice of the rule of the Government at home. This led him to return to England with the sole intention of doing nothing less than destroy the maritime strength of the nation by setting fire to the royal dockyards and burning the principal cities and towns, together with their shipping.

Money had been lodged in England for him by an American colonist, Silas Deane, and on arrival in this country Jack first lodged in Canterbury, where he employed a man to assist him in making his special incendiary canisters. Next, he visited the principal dockyards in the south of England, where he found the security arrangements almost non-existent.

At Portsmouth he took lodgings with a Mrs. Boxall, with whom he had a row and she turned him out, so he took two other lodgings, one at a public house and the other at a private lodging, where he particularly noted the amount of timber in the houses, the idea being that he would set both on fire before burning the dockyard, so that the local fire engines would be already occupied when the alarm went off in the dockyard.

On the 6th December 1776 he laid a gunpowder trail, augmented by hemp soaked in turpentine, in the rope house, and placed his special incendiary canister in the hemp house.

The next day he returned to the hemp house and tried to strike the matches which would light the candle in the canister, but they were damp and would not light, so he had to go away and get some better matches. This done, he hurried to the rope house and here at first things went as planned, but as soon as the gunpowder trail was alight he lost his nerve and beat a hasty retreat out of the dockyard and over the Portsbridge, abandoning his attempt on the hemp house and his scheme to fire the lodgings.

When he looked back at the town on his handiwork, it appeared as though the whole dockyard was alight, although he had failed in his full intention. Also, he had left a remarkable bundle in one of his lodgings which contained an English *Justin*, Ovid's *Metamorphoses*, a *Treatise on the Art of War and making Fireworks*, and a passport from the French Government.

Jack was arrested at Odiham in Hampshire and tried at Winchester.

He showed intelligence at his trial and questioned whether there really was any proof that he had set the rope house on fire; also whether the two landladies had seen enough of him to be able to swear to his identity. At the same time he repeated he was perfectly satisfied with how the trial was being conducted, he was most respectful to the judges and said he was quite prepared to accept the result whichever way it went.

After the judge's summing up, the jury almost immediately pronounced the prisoner guilty. The judge then said, 'I have only now to pronounce the painful sentence,' to which the prisoner interjected, 'Joyful, my Lord.' The judge's words ended, Jack the Painter added, 'My Lord, I am exceedingly well satisfied.'

Later that day he made a full confession of all his successful and unsuccessful attempts at burning, stealing and the like, from which it was clear that had he been better skilled with his fireworks and combustibles he could well have done very considerable damage.

At Portsmouth dockyard the sixty-four-foot mizenmast of the frigate *Arethusa* was put up as a gibbet, and on the 10th March 1777 the prisoner was brought from Winchester. The Commissioner of the Dockyard was Mr. Gambier, who wrote 'an exact account of the execution':

Having been carried in an open cart by the Hemp House and round the ruins of the Rope House, when he came opposite the Commissioner's house he desired to speak with the Commissioner, who thereupon went up close to him. He said, 'Sir, I acknowledge my crime and hope for forgiveness from God, through the merits of my Saviour Jesus Christ. I ask pardon of you, Sir, and hope for your forgiveness.' Upon the cart moving he said 'he had one thing more to observe as a caution to all Commissioners of the dockyards throughout England; to be more vigilant and strictly careful of them for the future, because it is in the power of a determined and resolute man to do a great deal of mischief.' As the cart stopped at the end of the Rope House, he looked attentively at the place of his perpetration, and said, 'I acknowledge my crime and am sorry for it.' He added, 'I recommend great care and strict vigilance at the dockyards at Chatham, Woolwich, Deptford, Portsmouth and Plymouth; and particularly at the Rope House at the latter.'

When, in October 1777, General Burgoyne had been defeated at the Battle of Saratoga, this precipitated the French entry into the American War of Independence, to take what advantage they could of the situation.

During the year 1778 the British Navy had failed to inflict any decisive defeat over the French Fleet.

France had been building up a first-class navy. French naval construction had long been of a high standard and the ships which were now at her disposal were well found and particularly good under sail. Much of her navy had been built by private subscription, notably one fine ship, the *Ville de Paris*, provided by the citizens of that city.

The British Navy, on the other hand, through neglect, was in no position to fight so well prepared an enemy. Keppel, who had been appointed to command the Fleet in this parlous situation, had great difficulty in getting to sea with a sufficient force, and then with one only partly trained. By last-minute superhuman efforts the Fleet was got ready, and on the 11th July Keppel was at sea in his flagship, the *Victory*, with thirty sail of the line and a handful of frigates. Curiously enough, on the day before Keppel had sailed, the French Fleet had left Brest with thirty-two sail of the line and a large number of frigates.

In these circumstances it was almost certain that the two fleets would sight each other very shortly and on the afternoon of 23rd July this, indeed, happened off Ushant. Keppel had formed his fleet into three squadrons. Sir Robert Harland, Vice-Admiral of the Red, commanded the van, Keppel was in the centre and Sir Hugh Palliser, Vice-Admiral of the Blue, was in the rear.

The remainder of that day and part of the next morning were taken up with manœuvring, until about eleven o'clock, when the two fleets approached each other on opposite tacks and a running fight ensued, in which Palliser's squadron in the rear took the heaviest blows. Keppel then turned his fleet so as to resume the action, but Palliser never got his squadron back into line, and night came, bringing the battle to an end. In the morning the French were seen to be sailing away over the horizon.

Keppel could not understand Palliser's failure to rejoin him, and besides making every signal he could think of, including ordering each individual ship to do so, he sent a frigate to convey a personal message to the Admiral of the Blue, but without avail.

So ended the Battle of Ushant, and Britain had failed to crush the French Fleet.

On the broad aspect of the situation resulting from the battle it can be said that all hope of retrieving the loss of the American colonies was now definitely gone for ever. With a powerful French Fleet aligned to their side and apparently the victor at sea, the colonists had little to fear. On the narrower planes, tongues soon began to wag in England as to the conduct of the action, but as Keppel, in his report, had not blamed Palliser by name, these whispers came to nothing very much at that time. Nothing could have been easier than for the Commander-in-Chief to censure his subordinate, but he desisted from doing so, believing it more in the interest of the country to keep the Fleet together without dissension than to hold post mortems. In fact, by so doing, the Fleet operated well into October before returning for a long refit.

However, the irreparable loss of the American colonies, and the French Fleet undefeated, once again set in motion, in the autumn, the whispers which had begun to stir in the summer.

The subsequent events might never have occurred had it not been that, in October, a few days before the Fleet arrived in Portsmouth harbour, the *Morning Intelligencer* printed an aaticle attacking the conduct of Sir Hugh Palliser.

Both Keppel and Palliser went to London on their arrival

in England, and it was there that Palliser called on Keppel and demanded that he should send a denial of these charges to the *Morning Intelligencer* for immediate publication. He had brought with him a written version of what he wanted Keppel to sign. The latter was furious and hotly refused to have anything to do with it.

Getting no change out of his late Commander-in-Chief, Palliser then went to the *Morning Intelligencer* himself and there and then wrote out his own version of the affair, which the paper published.

The storm which had been working up now burst across the country. It was not long before the matter was raised in both the House of Lords and the House of Commons. When the matter came up in the Commons, both Keppel and Palliser were in their seats, the latter on the Treasury Bench next to Lord North. Palliser spoke, defending himself and accusing his commander-in-chief. Keppel replied with such ability and conviction that when he marched out of the House, after delivering his speech, a large number of the Members followed him to indicate their strong and personal support.

Palliser, however, was still a Member of the Board of Admiralty and a personal friend of Lord Sandwich, with the result that a few days after the scene in the Commons, Keppel received a letter from the Secretary of the Admiralty informing him that he was to be court-martialled for his conduct off Ushant on 27th June 1778.

Here, then, was a unique situation. An officer third in command in a Fleet had arranged the court martial of his Commander-in-Chief. Naturally Keppel was dumbfounded and said so in his reply to the Admiralty. However, as he had a clear conscience, he informed the Admiralty that he would be ready with his evidence on 7th January 1779, the day appointed for the opening of the trial.

That morning, on board H.M.S. *Britannia* in Portsmouth harbour, the Honourable Augustus Keppel, Commander-in-Chief of the British Fleet at the Battle of Ushant, stood accused of four capital charges, amounting to a combination of cowardice and gross negligence, and one lesser charge. He was tried before a court consisting of admirals and captains, and the prosecutor was Sir Hugh Palliser, his former third-in-command.

Portsmouth took on an unaccustomed air. The trial of Admiral Byng was still very much in everyone's mind and people high and low came to the town to support Keppel by their counsel or their cheers. As a gauge of the popularity of the two contestants, Keppel's barge crossing the harbour on the opening day of the trial was accompanied by thirty boats full of cheering sailors, while Palliser's had four attendant boats. Keppel's followers included their Royal Highnesses the Dukes of Cumberland and Gloucester, the Duke of Portland, the Duke of Bolton, his great friends the Marquis of Rockingham and the Duke of Richmond, and many other well-known people, including Burke, Fox and Sheridan.

The trial opened in the *Britannia*, but after the first day was transferred to Government House. The account and minutes occupy one hundred and eighty-two large folio pages. The trial itself lasted five weeks.

As in the case of the court martial of Byng, the actual trial was not the concern of Portsmouth, but during it there were many dramatic moments, not the least when it was discovered that the log-book of the *Formidable*, Palliser's flagship, had been tampered with. When Keppel asked the master of the *Formidable* in court when he had first heard of this, Mr. Forfar replied, 'I heard it in a shop in Portsmouth yesterday. The woman in the shop was telling another person that there had been some leaves torn out of the *Formidable*'s log-book.'

At last, on the thirty-second day of the trial, Thursday, 11th February 1779, the court assembled for its finding. The session took on an air of tension, coupled with particular dignity, while the members made their way to their places. When all was ready the public and the accused were admitted. All eyes strained to see in which direction the Admiral's sword was pointing. It was a tense and dramatic moment. Then suddenly the suspense was broken, for there was the sword with its hilt pointing triumphantly towards the Commander-in-Chief. Cheers rang out through the court and no one suppressed them.

That evening Keppel was jubilantly followed through the streets of Portsmouth by bands and singing crowds.

*   *   *   *   *

Three years later Portsmouth was the scene of another naval drama—this time a very tragic one. There have been many accounts of the loss of the *Royal George*, with Admiral Kempenfelt on board. The following, written by a member of a gun's crew, comes as near to the truth as any, and is endorsed by the comments of an admiral:

In August 1782, the *George* was lying at Spithead in company with Lord Howe's fleet. There was the *Victory, Barfleur, Ocean* and *Union*, all three-deckers, close to her; the ship was in good repair, not at all leaky, and was to sail in two days to join the fleet in the Mediterranean. She had been paid, in consequence of being about to sail foreign, in golden guineas. On the twenty eighth of the month early in the morning, the seamen had been washing decks, and the carpenter had been ordered to let the water in, when it was found that the water cock, which was about three feet below the water line, was out of order, and it was necessary that it should be repaired. The foreman came off from the dockyard and stated that it was necessary that the ship should be careened over to port, sufficiently to raise the mouth of the pipe which went through the ship's side below, clean out of the water, that they might work at it. The following day, the twenty ninth, the weather was fine, with a strong breeze at west. The shipping (about forty sail of the line, and many frigates, and two or three hundred of sail of merchant vessels) were riding to the flood tide, with their heads towards Cowes. On examination it was found that the water cock must be taken out and a new one put in, to do which it was necessary to give the ship a parliament heel on her larboard side, as to raise the outside of the water pipe above water. Between seven and eight o'clock the whole of the larboard guns were run out as far as they could be, and the larboard lower deck ports were open. The starboard guns were also run in amidships, and secured by the tackles. The shifting of this great weight of metal brought the larboard lower deck port cills just level with the water. The men were then able to get at the mouth of the pipe to the water cock, on the starboard side, as it was clean out of the water, and for about an hour they were working hard at it, the ship remaining all on one side. About nine o'clock, just after breakfast, the hands had been turned up, when the last lighter, with rum on board, came alongside. She was a sloop of fifty tons, called the *Lark* and belonged to three brothers. She was secured to the larboard side of the ship, and the hands were piped 'clear lighter'. Some men were in the lighter slinging the casks; others at the yard tackle and stay falls, hoisting in; some in the spirit room stowing away; some in the waist, bearing the casks over and down the hatchway, all very busy clearing the lighter. Almost all the men were on the larboard side, and that brought the ship still more down to port. Then the water was not so smooth as at first, and it began to wash into the lower ports and of

L

course had no escape, so that there was very soon a good weight of water in the lower deck. There were mice in the ship and they were disturbed by the water entering their quarters and the men were catching them and laughing as they swam about.

The carpenter was the first to perceive danger. The casks of rum hoisted in and lying on the larboard side, before they could be lowered into the hold, made also a difference. So the carpenter went on deck to the Lieutenant, who was officer of the watch, requesting that he would be pleased to order the ship to be righted somewhat, as she could not bear it. But the Lieutenant gave a very short answer to the carpenter, who then went down below. He found the water came in so fast that he saw she was getting past her bearings, and he therefore came up a second time on the quarter deck to the Lieutenant and said to him, 'If you please, Sir, to right the ship; it is my duty to tell you she will not bear it any longer.' He spoke in a very positive way, as was his duty. But the Lieutenant answered, 'If you think, Sir, that you can manage the ship better than I can, you had better take the command.'

In the waist at the time were a good many men and they heard what the carpenter said and what the Lieutenant gave. They were all aware of the danger and felt very uncomfortable. There were plenty of good seamen aboard who knew what they were about almost as well as their officers and certainly better than the one who had the watch.

A few minutes afterwards, (he, the Lieutenant, had remained that time doing nothing, merely because he would not be dictated to by the carpenter), the Lieutenant ordered the drummer to be called to beat to quarters, that the guns might be run into their places, and the ship righted. The drummer's name was passed along quick enough for all were alarmed at their situation, for the ship had just then heeled over still more. All the men jumped down off the gangway as soon as the drummer was called, and hastened down to their quarters. The drum was not beat for the man had not time to get his drum. All hands were now tumbling down the hatchway as fast as they could to their quarters, that they might run their guns into their places and so right the ship.

I was stationed at the third gun from forward on the starboard side of the lower deck. I said to Carrol, who was the second captain, 'I say, let us try to get our gun out without waiting for the drum, for the sooner we right the better.' We bousted out our gun, which had run in amidships, but the ship heeled over so much that, do all we could, it ran in again upon us, and at the same time the water made a heavy rush into the larboard lower deck ports. 'The ship is sinking, Carrol,' I cried, 'lay hold of the ring-bolt and jump out, we shall all be drowned.' He made for the ring-bolt and I caught it, climbed out of the port and jumped into the sea. I never saw him afterwards.

I followed him as fast as I could out of the same port, which was the one belonging to our gun (the third from forward on the starboard side) and when I was outside I perceived that all the other portholes were crowded as full as they could be with heads of the men trying to escape and jamming one another so that they could scarcely move either one way or the other. I caught hold of the sheet anchor, which was just above me, to prevent my falling back in the board and perceiving a woman struggling at the port, dragged her out and threw her from me.

The ship was now lying down so completely on her larboard broadside, that the heads of the men in the ports disappeared all at once. They all dropped back into the ship for the portholes were now upright and it was just as if men were trying to get out of the tops of so many chimneys, with nothing for their feet to purchase upon. Just after the men fell inboard, there came a rush of air through the ports, so violent as to blow my hat off. It was the air from the hold and deck, which having no other vent, escaped, as the water which poured in took up its space. The ship then sunk, righting as she went down.

Much has been written and said as to the true causes of this tragedy. A retired Admiral gives perhaps the clearest true picture with his comments made at the time.

The *Royal George* did not upset until all hands were turned up to right the ship, and then five or six hundred men (about thirty or forty tons weight) must have gone over to the larboard side to get up the guns at which they were quartered into their proper places, and as the larboard lower deck ports must have been very near the water, the weight of so many men going over at once to that side caused the midship ports to dip a little under the water, and after that took place there was no hope left; nothing could then save her.

The ship turned over suddenly. Her masts went under water and continued so for nine or ten minutes. The starboard side of her bottom was then above water on which many hundreds of men and some women had scrambled and were making sad lamentations. This continued so long as the air in the hold supported the ship in that position, but as the water forced it out she sunk from under them. The vessel vibrating and the surge sweeping the people into the whirlpool.

On touching the ground she rebounded and finally settled. Then the masts came up again and as she lay on her larboard side side they inclined to the southwards towards the Isle of Wight at an angle of about 45 degree. The main top was then eight or ten feet above water.

The ships at Spithead immediately fired signals of distress. There was no want of assistance and if the ship had continued afloat a short time longer most of those who had got on the bottom might have been taken off, for the boats from the men-of-war lying to the westward with wind and tide in their favour were soon on the spot. But alas too late, as those that could swim were drowned by those who could not. The upsetting of the *Royal George* while at anchor at Spithead was not believed in London by many experienced naval officers and others until it could no longer be doubted.

The water cock should have been put to rights before the shot was put aboard. But if the Lieutenant of the Watch had given the order to right the ship when the carpenter first spoke to him nothing amiss would have happened, as three or four men at each tackle of the starboard guns would have very soon bounced the guns all out and have righted the ship.

The wind was from the north west, only a bit of a breeze, and there was no sudden gust of wind which made her heel over just before she sank. It was the weight of metal and the water which had dashed through the port holes which sunk her, and not the effect of the wind on her.

Professor Lewis gives the interesting opinion that the woodwork holding together the copper sheathing was rotten and the ship's bottom fell out with the weight of the water.

Of the twelve hundred people on board at the time, only three hundred were saved. The disaster was all the more tragic as the ship was sailing the next day, so many wives and sweethearts were on board, together with a good many young children. The *Royal George* had always been a flagship and this time she was flying the flag of Admiral Kempenfelt. He was trapped in his cabin and never had a chance. There was scarcely a Portsmouth family which did not lose a relative or close friend.

9

Prelude to Victory

Thirty-two-gun frigate ship

During the eighteenth century the defences begun by de Gomme in the reign of Charles II were steadily enlarged and improved (see plan 1). In addition, the secondary town of Portsea was given ramparts and a moat similar in design to the parent town, but on a much more massive scale.

These defences did not stop where de Gomme's plans had ended, because a new factor in land warfare had appeared. This was the mobile gun which commanded entirely fresh thinking in defensive works. It had become possible for an enemy to land artillery along the coast and attack the Island of Portsea from the north. Consequently, in 1747, a continuous rampart and moat had been constructed along the whole northern face of the island and the Portsbridge had been entirely reconstructed. A new fort, Cumberland, had been built to prevent the entry of hostile shipping into Langstone Harbour.

To improve the defences of the entrance to the town, the Landport Gate (No. 17) was removed from a point at the north end of the High Street to a position halfway between the Town Mount Bastion (No. 15) and Guy's Bastion (No. 19). It had a drawbridge to its ravelin and a further bridge to the glacis; being built of white Portland stone, it made a handsome entrance gate. When a sovereign visited the town, the gate was closed and the keys were delivered to the Sovereign, who returned them to the Garrison Commander, giving the order to 'Throw open the gates of Her Majesty's Fortress that the Queen may enter', and this ceremony is continued to this day.

Many of the new fortifications were built by convicts who were housed in former men-of-war, which were shorn of their masts and moored in both Portsmouth and Langstone harbours. The convicts with severe sentences were deported to the New World but with the outbreak of the American War of Independence it became no longer possible to deport them there. Accordingly it was decided to send those with deportation sentences to Australia, and the prison hulks in Portsmouth harbour became 'a transit camp' for many of these sailings.

On 13th May 1787 the first batch of deportees for Australia left Portsmouth under the charge of a company of Marines, some of whom took their wives with them. There were six ships in all and the squadron was commanded by Captain Phillips. The voyage lasted thirty-six weeks and before the destination was reached their numbers had been increased by seven children.

Captain Phillips' orders were to land in Botany Bay but, seeing a magnificent harbour slightly to the north, he landed there on 26th January 1788. Thus Portsmouth sailors and Marines founded what is now the great City of Sydney, which is sometimes referred to as a daughter of Portsmouth.

The Marines, who remained with their wives, were the first representatives of constituted British authority in Australia and the work they did there was the laying of the foundations on which the Commonwealth of Australia has been built up.

Although Plymouth took a part in this colonisation, Portsmouth, because of its supremacy as a naval port and its favourable geographical position, was the principal point of departure for some fifty years. Accompanying these squadrons were geographers, and naval and military officers who became Governors of territories. Names on the map of Australia testify to the work of many of these men. The Bass Straits were named after Surgeon Lieutenant Bass, who lived in Southsea.

The Murray River took its name after Captain Murray of the Marines and others were Ross and Jackson. Captain Collins, a Marine from Portsmouth, founded Hobart in Tasmania.

As for the convicts, the hardened criminals continued their life of crime and became bush-rangers, but the majority took to the country and ended their days as well-to-do farmers, while a few less enterprising took posts as servants of the Marines.

At the beginning of the last decade of this memorable century Pitt was telling the country there would be no war for fifteen years. The American War had ended with the Treaty of Versailles in 1783, by which Great Britain acknowledged the colonists' independence. France and Spain remained hostile and it should have been clear to the Government that much would depend on sea power to hold the remainder of our vast colonial empire, but reductions in armaments had been proposed and in consequence Portsmouth lay comparatively idle. Nothing was building in the dockyard except the *Swift* of 329 tons.

There were, however, courts martial from time to time, and when on the 19th June 1792 mutineers from the *Bounty* arrived at Spithead there was really something to revive interest in naval affairs.

The *Bounty* sailed from Spithead on the 23rd December 1787, under the command of Lieutenant Bligh, a Cornishman. There were two master's mates, one of whom was Fletcher Christian. The object of the expedition was to convey bread-fruit trees from the Society Islands to the West Indies, as a useful source of new food there.

The job having been completed, the *Bounty* was making her way home when, on the 28th April 1789, when the ship was in the Friendly Islands, the crew mutinied, and Bligh was set adrift with a number of officers and ship's company in an open boat, and Fletcher Christian sailed away in the *Bounty*.

Some of the mutineers landed in Tahiti, others in Pitcairn Island. On the 23rd March 1791 H.M.S. *Pandora* arrived at Tahiti and took off the mutineers from the island. After a series of adventures in which the *Pandora* was sunk, the mutineers arrived at Spithead in another ship on the 19th June 1792. They were tried by court martial in Portsmouth on board H.M.S. *Duke* on the 12th September 1792. There were ten men in all. On the 28th October 1792 three of these men were publicly executed in the presence of parties of seamen from every ship in the harbour.

When Pitt made his optimistic speech forecasting fifteen years of peace for Britain, the French Revolution was already a fact, and within twelve months Britain had embarked on the final struggle against France which was to last until 1815.

At first, allied with Britain were Austria, Prussia, Holland, Spain and Sardinia, but by 1797 this country stood alone. In all this anxious time the Navy, commanded by officers of exceptional ability and considerable experience, showed the way to the eventual defeat of Napoleonic France through sea power.

England might have been deprived of the greatest of these by an earlier event best described in a letter by his own hand.

To William Locker Esq.

Portsmouth, April 21st, 1784.

. . . And yesterday, to complete me, I was riding a *blackguard* horse that ran away with me at Common, carried me round all the Works into Portsmouth, by the London gates, through the Town out at the gate that leads to Common, where there was a waggon in the road,—which is so very narrow, that a horse could barely pass. To save my legs, and perhaps my life, I was obliged to throw myself from the horse, which I did with great agility: but unluckily upon hard stones, which has hurt my back and my leg, but done no other mischief. It was a thousand to one that I had not been killed. To crown all, a young girl was riding with me; her horse ran away with mine; but most fortunately a *gallant* young man seized her horse's bridle a moment before I dismounted, and saved her from the destruction which she could not have avoided. . . .

I am yours, most sincerely,
Horatio Nelson

The first encounter with the Revolutionary Fleet took place in 1794 and lasted five days, culminating in the Battle of the Glorious First of June when Lord Howe, at the age of seventy, defeated de Villaret Joyeuse, who had put to sea to guard a large convoy carrying corn from America, which was desperately needed to make up for the disastrous French harvest of the previous year.

The victory was one of the most complete in British naval history and on the 17th June the victorious Fleet arrived at

Spithead, together with the prizes. The *Evening Post* takes up the story . . .

This morning the conquering fleet, with their prizes, appeared in the offing. Crowds of people were soon collected on the ramparts, and when the *Queen Charlotte* dropped anchor at Spithead, the guns on the batteries were fired. About thirty minutes past twelve, Earl Howe landed at the new Sally Port, when a second discharge of artillery took place. His Lordship was received with the reiterated shouts of the people, collected together in astonishing numbers; a Captain's guard of the Gloucester militia was drawn up on the lower end of the grand parade, with the band of the Regiment playing, till his Lordship came up to them, 'The Conquering Hero Comes!' The streets, tops of houses, balconies, windows, grand parades, and the ramparts from the Queen's battery to the main guard, were entirely crowded beyond all example, and their shouts rent the air.

As his Lordship passed to the Governor's house, when he could be heard, he repeatedly thanked the people for the great respect shown him, observing that the brave British seamen did the business!

As soon as his Lordship entered the Governor's house, the Marines and Gloucester Bands, on each side of the entrance, struck up 'Rule Britannia', 'Britons strike home', 'God Save the King'. &c. and the preparations for a third grand illumination, surpass, if possible, those of last night and the preceding.

Nine ships of the line of Earl Howe's fleet are ordered into Plymouth, and the rest, viz.

Royal Charlotte,	*Royal George,*	*Queen,*
Bellerophon,	*Russel,*	*Caesar,*
Leviathan,	*Bellona,*	*Barfleur,*
Invincible,	*Thunderer,*	*Brunswick,*
Alfred, with the six prizes,		

are all come into this port. Our ships seem to have suffered greatly in their masts and rigging, and several of them have sustained considerable damage in their hulls; but the killed and wounded of the British, considering that it was the severest fight that ever happened since nations warred against one another on the ocean, is far less than can be expected, and bears no sort of proportion to that on board the enemy's vanquished ships.

This day Earl and Lady Howe, with a great party, dined at Admiral Sir Peter Parker's, our very popular and worthy Port Admiral, who entertained his distinguished guests in the most sumptuous style, and such as evinces his usual hospitable and elegant taste.

Later, on 26th June, their Majesties came to Portsmouth to honour the Fleet. This memorable occasion is vividly described in the Annual Register . . .

Their Majesties arrived here on Thursday morning, in pursuance of the resolution they had announced of visiting the fleet, and were received by the governor and Lord Howe, and conducted to the dock yard, whence they proceeded to Spithead with the Royal Family. Lord Howe's flag was shifted to a frigate, and the Royal Standard hoisted on board the *Queen Charlotte*, on board which His Majesty, the Queen and the Royal Family remained till six o'clock. The Lords of the Admiralty hoisted their flag on board the *Queen*, Admiral Gardner's flag being removed on the occasion. The whole garrison was under arms; the concourse of people was immense. The King, with his own hand, carried a valuable diamond-hilted sword, from the Commissioner's house down to the boat, which he presented to Earl Howe, on board the *Queen Charlotte*, as a mark of his satisfaction and entire approbation of his conduct. His Majesty also presented a gold chain, to which a medal is hereafter to be annexed, to Admiral Sir Alexander Hood and Rear-Admiral Gardner. The like honour was conferred on Lord Howe's first captain, Sir Roger Curtis. The wounded Admirals, Bowyer and Pasley, who consequently could not attend, have been distinguished with similar marks of favour. The Royal Family, in the evening, on their return from Spithead, rowed up the harbour to view the six French prizes, which are at moorings there. On Friday, the King first gave audience to the officers of Lord Howe, and afterwards indiscriminately to all the other naval and military officers. Some marks of distinction were conferred. On the levee being ended, the Royal Family returned to the Commissioner's house in the Dock-yard to dinner. The town was brilliantly illuminated in the evening, and every possible demonstration of joy manifested. On Saturday, the Royal Family attended the launching of the *Prince of Wales*, a fine second rate. Four flags were flying on board the *Prince of Wales* during this ceremony; the Royal Standard, the Admiralty flag, Sir Peter Parker's white flag as Port Admiral, and the Union flag. The cheering of the multitudes, in honour of the royal visitants, wherever they appeared, made the air ring; and bands of music continued playing in the yard and on board the ships and yachts up the harbour. Immediately on the *Prince of Wales* being brought up to her moorings, Their Majesties, Prince Ernest, and the Princesses, embarked in order to go on board the *Aquilon* frigate (Captain

Stopford), at Spithead. As the barges approached the ships at Spithead, the firing of two guns from the *Queen Charlotte* were, as on a former marine trip, the signal for a general salute; every ship, in consequence, fired twenty-one guns, and the crews cheered as the barges passed. On Their Majesties going on board the *Aquilon*, and getting under sail, the like salute was fired; and the bands of the different ships played martial symphonies for the greatest part of the day. The *Aquilon*, after sailing round the fleet, stood away towards the Needles. Owing to there being very little wind, soon after the *Aquilon* frigate had got to the eastward of Cowes point, she, in going about, touched the ground, by which accident they were stopped an hour or two; and night coming on, Their Majesties and all the royal party took to their barges. The *Aquilon*, on the rising of the tide, was got off without receiving damage. On Monday morning, Their Majesties, Prince Ernest and the Princesses, went on board the *Niger* frigate, and sailed for Southampton, where they landed in the afternoon, and immediately proceeded in carriages for Windsor.

The war did not go well on land, however, and by early 1797 all our allies had either deserted us or had been forced to fight for the other side, and amongst these was Holland, another naval power. Now at last it was clear to all that the whole future of England, and the Colonial Empire, depended on the Navy. In February the shape of things to come was clearly shown to the world when Sir John Jervis, with Nelson commanding the *Captain* in his fleet, soundly defeated the Spaniards at the Battle of Cape St. Vincent. It was at this moment of encouragement and hopefulness that a national disaster not of the enemy's making threatened our supremacy at sea.

Lord Howe had asked to retire following the battle of the Glorious First of June. He had pleaded ill-health and age, but the King and the Board had insisted that he remain in command. They allowed him to absent himself from the Fleet for as long as he liked, leaving his second, Lord Bridport, in command. It was during one of these protracted periods of Lord Howe's absence when in April 1797 it was discovered that a plot was hatching in the Fleet, then lying at Spithead, to enforce the demands of the men of the lower deck. Petitions had been sent to the Board supported by personal letters to Howe, but the grand old man, who had the hope of retiring in mind, had not acted on them.

There were many grievances. Pay had not been raised since Charles II's day, while prices had risen thirty per cent. This was bad enough, but the tickets with which the man were paid were hard to cash ashore and some men, after as much as four years' service, and having sent their tickets home, found that their wives had been forced to trade them for much less than their value. The Press Gang was loathed, and as there was no shore leave, for fear of men deserting, pressed men found their lives virtually ruined. Thousands succeeded in deserting and thereafter lived in fear of arrest and possible death. It might be though that the 'cat' was part of the trouble, but this was not so. The men recognised that discipline had to be enforced, and in any case many captains kept order entirely through the strength of their own personalities. Besides the pay, the food was thoroughly bad, and even in harbour fresh food was seldom brought off. The stopping of merchantmen in the channel on their way home after a long voyage, when able seamen would be taken off for service in the Fleet, perhaps never to see their families again, was an added cause of discontent, but the last straw was an application by the soldiers for a rise of a shilling a day which was granted immediately. Behind the minds of the men was always the fact of the French Revolution which had been fought and won to redress grievances.

Lord Bridport was ordered to take the Fleet to sea to blow the trouble out of the men's heads, but when he made the signal ships' companies manned the yards and cheered. Similar but more serious trouble broke out at Yarmouth and the Nore, where Admiral Duncan was based for the purpose of blockading the Dutch Fleet in their ports. Some ships actually on duty off the Dutch coast sailed for home.

At Portsmouth the men's delegates virtually took over the Fleet. They imprisoned their officers and conducted the administration of the Fleet from Lord Howe's cabin in the *Queen Charlotte*. Violence was avoided whenever possible, and officers were treated with respect and demands were made with politeness. Here and there, particularly when an officer resorted to arms, the men retaliated with force, but continued to use moderation as soon as the opportunity was presented.

Negotiations with the Board's representatives who had come to Portsmouth under these extraordinary circumstances came to nothing. Meanwhile anxiety over the movements of the

French Fleet brought the Board almost to desperation. At this point the King suggested that Lord Howe must be sent down to Portsmouth. Suffering agonies from gout, Howe made the journey, and there followed one of the most remarkable scenes ever enacted in a British Fleet.

Before coming to Portsmouth Howe had obtained the King's Pardon and had extracted from the Board a promise of a rise in pay, and on other matters he had secured a free hand. He determined to visit every ship. As his barge came alongside each ship, careful hands lifted him on to the ladder and carried him on board. There every head was bared and the men stood in silence. This was not so much a meeting of their commander-in-chief with mutinous men, but a family waiting to hear what their father had to tell them. Firstly Howe asked for their loyalty, and this he received in full measure. Having obtained their hearts he told them they had done wrong, but he recognised they had grievances. He told them they would have their pay rise and he would see to it that other hardships and causes of discontent were removed. In an afternoon the mutiny was over. On May 18th the British Fleet once more put to sea. Portsmouth had been the focal point of one of the gravest moments in our history.

Ashore Lord Howe was faced with a task which he found very distasteful. The mutineers had given him a list of over one hundred officers, mostly midshipmen, who they wished to be removed from the Fleet. The men thought they were unjust in their enforcement of discipline. This he had agreed to with great reluctance, and recommended to the Board that these officers should be kept on full pay and gradually infiltrated back into the Fleet. The Board agreed.

The town which Lord Howe then said goodbye to for the last time was like no other in the kingdom. Its unique position had made it the heart of the British Navy. There was invariably a mass of shipping at Spithead and on fine evenings the inhabitants promenaded along the defensive ramparts looking at the ships and listening to the military bands which played on the Governor's Green. There was much unwritten etiquette in naval circles. Senior officers stayed at the 'George' in the High Street, Lieutenants frequented the 'Fountain' further down the street and on Point, not far from King James's gate, was the 'Blue Posts' where the coachman informed Peter Simple, 'the midshipmen leave their chestesses, call for tea and toastesses and sometimes forget to pay for their breakfastesses'. Here too on Point were taverns, good and bad, pawnbrokers, money lenders, tailors, pastry shops, all mingled in a maze of narrow streets with questionable lodging houses, where the Polls of Point plied their trade and at night time in the taverns and alleys there took place the worst scenes of drunkenness and debauchery ever known. Pinckards summed up the scene on Point when he wrote: 'Portsmouth is not only filthy and crowded, but crowded with a class of low and abandoned beings who seem to have declared open war against every habit of decency and decorum.'

When an expedition was embarking the scenes in the town and Point surpassed all description. The hostelries were overflowing. The 'Arethusa', the 'Mars' and the 'Neptune', with a dozen others, all named after ships, burst their sides with sailors and soldiers having a last fling ashore. In the streets porters carrying luggage struggled against parties of drunken sailors arm in arm obstructing all traffic, while midshipmen did their best to lure them to the boats waiting at the Camber. There, overloaded boats upset, boatmen wrangled over fares, men greeted old friends and others said their last goodbyes, while traders in liquor of every possible description made their last sales.

As a contrast, somehow through all the confusion, a captain would leave in his long boat with the same dignity which he had received on his departure from the Port Admiral's House. When a front-line regiment embarked the bearing of the marching men and mounted officers was magnificent as they swung down the High Street with colours flying and bands playing, followed by a vast and motley crowd including fiddlers, pickpockets, fortune-tellers and barking dogs.

When the third *Victory* was destroyed by fire in the dockyard in 1721, a fourth had been laid down on the Thames and was launched in 1737. She was described as the finest and most powerful ship-of-war ever built in a British dockyard. Many experienced seamen considered her sides were too lofty, making her unweatherly. Perhaps it was because of this suspected defect in design that she was the only *Victory* which was an unhappy ship. Nevertheless, when Admiral Sir John Balchen, a very popular officer, hoisted his flag in her, many midshipmen and young volunteers of all ranks rushed to serve in her. In consequence she had a complement of over a thousand men in her when on October 4th, 1744, she foundered in a hurricane somewhere between the Scillies and Alderney. No bodies were ever found; only some wreckage and midshipmen's chests.

Twenty-one years later, on the 7th May 1765, the fifth *Victory* was built and launched, this time at Chatham.

It will be remembered that in 1778 this ship had been Keppel's flagship at the fateful Battle of Ushant. The *Victory* again was seen at Portsmouth in 1791 when a large fleet collected at Spithead under its commander-in-chief, Lord Hood. Pitt visited Lord Hood that summer and went on board the *Victory*. Later in August Lord Hood struck his flag, but not long afterwards he again selected the *Victory* for his flagship in the Mediterranean. In 1795 the ship returned to Portsmouth and was surveyed, but taken to Chatham, the port where she was built, to refit. The next time Portsmouth saw this famous ship was in early May 1803 when she came round and anchored at Spithead. Then, on the 18th of that month, at 3.30 p.m. Vice-Admiral Lord Nelson's flag was run up in the ship for the first time, and shortly afterwards the Admiral went on board. Then followed Nelson's famous search for the French Fleet, his blockade of Toulon, and his remarkable chase to the West Indies and back. All this took two years, during which time he had not set foot on land. It was on Sunday, the 18th August 1805, that Nelson landed at Portsmouth, amid cheering and adoring crowds. He then proceeded to his home at Merton Place, south west of London, where he had hoped to rest for some time and enjoy the companionship of Lady Hamilton and play with his adored little daughter, Horatia. Events were moving fast, however, and by the second week in September the *Victory* was again anchored at Spithead, and on Saturday the 14th she moved to St. Helens to await the Admiral. At 11.30 the *Victory* hoisted his flag, while Nelson was attending to last-minute business in the 'George' Hotel in the High Street. It was two o'clock in the afternoon before he was ready to go on board, but by then the street in front of the hotel was already blocked with people waiting for a sight of him. It was a moment of great portent for him when he stepped out of the 'George' to walk to the barge. He had never forgotten the fortune-teller who, many years previously in the West Indies, had told him his fortune up to the age of forty-seven, and had then looked up and said to him, 'I can see nothing more after that.' This premonition was much in his mind, besides his sadness of having to leave Merton so soon after his two years of absence. Lord Nelson's age at this time was forty-seven.

The crowd in the High Street was so great that it seemed doubtful whether he could in fact, even with the help of marines and his coxswain, walk to the Sally Port, so, accompanied by Captain Hardy, he decided to slip out of the 'George' by the back way into Penny Street and send a message to the barge to await him further along the shore. This way led him along the north side of Governor's Green and then by way of the King's Bastion to the Spur Redoubt and thence on the beach. Some people were already making their way to the beach by this route as they realised, owing to the crowd in the High Street, that they had no hope of seeing their hero, and had decided to compromise by going to the beach to watch the barge being rowed on its way to Spithead and St. Helens. As soon as they saw Lord Nelson, this time, instead of cheering, these people were overcome by an awed silence. Men doffed their hats, women knelt in prayer, and a few tried to touch his hand. All had a terrible foreboding that this might be the last time they would see him alive. Lord Nelson, feeling the tension of the moment, sent a message to let the people in the High Street know that he was not passing that way, but would be embarking off the beach near the King's Bastion. In no time, the present small stream of people following his route swelled to a surging crowd, but still no one cheered. Turning to Captain Hardy, Nelson said, 'I used to have their huzzas, but now I have their hearts.' As he stepped into the waiting barge men and women waded into the sea and only then, when he raised his cocked hat to bid them goodbye, did a cheer go up, but even this did not really break the almost anguished anxiety of all who were privileged to be there. As the barge made its way to Spithead the crowd mounted the ramparts to have a better view until it was no longer possible to distinguish one boat from another in the mass of shipping collected at Spithead and St. Helens.

The news of the Battle of Trafalgar was received in Portsmouth in the same way as in all towns and villages throughout the country. There was profound relief that a major victory had been won, but overshadowing all was the tragedy of the death of the victor and hero, Lord Nelson.

It was at 1.30 on the 4th December that the inhabitants of

Portsmouth once again saw the *Victory* as she anchored at St. Helens, with the Vice-Admiral's flag at half-mast, showing that Lord Nelson's body was on board. After taking on provisions and landing a few local men, the *Victory* sailed for the Medway on December 10th, and Portsmouth people imagined that the ship had also sailed out of their lives. Little did they think then that in years to come this famous ship would be the greatest treasure which any city in the United Kingdom could possibly have, and would be theirs for all time.

M

10

One Hundred Years of Peace

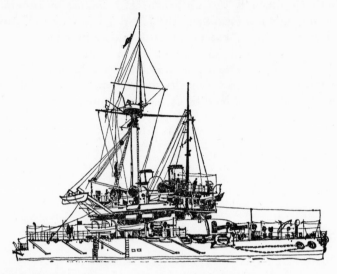

H.M.S. Devastation

During the hundred years which followed Trafalgar, Portsmouth and Portsea changed from an important and picturesque naval base full of sailing ships, to the greatest naval port in a vast empire, fully mechanised, harbouring ironclads and covering the port with coal dust and smoke. No longer did the sound of the adze predominate. Its place was taken by the steam hammer and the riveter. The stage-coach was replaced by the railway, night shifts in the dockyard worked by gas light and trams conveyed the workers to the yard. Off the Isle of Wight the sound of heavy gun-fire heralded the age of battle fleets and big guns. The presses of the *Portsmouth Telegraph*, established in 1799, which later became the *Hampshire Telegraph*, covered these events for an amazed public.

But the old age did not pass away in just a decade. It was a slow process in the first half of the century. The first to go were the personalities, and the last of these was Lord Collingwood. He had led the leeward squadron at Trafalgar and like Lord Howe before him had begged to be relieved of his command and allowed to spend his remaining days at home in England, but again the government of the day would not listen to the pleadings of another of their most trusted Commanders. Collingwood remained in the Mediterranean, hardly going ashore during five years' service and gradually failing in health until, in the spring of 1810, he sailed for home in the *Ville de Paris*, but he died before passing through the Straits of Gibraltar. His body was transferred to the frigate *Nereus* and, as on the occasion when the *Victory* brought home the body of Lord Nelson, she anchored in St. Helens Roads to land a number of men and to pick up fresh provisions. She sailed the same day for the Nore, and so the last of the great admirals of the sailing era passed out of history and the story of Portsmouth.

At last comparative peace had come to Portsmouth and this breathing space provides an opportunity to look round Portsea Island. The town inside the fortifications had been filled to the brim and there was no more room for development, neither was there any more room in Portsea inside the ramparts, so houses were springing up around the Landport and to the eastward of the town fortifications, the latter heralding the birth of Southsea. Many of the new roads adopted famous names commemorating Portsmouth's links with the past. Copenhagen Street, Nile Street, Trafalgar Street and Waterloo Place recalled these famous battles. As the century developed further building encroachments swamped the old manors of Froddington (or Fratton), Kingston, Stamshaw and Buckland but the settlements at Copnor, Milton and Eastney remained agricultural for some time to come.

By 1820 the population of Old Portsmouth was seven thousand and Portsea thirty-eight thousand. Happily the Government had bought Southsea Common from the Lord of the Manor and nothing could be built on it. It remains one of Portsmouth's greatest assets.

In the early summer of 1814 Frederick William III, King of Prussia, and the Tsar Alexander I of Russia, were in England on a visit to the Prince Regent. As the defeat of Napoleon had been brought about chiefly through the efforts of the British Navy, it seemed appropriate that these two Allied potentates should visit Portsmouth and the Fleet to see for themselves the naval base from which the British naval operations had been mounted and to have a first-hand sight of the ships, many of which had taken part in the principal fighting.

A contemporary wrote: 'Those who were not present will feel pleasure in tracing those scenes which, for splendour, importance and effect, were never before equalled in Portsmouth, and rarely in any other place.'

The preparation began some days before the royal visitors were expected, during which time excitement was increased by the news that the veteran Marshal Blücher would also be present. Both the Civic Departments and the inhabitants of the town vied with each other in their arrangements for the great occasion. As regards the latter, the lodging-house keepers soon saw the advantage they could make out of the celebrations, and offered rooms for prices ranging from five pounds to as much as fifty pounds for a few days' stay.

The first person of importance to arrive was His Royal Highness the Duke of Clarence, later William IV, who was an Admiral of the Fleet, and hoisted his flag in the *Jason* which, on Saturday, 18th June, with the State yachts *Royal Sovereign* and *Royal Charlotte* had been brought round from the Thames. He was given a seventeen-gun salute and was attended by Rear-Admiral Blackwood, who was Captain of the Fleet.

Monday, the 20th June, was a day of dress rehearsal. While the Fleet was busy with 'spit and polish', the Army took up their stations. Between eleven and twelve thousand men took part, including Royal Marines, the Portsdown Yeomanry and the Portsmouth Volunteer Artillery. There was also a considerable body of cavalry, including Hussars and Light Dragoons.

During the week-end Lord Melville, the First Lord of the Admiralty, and Members of the Board arrived. The flag of the First Sea Lord was hoisted in the *Ville de Paris* at Spithead and saluted with nineteen guns by the whole fleet. During the following forty-eight hours there was much flag shifting. The Navy had to deal with the royal standard of the Prince Regent, the Union flag of the Admiral of the Fleet, the flag of the First Sea Lord, the flag of the Commander-in-Chief of the Fleet and the Admiralty flag. As these V.I.P.s arrived and were received, their flags were hoisted and struck and re-hoisted as the situation required. Unfortunately this complicated business proved too much for contemporary writers to set down clearly, but at all events the honours due were paid correctly by the Fleet, the naval saluting being augmented sometimes by the army batteries on shore.

His Royal Highness the Prince Regent was expected to arrive on Tuesday, the 21st, but he did not appear, nor was there any news of him, so a guard had to be placed on Portsdown Hill in case the Prince made an appearance in the night.

No doubt by day, information would have been received quickly through the semaphore on Southsea Common, by which, together with the other fourteen stations between London and Portsmouth, it was possible to get a brief message through in clear weather in five minutes.

In the event of his arriving by night, the guard were to receive His Royal Highness and then fire three rockets to warn the town and Naval and Military Commands that the Prince had arrived. Whatever the hour, a salute of a total of sixty-one guns was to be fired immediately. Hearing of this, a group of wags set out for Portsdown Hill with three rockets which, had they let them off, would have started the whole proceedings, but they lost their nerve and disagreed among themselves about the plan, and thus a chain reaction of almost disastrous consequences was averted.

Nothing happened during the night, and in the forenoon of Wednesday, the 22nd, a message was at last received, saying that the Prince Regent would arrive between five and six in the evening. As soon as this news was known for certain, hundreds of people flocked into the town and filled every point of vantage. Some had come from as far as Wales, and their carriages congested every street. The weather being fine, the ladies put on their finery and evidently struck a high note with one reporter, who delighted in the sight of so many 'lovely ladies'. By mid-afternoon the troops were all in their positions, which stretched for three miles without a break from the Grand Parade to Hilsea Barracks.

While accommodation was a problem for the high-class visitors and some even slept in hay lofts, the arrangements for the principal visitors had been carefully thought out. His Royal Highness the Prince Regent was to take up his residence at Government House; the Emperor of Russia and his sister, the Grand Duchess of Oldenburgh, were to reside with the Honourable Commissioner Grey in the dockyard; the King of Prussia, his two sons and nephew, the Princes, were to occupy the house of the Lieutenant Governor, who had moved elsewhere temporarily; Marshal Blücher and Count Platoff (if the latter arrived), were to have the rooms of the bank of Messrs. Goodwin & Company on the Parade.

At about 4 p.m. the artillery on Portsdown fired a salute of twenty-one guns and this was followed by the Fleet announcing

the arrival of the Prince Regent. Everywhere people crowded
to get the best positions. Some enterprising people had put up
special stands, and positions on these could be obtained for
prices from two shillings up to one guinea. Many resisted the
temptation to buy, as they sensed that without any form of
crowd control these stands could easily collapse.

All along the route from Portsbridge the crowds cheered,
hats and handkerchiefs were waved in the air, and military
bands played the National Anthem. About two miles from the
Landport Gate the royal coach was met by a party of rope-
makers who by tradition escorted the royal visitor to the gate.
They were wearing white jackets and purple sashes, and
carrying wands and national flags. This party ran before the
royal coach until it halted at the gate, which had been shut.
The Lieutenant Governor then presented the keys to His
Royal Highness. The Prince smilingly received them and then
handed them back, giving the command, 'Open the gates of
His Majesty's fortress!!' Meanwhile the guns on the ramparts
had fired a triple salute, which was taken up by the ships of the
Fleet.

Upwards of eighty naval officers of senior rank met the coach
in the High Street and preceded the royal party to Government
House. The outriders, the Hussars, the special escort of naval
officers, flanked all the way by the soldiers lining the streets,
made a dazzling spectacle. This was crowned by the sight of the
Prince, his brother, the Duke of Cambridge, and Major-
General Bailey, the Grand Equerry. On their arrival there were
tremendous cheers from a vast crowd surrounding Government
House and on the ramparts. These cheers were redoubled when
the Prince appeared on the balcony for a few minutes. Back at
the Landport Gate the crowds pressed to enter the town, but
no more could be allowed in, and there was great disappointment when the gates were shut. People nearest the gate were
nearly suffocated by the press of those trying to get in, and all
were astonished at being barred entry.

At seven that evening the Prince gave a dinner party for
forty guests, who included the Members of the Board of
Admiralty, all the flag officers of the port and ships present,
the general officers and many people of distinction.

At 8 p.m. the King of Prussia arrived, entering the Landport
Gate in an open chaise and four, drawn by Royal Artillery
horses and escorted by Dragoons. This cavalcade moved at the

gallop and had been preceded by the royal princes, whose appearance was equally dramatic. Lord Cavendish Bentinck saw the King safely to the residence of the Lieutenant Governor in St. Thomas's Street.

The Emperor of Russia, with the Grand Duchess of Oldenburgh, came at about 10 p.m. and drove through Queen Street to the dockyard, where they were received by the Honourable Commissioner Grey and his lady. A number of senior people connected with the dockyard made up the reception party. The Emperor was attended by the Earl of Yarmouth and the Russian Ambassador.

While the arrivals of these potentates caused considerable excitement, the people of Portsmouth were extremely anxious to give a rousing welcome to Marshal Blücher, but he proved to be elusive. There were many false alarms, as one contemporary writer vividly described:

The populace had not discovered Blücher, and every coach which came in was cheered and followed, under the impression that the veteran hero was the inmate. Some asserted that he had already arrived and that they had had the honour of shaking hands with him. In this confused state of the public mind, the Duke of Saxe-Weimar appeared on the Parade, and though he bore not the least resemblance to the Silesian Hero, still he being habited in a splendid foreign uniform, hundreds crowded round him, chanting, 'Blücher, Blücher'. The people snatched his hands to shake them and took him by the arms. The Duke bore all with the utmost good humour and made as speedy retreat as possible. Blücher was more than sixty miles away.

By this time all the illuminations were burning. Crowds wandered through the streets admiring the ingenuity of design and the colourful tableaux. From the descriptions by contemporary writers, these must have been the greatest displays Portsmouth had ever done. Every official residence was decked with crowns, initials of the visitors, and rows of lanthorns. Every public house had something different. There were representations of Napoleon chained to a rock. One had Nelson's famous signal in lighted letters, and the Farlington Water Works displayed a nymph in a recumbent position and intertwined around her were the pennons of England and France, with the words, 'Continue peace till fountains cease'. Portsea and Gosport were in no way behind in their own displays, some depicting Peace, and Mr. Ambrose portraying War tired of his toils resting for breath on the Altar of Peace. Meanwhile at Spithead the Fleet kept up a programme of illuminations all night and fired salutes from time to time.

The next day, Thursday, the 22nd, the whole royal party, attended by countless noble and important people, including the Board of Admiralty, inspected the dockyard and then went off to the Fleet, where ships were inspected, frigates carried out manœuvres and banquets were held. The Emperor of Russia astounded everyone by sitting down to food on the messdeck and prevailed on the Duchess of Oldenburgh to do the same. Before leaving the Fleet, the Prince Regent ordered, 'Splice the main brace', and on the return journey salutes were fired from Southsea Castle and the ramparts.

That evening the Prince gave a dinner party at Government House for 120 people. This was a magnificent affair, and when it was almost through, the elusive Marshal Blücher suddenly turned up at the 'Crown' Inn. This was the signal for the crowd to go nearly mad. Blücher had to appear at his window. He had a glass of wine in his hand and drank to the people. Then he proceeded by carriage to Government House, a journey almost halted by the seething crowds, only the military in force getting the way clear. His arrival at Government House broke up the dinner, happily just ended, and the crowd shouted and cheered until the Marshal and the Prince Regent came out on the balcony. Later, the Prince said he had ex-perienced nothing like this, even in London.

The next day, Friday, the 23rd, was the turn of the cavalry to line the streets. At ten o'clock the royal party again went to the dockyard and carried out further inspections, including storehouses, rigging lofts, rope houses, copper mills, 'on all of which the royal company bestowed their highest encomiums'. Then, embarking at King's Stairs, the party were taken to the yacht *Royal Sovereign* at Spithead. Immediately on their arrival the whole fleet got under way and carried out manœuv-res under full sail off St. Helens. Hundreds of boats had put to sea to witness this magnificent sight and the beach at Southsea was crowded with spectators.

While this great spectacle was being presented the focus of the populace suddenly changed to the 'George' Inn, where the Duke of Wellington had arrived. Fleet manœuvres were instantly forgotten and the crowd left the beaches and filled the High Street. The Duke quickly made his way to Government House and frequently appeared on the balcony, sometimes addressing the crowd who, together with hundreds of foot soldiers, shouted their welcome, while the mounted soldiers twirled their sabres in the air.

That evening the Prince Regent gave a ball and supper at the 'Crown' Inn. There the Duke of Wellington and Marshal Blücher could be seen in close conference. Neither danced.

Next morning, Saturday, the 24th, the Prince Regent held a levée, and after receiving a loyal address from the Mayor, Henry White, conferred the honour of knighthood on him. Vice-Admiral George Martin, Henry Peake,[1] Surveyor of the Navy, and Captain Burton, of the 2nd Queen's Regiment, who had commanded the royal guard of honour, were also knighted.

During the remainder of the day the various parties left the island. On reaching the top of Portsdown Hill, the Prince Regent, the Emperor of Russia and the King of Prussia reviewed troops from the garrison.

Somewhat unexpectedly, Marshal Blücher returned to Portsmouth, and finally set off on his own in a coach-and-four. The inhabitants, whose mood was still one of gaiety and excitement, made every use of this final opportunity, and, taking the horses out of the shafts, themselves dragged the coach as far as the Landport Gate, to the delight of the Marshal.

Thus ended an event which was unique. During the entire week business had been suspended, and every night people in their thousands shut up their houses and came into the Old Town so as not to miss any of the spectacular scenes. For once the weather smiled on an important ceremonial occasion and was perfect throughout. Certainly there had been nothing like this before, and no royal visit has since surpassed it in excitement and splendour.

Little did these reigning monarchs and military leaders think that in a short space of time their rejoicing would prove to have been premature, and for Wellington and Blücher the hundred days of anxious campaigning would have to be endured before Napoleon would finally be defeated at Waterloo almost exactly one year later.

The final defeat of Napoleon on the 18th June 1815 brought to an end the war on land, in the same way as Trafalgar ended the war at sea. In Portsmouth the inhabitants recalled seeing

1. Great-great-grandfather of the Author.

Wellington and Blücher and felt they could picture the scene at Waterloo at the end of that memorable battle better than most people. Their minds, however, were not altogether filled with these thoughts. Something very significant had taken place precisely one week earlier. A steam vessel had entered the port. This event was highlighted in the local press, and justifies a verbatim account which read:

A STEAM VESSEL.—A vessel of this description suddenly made its appearance here yesterday, and coming into the Harbour immediately against the wind, produced, with a little surprise, a considerable degree of curiosity. She was built lately on the Clyde, and was brought here for the purpose of shewing the uses to which she may be applied. She is a very neatly fitted vessel, has the appearance of a yacht, is 75 tons burthen, answers to her helm with all the celerity of the best sailing vessels, and goes through the water at the rate of from seven to eight miles an hour—which is produced from the steam from the engine erected in her, it being of 14 horse power: one ton of coals is sufficient fuel to produce the necessary force of steam for impelling her 100 miles. She came to this place from Plymouth Sound in 23 hours. The machinery in her, we suppose, is constructed upon the common principles of most steam engines: the steam produced by the boiling water is condensed into a piston or pipe, which acts upon two wheels that are fixed upon the sides of the vessel, and these touching the sea, propel her forward in any direction, at the rate mentioned. It was intended, had the wind not been fair, that she should have towed the *Endymion* frigate out of the harbour this morning. The vessel went out by herself at between nine and ten o'clock, when Admirals Sir Edward Thornbrough, Halkett and Fleming, Capts. Boger, Tower, &c. went on board to ascertain her qualifications. She continued to work about Spithead nearly two hours, when she departed for Margate and the River. The Admirals, with Lady Thornbrough, Sir George and Lady Bingham, Mrs. Beaumont, &c. who were much gratified by the experiments made, afterwards proceeded on board the *Curaçao*, with Capt. Tower, and partook of an elegant and sumptuous repast.

On the whole, however, these were leisurely times and life was altogether less exciting. The Portsmouth and Arundel Canal illustrated the mood, as men's minds were concentrated more on trade than defence. The idea of the canal sprung from the acute need for improved transport methods to aid industry and trade.

One answer to the problem was introduced by the third

Duke of Bridgewater who, after seeing the way in which canals were used on the Continent, obtained an Act of Parliament in 1759 for a canal from his Worsley coal mine to Manchester. From then on canals in the midlands and north were rapidly constructed, and conveyed coal, wool and all manner of goods to and from the factories, the mines and the ports. With these examples before them, merchants in the south jumped to the construction of canals, feeling assured of cheaper transport, wider trade and greater profits. But what was best for the north did not necessarily apply in the south, which was primarily agricultural. Besides, at the height of canal promotion in the south, the Napoleonic Wars were raging, and this had given a stimulus to agriculture.

Canal building began to affect Portsmouth when the London–Croydon Canal was constructed and plans were going ahead to extend this waterway into Surrey, Kent and Sussex.

First talk of a London–Portsmouth canal had taken place as early as 1803, and for the next ten years more talk and endless negotiations with company promoters and industrialists who were lobbying Parliament, supported by exhaustive figures showing the estimated profits of the various schemes, at long last brought the project to fruition. Actual work was begun following the petition sent to Parliament in 1817 and which received the Royal Assent on July 7th that year.

The canal was to run from the 'Ship and Anchor' at Ford, on the river at Arun below Arundel, to the Salterns at Birdham and thence to Itchenor through Yapton, Barnham, Drayton, Merston to Hunston, where a wide branch turned north to Southgate in Chichester City, then to Birdham and Chichester harbour. From the harbour the ships and barges could use either Thorny or Emsworth Channels to Langstone Channel, through Langstone Harbour, finally entering Portsea Island at Eastney Creek, which was to be built large enough to take ocean vessels.

The entrance on to Portsea Island was through a large sea lock near Milton, from which the canal would run westward for two and a half miles through Fratton to the Halfway Houses on the main London road leading from Portsmouth.

Commissioners were appointed to settle differences between the Canal Company and landowners. The principal supporters of the Company were the Duke of Norfolk and the Earl of Egremont.

The French prisoners of war and other labour completed the canal in three phases, so the Portsmouth and Arundel Canal Company staged three opening ceremonies.

The first ceremony took place on Tuesday, April 9th 1822, when the deep wide section of the waterway which led to the city of Chichester was opened. The *Egremont,* the Company's steamship, left Eastney Creek, off Milton, at eleven o'clock in the morning with several other vessels in tow. These consisted of three barges of forty tons each, two sailing vessels and eleven rowing boats, the whole of which, including the steamship, extended a hundred and fifty yards in procession and carried one hundred and thirty-two passengers. On board were tradesmen engaged from Portsea, Portsmouth and Gosport, 'who were in the habit of receiving goods from London', and some locals who were interested in the project.

John Williams, chairman of the Company, had planned an early start in order to take advantage of the tide, but events did not take place as scheduled. Just before sailing at 9 a.m. a man named Burnett appeared on the deck of the *Egremont* and offered his services as a pilot, claiming knowledge of the route through Langstone Harbour and Hayling Channel. His offer was accepted by Williams, who was relieved to be able to take the opportunity to spend more time with his guests.

Burnett began his duties by advising a later start than planned, because of the shallow depth of water he estimated would be in Hayling Channel. This was accepted, and when eventually the procession arrived at the entrance to the Channel, Burnett expressed further doubts about the depth of water and delayed another hour. It was nearly 5 p.m. when the ships were off Chichester Harbour, and at this point Burnett put the whole procession aground. The Portsmouth representatives sat it out until the turn of the tide, while ahead of them pleasure craft, trading vessels and fine yachts secured in the heart of Chichester, to the cheers of dense crowds, augmented by the rousing music of numerous bands and cannon fire salutes. To crown their disappointment, the Portsmouth contingent were late for the magnificent dinner which followed.

The Portsea Island section of the waterway took a further six months to complete; then on the 19th September, after four years of giving financial and moral support, the inhabitants of the island took a day's holiday to see the opening of their section of the canal. The whole three miles were crowded on both banks. The Company steamship, the *Egremont*, once again led the procession, crowded with civic personalities and followed by barges filled with passengers. With a band on board playing lively music and the whole procession decorated with coloured flags, it made a grand day's holiday.

At first the Company was confident that the canal would win the vast trade which was anticipated, but the mechanical age was gaining momentum every year. Improved communications began to take their toll of the traffic almost as soon as the complete waterway to London was in operation. By September 1826 Lord Egremont had relinquished all his shares to the Company, 'that it may put the canal back into the good care originally planned'. But the writing was too clearly on the wall. In 1824 the total tonnage in the canal to and from London had totalled 3,650 tons, but in 1826 it had dropped to 1,321 tons. It had been hoped that the time of four days for the whole journey could be maintained, but an article in the *Morning Chronicle* of June 4th, 1826, indicated that such a time was an exception and the usual journey took considerably longer. Even the use of 'fly-barges', lightly laden and travelling all day and night, was unsuccessful, for there was delay in changing horses and passing through locks.

The Portsea Island section of the canal fell into disuse about 1830. Fortunately for Portsmuthians they all got their money back in the course of time, and in some cases with interest, as the land increased in value with the coming of the railway and the ever-pressing problem of housing development. Perhaps the greatest loss from the failure of the enterprise was the charm which the canal had given to Portsea, with its green banks, colourful barges and coastal shipping.

Another form of transport which would cease before the century was out was the coach. One of the colourful coachmen of Portsmouth was Mr. Alderman Nance, who was mayor in 1854. For some time he drove the famous Tantivi coach between Portsmouth and London, and once made the journey in the short time of five hours and forty-two minutes, a record which was never broken. The coach journey started in Portsmouth from the 'Blue Posts' Hostelry, which was owned by his father.

With the air of peace prevailing, life in the dockyard had also become leisurely. The *Princess Charlotte* of a hundred and ten guns was begun in 1812, but was not launched until 1825. The *Indus*, begun in 1819, was not completed until twenty years later. But the building was as good as ever. The *Lacedemonia*, built at the same time as the *Princess Charlotte*, was a classic example of the perfection to which sailing men-of-war had advanced down the ages. She had lovely lines, handled like a gazelle, and with her sides painted black with white ports was remarkably trim and smart. The *Queen* (3,104 tons) built in 1839 marked the zenith of the battleships of the sailing era. She was with the Fleet in 1854 and returned to Portsmouth in 1859, when she was converted to steam and became a 'screw' battleship. She retained her eighty-six guns. The fitting of a screw was the result of a trial carried out in 1842 at Portsmouth when the *Rattler*, screw-driven of seven hundred and seventy-seven tons and two hundred horsepower, was lashed stern to stern with the paddle yacht *Electro* of the same displacement and horsepower. Both ships were driven away from each other at full speed, and the *Rattler* succeeded in towing the *Electro* after her.

The last sailing ship to be built in Portsmouth dockyard was the *Leander*, launched in 1845, in spite of the dockyard having built the *Hermes* in 1825, a steamer of seven hundred tons and carrying six guns. Also, a steamship service had run between Portsmouth and Ryde before 1828. From 1835 the Ryde service was run by the Portsmouth and Ryde Steampacket Company, who also ran trips round the Isle of Wight. The Ryde service began under sail in 1775, when hired wherries were available and acted much as they pleased until 1809, when charges were laid down, and three years later there were restrictions based on weather conditions. By 1817 there was a regular twice-daily sailing. In 1823 the *Prince Coburg*, a steam paddle boat, was plying to Cowes from Southampton.

The final change from sail to steam began in earnest in 1855, four years earlier than the conversion of the *Queen*, when the *Marlborough* (4,000 tons), originally designed as a sailing ship, was converted to steam while still on the stocks. From then on development proceeded at a hot pace.

In 1871 Portsmouth built the *Devastation* (9,380 tons),[1] the

---

1. When the *Devastation* was completed it was decided to give the size of men-of-war by their displacement, that is to say, the actual weight of the ship. Previously the tonnage had been expressed as a measure of cubic capacity of the ship. This caused some confusion at the time, but not nearly so much as has been caused to historians in the last hundred years when comparing the sizes of ships ancient and modern.

first large man-of-war equipped entirely without sail power. Her main armament was four twelve-inch guns, all still muzzle loaders, and four ten-inch breach loaders. The experts had not yet made up their minds whether to change altogether to breech loading, and did not come to a final decision in favour of breech loading until 1879. The next big ship to be built was the *Inflexible* (11,850 tons) in 1876, with four immense sixteen-inch guns and an armour belt twenty-four inches thick. This ship was not fast enough for the rapidly developing Navy, so the *Trafalgar* (11,940 tons), built in 1886, was given four thirteen-point-five-inch guns and, to the satisfaction of the designers, very nearly touched seventeen knots.

By 1895 the rapid changes in design and materials had ceased and ideas had become consolidated. When Portsmouth built the *Majestic* in 1896 a stage had been reached where thirty ships of this class were built in the space of eight years with no changes. To meet such a construction programme all the Royal yards had to be brought in, and contracts put out to private firms. The *Majestic* class carried four twelve-inch guns and twelve six-inch, and could do seventeen and a half knots.

Not only battleships, but the whole of the Navy was transformed in the century. Other new classes of ships came into being and Portsmouth yard built armoured cruisers and protected cruisers. Some of this transformation was due to the advent of the torpedo. Battleships carried this weapon and so did torpedo boats, and destroyers were built to meet the threat to the battle fleet by the latter.

In the hundred years between 1805 and 1905 Portsmouth dockyard built one hundred and sixty-three ships, directly contributing to the greatest transformation in the history of naval construction. All this staggering development in the nineteenth century strains the imagination as to what the dockyard must have endured to keep pace, and underlines the skill of the constructors and engineers and the men on the drawing boards; the fitters, turners and welders and all the variety of trades which make up a large maritime construction yard.

One man considerably eased the problems of those who strove to make the dockyard efficient. This man was Marc Isambard Brunel. He started life in the French Navy, escaped to America in the Revolution, and became Chief Engineer of

New York. Learning that there was a monopoly of pulley-block making in England, he came over with his own designs, which were adopted by General Sir Samuel Bentham, Inspector General of Navy Works. Brunel worked in the dockyard from 1803 to 1808, installing forty-three of his machines. Nearly fifty years later these machines were making one hundred and thirty thousand blocks of all sizes every year. Four of these machines are still in current use.

By 1860 the size of the dockyard had already reached ninety-nine acres, which included eleven docks and two large basins, and four years later the whole area was more than doubled, bringing the total to two hundred and sixty-one acres. Considerable excavation had to be carried out to make a third basin and increase the number of docks. The work was largely done by convict labour, and the excavated material was dumped for reclamation around Whale Island, increasing the size of the island from eleven and a half acres to seventy-four.

These great changes imposed a considerable strain on the personnel of the Navy itself. The experiments, the training of officers and men, the fatal accidents and all the time the anxieties of what was going on in other countries, could only have been gone through by men of great resolution. The guns used by Nelson at Trafalgar differed only in name from those used by Drake when he fought the Armada, yet in this astounding nineteenth century, a sailor who started his career in a wooden ship solely equipped with sails ended his time in an iron ship carrying guns of twelve-inch calibre and over.

Meanwhile the successive commissioners struggled not only with the administrative details of the vast expansion, but with the usual flood of problems in which the position involved them.

Pay was always a difficult matter, not only with rising costs, but with the greater responsibilities of dockyard officers in particular. In 1801 the master shipwright earned £600 per annum in peace time, and £720 in war, and the dockyard surgeon £300 and £360 respectively. Both thought they were underpaid. Mr. Robert Smith, on being appointed 'Tapster of H.M. Dockyard' for selling beer, complained of his small return. There was always some difficulty with the administration of the tap houses. Captain the Honourable Sir George Grey, Commissioner, let this matter run, but his successor,

Rear-Admiral Sir F. L. Maitland, who took over in 1832, closed them once and for all time. One thing Sir George did not allow to run on was the custom of keeping hens, rabbits, pigeons and all sorts of livestock in the yard, and he banned all this, except for permanent residents.

Some of the problems were brought to the Commissioner in the very nicest way. In 1807 the Mayor, John Carter, attended by aldermen, the Town Clerk, the Coroner and other principal civic officers, arrived one morning at the dockyard gates to assert the right of judicial process and the exercise of the office of coroner. Sir George would not let them in until he had assurances that they were not claiming jurisdiction over the soil of the dockyard. This point having been established, the proceeding took the form of a 'get together' in every sense of the word. Opportunity was taken to discuss the work going on for the erection of a monument on Portsdown Hill, 'to the memory of the late Lord Nelson by the Officers, Seamen and Marines of the Fleet'. Their interest was mutual, and a site was selected on Portsdown Hill which overlooked Portchester and the entrance to Portsmouth Harbour.

Royalty arrived from time to time and needed considerable attention. In 1802 His Royal Highness the Duke of Kent embarked for a voyage to the Continent. Arrangements had to be made for his suite, which consisted of one major, two captains and one parson as his personal attendants, as well as three male upper servants and two female under servants. A cook and his wife, both coloured, came along, and there were eight livery servants. Finally for good measure His Royal Highness brought his own band, which was supplied partly from the 1st Battalion the Royals and partly from the Royal Artillery.

Not all launchings went to plan. On Wednesday, 4th September 1825, the *Princess Charlotte* of one hundred and ten guns was launched by His Royal Highness Prince Leopold. In order to assist the crowds in getting to the slip, three light bridges had been placed across the gates of the locks which lay between the dockyard main gate and the *Queen Charlotte* slip. One of these locks was large and more like a basin. Ten minutes before the launch the bridge crossing the gates of this lock was crowded with people, when suddenly the lock gates gave way. A tremendous wave of water carried all before it, including the bridge and the people. The force was so great

N

that many people were carried to the far end of the dock and dashed against the wall. Then, when the wave rebounded, others who were clinging to wreckage were swept across the basin again. There were many brave deeds done that day. Men jumped into the cauldron of swirling water to rescue women and children, many of whom had been stunned when they hit the lock wall at the far end. In consequence only sixteen people lost their lives, but there were three times as many with fractured ribs, arms and legs. The cause of the accident was the abnormal high tide, which exerted a pressure calculated to be over five hundred and twenty tons on lock gates which were weak in their original construction.

Those who returned to their homes using the dockyard main gate crossed the Hard. This short stretch of road leading from the dockyard towards old Portsmouth was already becoming known outside the town. Thousands of sailors passed this way every year and hundreds of dockyard workmen made their daily journey to and from work along its route. In 1817 thirty people were paying rates along the Hard and in 1823 the street Directory mentioned the 'Keppel's Head' for the first time. In the same year Mr Seagrove, the naval tailor, was listed in the Directory. This business later became Gieves, Mathew and Seagrove and in more recent times has become Gieves, known all over the world and famous for its service to naval officers.

William IV, who joined the Navy as a midshipman and had risen to the rank of captain and been created Duke of Clarence, when heir apparent would sail in his yacht the *Royal Sovereign* to Portsmouth to inspect the dockyard and naval establishments. He would go round almost unattended, and gave great pleasure to all and sundry, chatting away to whoever engaged his attention. Sometimes when he gave a ball on board his yacht, dressed in his full regalia, people could hardly believe this was the same elderly gentleman who had talked to them earlier in the day. He annoyed the Navy by introducing red facings to uniforms instead of blue. This decision was later rescinded by Queen Victoria.

In 1827 William was created Lord High Admiral, an office which had lain dormant for one hundred and twenty-seven years. This appointment brought him in his yacht to Portsmouth again, where he inspected the ships 'in Ordinary' and reviewed the Royal Marines. Typical of his genial character,

he accepted an invitation to dine with the Mayor and Corporation, but when he became king he did not visit Portsmouth
again.

Queen Victoria made her first visit to the town of Portsmouth on 28th February 1842. The inhabitants marked this
opportunity to welcome their youthful Queen by erecting three
magnificent triumphal arches. The first was at Mile End, the
second at the east end of Union Road, and the third at the
west end leading into Lion Gate Road. Flags were flown from
every building and the town was made as gay as possible.
Rain spoilt much of the pageantry and some of the decorations,
but the Queen enjoyed the visit. She was received by the
Governor, Sir Hercules Packenham, at the Lion Gate leading
through the Portsea ramparts into the dockyard, where the
ceremony of the keys of the garrison was performed. She
wrote about the visit to Viscount Melbourne:

. . . Our excursion was most successful and gratifying. It rained
very much all Monday evening at Portsmouth, but nevertheless we
visited the *St. Vincent* and the *Royal George* yacht, and the Prince
went all over the dockyard.

It stormed and rained all night and rained when we set off on
board the *Black Eagle* for Spithead on Tuesday morning. It however
got quite fine when we got there and we went on board the *Queen*
and a glorious sight it was; she is a magnificent ship, so wide and
roomy, and though only just commissioned, in the best order. With
Marines, her crew is near upon a thousand men. We saw the men
at dinner and tasted the grog and soup, which pleased them very
much.

Captain Rice had handed the grog to the Queen in a glass,
but she said she wanted to have it 'as the men did', so he
took a can of grog from the nearest mess table and presented it
to the Queen on bended knee. The royal party stayed at
Admiralty House for the visit. The Duke of Wellington was
among the guests and possessed himself of a large umbrella
which he held over the Queen whenever she had to walk in the
open.

The Gosport Railway Station was opened in 1841, and the
Portsmouth Station did not come into being until 1848,
therefore the Queen came, in the first place, to Gosport by
train, and when a special small Royal Station was constructed
in the Clarence Yard, she found it convenient to use this route,

boarding the royal yacht lying alongside the Clarence Pier. In so doing, she could go to and from her island home with the minimum of protocol.

When, in 1844, Louis Philippe, King of France, came to England to stay with Queen Victoria at Windsor, it was found convenient to receive him at the Royal Station in Clarence Yard, where he joined the train which took him as far as Farnborough.

Queen Victoria had previously stayed with the King at the Château d'Eu, two miles from Treport, and this was a return visit. Louis Philippe came over in October, bringing with him a squadron of battleships. In Portsmouth, on the other hand, orders were received that no show of military strength was to be made, the emphasis being on friendliness and peace. This gave no trouble to Portsmouth, where the guns of the fortifications had been neglected and were virtually non-existent or useless. Only frigates and some yachts were sent to Spithead to meet the French squadron, which was under the command of the Prince de Joinville. This officer had a chip on his shoulder about England, and when he saw the meagre military display he made up his mind that this would be the time to attack her. He made his views public on his return to France, and started yet another invasion scare in this country.

Louis Philippe having landed at Clarence Pier, spent three pleasant days at Windsor and returned, this time accompanied by the Queen and the Prince Consort, together with the Duke of Wellington. When the royal party arrived it was too rough for the King to go off to his flagship at Spithead, and as he had to get back to France to keep some important engagements it was decided to send him back via Dover. The whole party waited in the parlour of the house of the Superintendent of Clarence Yard, for which honour he had had no warning and had made no preparations. As the household staff feverishly made arrangements for trains to take the King of France to London and thence to Dover, the rain beat down and the wind blew harder than ever. Eventually, the King got away from Gosport Station and arrived at Nine Elms, Lambeth, then the terminal of the Gosport line at about 10.5 p.m. Transport was laid on to take him to New Cross for the train journey to Dover. When he got there he found the station was on fire, but the hastily prepared royal train had been moved clear and he finally arrived at Dover at 2.30 a.m. the next morning. Meanwhile the Queen and the Prince Consort stayed the night on board the royal yacht and left next morning to go on board the French flagship and thence to Osborne. It should be said, what with the wind, the rain and the fire at New Cross Station, it would have been understandable if the French king had shown some agitation, but he remained calm and delightfully courteous throughout, remarking that he hoped the burning station was fully insured.

In this century Fleet reviews became popular. Queen Victoria reviewed the Fleet seven times from the deck of the royal yacht. By far the biggest review was held in 1856, to mark the end of the war with Russia. It was a perfect day, and people said it could really be the Mediterranean instead of the Channel. It was estimated that six hundred thousand spectators came to see the two hundred and fifty-four naval ships drawn up in two lines at Spithead. The Queen made a special gesture by walking past lines of severely wounded sailors and soldiers drawn up in the dockyard. She was deeply moved by some of the pathetic sights on parade.

The Queen, the Prince Consort, the Prince of Wales, Prince Alfred, the Princess Royal and Princess Helena came from Buckingham Palace, boarding the train at Vauxhall and alighting at the Royal Station at Clarence Victualling Yard.

Two years later the Queen stepped on Portsmouth soil proper for the second time when, in August 1858, she presented Victoria Crosses to twelve officers and men before four thousand troops and twenty thousand spectators drawn up on Southsea Common.

In the life of a seaport like Portsmouth there were always incidents taking place, less spectacular than Fleet reviews and launches, some humorous and some tragic. For instance, something was always happening on Point, and on Saturday, 24th June 1809, the beach was alive with activity. The second battalion of the Eighth Regiment had arrived from foreign service the day before and had left much of their baggage and stores on the beach. A party of soldiers was endeavouring to sort out the muddle, while nearby an old Irishwoman, the wife of a local soldier, was doing her washing together with a friend of hers who was smoking a pipe. The friend offered her a pull, but the pipe did not draw very well, so the woman knocked it out on the pebbles. In a moment some loose gunpowder started to burn, and before this could be controlled the fire spread to a keg of powder, which blew up with tremendous force. Thirteen soldiers were instantly killed, others were blown into the sea or had their arms and legs blown off. One human body minus arms and legs struck the Customs House and another smashed against the 'Union' Tavern, covering the whole frontage with blood. Some bodies were found deposited on the roofs of houses. Fortunately a few brave men ran down to the beach and rolled the remaining kegs of powder into the sea. At last, when quiet and some order had been restored, a search was made for the woman. She was found to be unhurt, and attributed her safety to her large wash-tub, which had been blown on top of her, and from which she had had difficulty in extricating herself.

Then again, in a garrison town, where an officer's honour counted so highly, duelling was not unknown, and in 1845 what was reputed to be the last duel fought in this country took place on Browndown on the Gosport side. About this time it was the custom of the elite and beauty of the neighbourhood to go to the Assembly Rooms on Southsea beach on Sundays to hear music, bathe, dance and read the newspapers. There were always plenty of officers there from the Navy, marines and garrison regiments. Captain Seton, of the 11th Dragoons, had taken a fancy to the wife of Lieutenant Hawkey, of the Royal Marines, having met her at the rooms. It was not long before they were going to 2 King's Terrace, the lady's lodgings, at times when Lieutenant Hawkey was away. Hawkey soon found out what was happening and challenged Seton to a duel.

All the customary procedure of duelling was carried out, and in due course the two officers with their seconds and other attendants arrived at Browndown. On being given the order to fire, Seton's bullet missed and Hawkey's gun did not go off. The second time Seton missed again, but Hawkey's shot struck Seton on the left hip and penetrated the groin. Hawkey fled from the scene and Seton was taken to the Quebec Hotel, where an operation was performed. A few days later Seton died. Hawkey was subsequently found and tried at Winchester, where the jury acquitted him, partly on the grounds of provocation and partly because the jury considered that death was due more to the clumsy work of the surgeons than the bullet.

On the cultural side Portsmouth could claim three worthy

sons. The name of John Pounds is associated with what used to be known as the Ragged Schools. He was born in 1766 of very poor parents and was apprenticed to the dockyard as a shipwright. Unfortunately, at the turn of the eighteenth century, he broke his thigh in an accident and was forced to look for other employment. He set up as a cobbler in a little wooden house in St. Mary Street. He was a man of great heart and sympathy with the lot of others, and took under his charge his brother's boy, who was sickly, suffered from rickets and had club feet. First of all he devised a contraption of leather and iron which he fitted on the boy, who was then able to walk. He then taught the boy to read. Friends and neighbours began to send their children to John also to learn to read. From then on more and more children came and the curriculum broadened to simple sums. Not only did he give these children learning, but often rationed himself to share his scanty meals with them. Crowded together on stools and boxes, with his cages of tame birds all around, he cobbled and taught, seeking no reward, and was deeply moved when old pupils came back from the sea or the forests to thank him for the start he had given them.

The example set by John Pounds stimulated others to carry on his work, not only in Portsmouth, but all over the country. The Ragged School movement spread rapidly, and in 1844 the Seventh Earl of Shaftesbury became President of the Ragged School Union. In 1905 the Shaftesbury Society opened a new Gospel Hall in the East End of London and called it 'John Pounds Mission'. In Portsmouth the 'John Pounds Memorial House' in the High Street perpetuates his name.

Charles Dickens was born in a house in Portsea, now 393 Commercial Road, Landport. It was the evening of Friday, 7th February 1812, when Charles Dickens' mother put on a dance frock and attended a ball at the Beneficial Society's Hall. She returned home late at night, but before morning her son was born. John Dickens, Charles' father, was a clerk in the pay office in the dockyard, and arranged for the child to be baptised at St. Mary's, Kingston, the parish church of Portsea. John moved his family to London when the baby was two years old, and Portsmouth saw no more of its famous writer except on the very few occasions when he came down to hold one of his popular 'readings'.

The third Portsmouth-born man of letters to grace this century was the novelist and poet George Meredith. His birthplace was 73 High Street, where he was born on the 12th February 1828. He was the grandson of a famous and much respected naval tailor. Like Charles Dickens, he left the town at an early age.

A fourth writer, who was also a doctor, spent eight years of his life in Portsmouth towards the end of the century. He was Conan Doyle, who practised in the town from 1882 to 1890.

The stamp of culture in any form had unfortunately left the Free Mart Fair a very long time ago. An attempt to abolish the fair was made in 1841, but this failed. However, at long last, in 1846, its abolition was included in a Local Improvement Bill and received the Royal Assent the following year, and the 'Open Hand' was withdrawn.

The fair had run for over six hundred years, and it must be acknowledged that it gave some measure of prosperity in its early days. Later, it brought fun and laughter to people of few pleasures as we know them today. But it had outlived its purpose, and in Portsmouth, where the habits of sailors were not always of the best, it fell prey to the worst types of depravity, which the authorities seemed unable to suppress.

Also, in 1837, the Royal Naval Academy, as such, in the dockyard was closed. Instruction of young naval officers, naval instructors and constructors went through many vicissitudes at Portsmouth until the Cadet Training Ship *Britannia* was moored at Dartmouth later in the century, and the Royal Naval College was opened at Greenwich.

The invasion scare of 1844 started by the Count de Joinville was revived in 1859 and brought a change in the face of Portsmouth. A Royal Commission was appointed to look into the defences of the port. It decided that with the improved range and size of guns the defences must be pushed further out away from the dockyard and military establishments. This was a vast and ambitious scheme and marks the pinnacle of years of military garrison. Five forts were built along the line of Portsdown Hill and one at Fareham. All had their guns facing landward to protect the town and naval arsenal from the rear. Gosport and Stokes Bay were given six. The castle at Southsea was augmented by two to the eastward. To meet the threat of an attack by ironclads from seaward, four forts were con-

Above   The Cathedral Church of St. Thomas à Becket, Portsmouth.
Below   The Garrison Church, Portsmouth; all that remains of the *Domus Dei*.

Coronation Review at Spithead, Portsmouth, 1911

Part of Portsmouth Dockyard, showing H.M.S. *Victory*

Royal Yacht *Britannia* entering Portsmouth Harbour. View shows
Henry V Round Tower. Point with the Camber in background.
Fort Blockhouse is seen in the foreground.

structed at Spithead and the approaches. They were named Spit Sand, Horse Sand, No Mans and St. Helens, and remain as familiar outposts to the harbour of Portsmouth. Nine thousand tons of Portland stone were brought to make artificial islands for the foundations and each fort had its own artesian well. On the Isle of Wight seven forts were built and for good measure there was one more on the mainland at Hurst. These were all subsequently referred to as 'Lord Palmerston's folly'. To support the forts on Portsdown Hill, the Hilsea lines begun in de Gomme's time, were enlarged and strengthened. The gunpowder was kept in a vast magazine at Tipnor on the north-west shore of Portsea Island.

All this required manning. Thousands of artillery men were billeted at the forts or in the town, and the military garrison was increased to near divisional strength, to make Portsmouth the most guarded port in the Empire. The Gunwharf Barracks, together with Colwort, Clarence, Victoria, Mill Dam, Cambridge and Anglesea were filled to bursting-point.

Through this development Portsmouth began its own destruction from the historical point of view. During the 1870's and 1880's the old town defences, now redundant from the military aspect, were demolished except for the seaward line. With them the gates, which were of considerable beauty and historic interest, were either demolished or removed to other sites, except the Landport Gate, but even this historic entrance to the old town was stripped of much of its charm, only the central arch remaining. It was said at the time that had Portsmouth preserved the old ramparts, with its glorious range of elm trees, and cared for the gates and moat, this would have been not only of the greatest historic interest to generations to come, but it would have made Portsmouth one of the most beautiful towns in England. Had the Portsmouth–Arundel Canal also been preserved, the beauty and interest of Portsmouth, with its historic fortress and waterway, would have been one of the great show places of modern times. Portsmouth people may have temporarily lost their sense of heritage at this time, to the everlasting regret of later generations.

It was natural that naval affairs predominated the town, but steady progress was made on the civic side, much of which was unspectacular, but the Corporation made up for this by building the magnificent Town Hall, the foundation stone of which was laid by the Mayor, Alfred Blake, on the 14th

October 1886, and the building opened by the Prince and Princess of Wales on the 9th August 1890.

One of the earliest celebrities to be welcomed and entertained in the new building was Captain Scott on his return to England from the Antarctic in the *Discovery* in 1904.

In fact, at the turn of the century the town was acquiring some fine and important buildings. The Naval Barracks were completed in 1903, thus ending years of accommodating sailors in rotting hulks in the harbour, and Agnes Weston built her famous Sailors' Rest in Edinburgh Road.

In 1891 it was felt that two big ships shortly to be launched commanded Her Majesty's presence at the ceremony.

At the high-level station at Portsmouth and Southsea there is a branch line which runs to the dockyard. This solely serves the yard and joins up with the complicated network of lines running like a spider's web, the threads of which pick their way amid the three hundred acres of workshops, offices, docks, basins and wharfs. It was possible, therefore, to explain to the Queen that if she would launch the *Royal Sovereign* and the *Royal Arthur*, two ships with very appropriate names, Her Majesty would not be required to drive through the streets of Portsmouth, or cross the water from Clarence Yard, but could be taken by train alongside the launching site and only alight on Admiralty property. The date was February 28th and if the weather was unkind the Queen could be under cover. Her Majesty accepted.

The *Portsmouth Evening News* introduced the event in these words:

Portsmouth, the scene of so many incidents inseparably connected with the history of the nation, and which figures more or less conspicuously in almost every war which has taken place since the invasion of the Romans, was on Thursday once more the centre upon which the eyes of the country were fixed with no small degree of interest. Royal visits are common in Portsmouth, Emperors, Kings and Princes, with their feminine equivalents, continually arriving and departing from the port or taking part in some ceremony connected with her national position as the Chief Headquarters of the first line of defence of this vast Empire. The presence of the Queen in Portsmouth, however, except when embarking or disembarking on her departure or her return from the Continent or (on exceptional occasions) when passing between the mainland and her marine residence at Osborne, is exceedingly rare, so that her official visit on Thursday must be regarded as one of peculiar interest, apart from the exceptional incident of the launch of two of the most important warships in their respective classes ever yet constructed in the national dockyards.

Double launches, though exceptional, are not unknown in Portsmouth, two vessels not of heavy tonnage having been simultaneously launched here many years ago; nor is the presence of the Sovereign on this occasion singular, Her Majesty having attended the launch of the *Marlborough*, in 1850. On that occasion she occupied a platform by the waterside near the stern of the vessel and the latter, on being released, heeled over to starboard and stuck on the ways right over the Royal platform, an accident which so startled Her Majesty that she has never since been present at a similar function until now.

The Prince of Wales arrived separately, also travelling by train, which took him through the high-level station and along the branch line to the North Railway Jetty in the dockyard. Shortly afterwards, at 12.25, the Queen's train passed through the crowds climbing on to every vantage-point to see and to cheer. The train took her to the rear of the launching platform where the *Royal Arthur* rested on the stocks.

The crowds around the slip were particularly dense, because this was going to be the better spectacle of the two ceremonies, the *Royal Sovereign* having taken the water on the previous Tuesday and was floating in a basin near the *Royal Arthur* in thirty-two feet of water and held in position by a special cable.

Every person directly concerned with the launch of a man-of-war was present on or near to the platform. The Board of Admiralty were there in full, the Commander-in-Chief and officers of the Fleet, the Mayor of Portsmouth and his aldermen, and the Bishop of Winchester and a concourse of clergy from the diocese. Senior army officers from the garrison and Members of the Government also claimed reserved seats. This great gathering was doubled by the presence of their ladies, and, so to speak, bringing up the rear, were foreign attachés and their ladies.

The most striking feature of the *Royal Arthur* was her immense phosphor-bronze ram.

The religious service having been completed, the Queen pressed an electric button, releasing a garland and a bottle of champagne. Unlike the *Marlborough*, the *Royal Arthur* behaved perfectly, and as the band of the Royal Inniskilling Fusiliers played 'Rule Britannia' the 7,700-ton man-of-war glided gracefully into the water, to the deafening cheers of the crowd.

Vast precautions had been taken to prevent a repetition of the terrible disaster when the caisson gave way at the launching of the *Princess Charlotte*, and it took some time to shepherd the crowd to the basin where the *Royal Sovereign* was berthed. The Queen, delighted with the spectacle of the ship, happily made her way to the second platform. Here were two electric buttons: one to 'let go' the special berthing cable signifying a launch, and the other to release another garland and bottle of champagne. This ceremony, less spectacular, but quite impressive, also went off perfectly, music being provided this time by the band of the Royal Marine Light Infantry.

The two ceremonies over, it was the intention that a number of senior officials responsible for the arrangements and the construction of the two ships, should be presented to the Queen, but Her Majesty, seeing the crowds surging towards the royal platform, became alarmed and left abruptly for the royal train, which had been manœuvred to the rear of the basin. In a short space of time the South Western Railway Company had drawn the train through the dockyard over the high-level station at Portsmouth and Southsea and into the Hampshire countryside.

On the 23rd January 1901 Queen Victoria died at Osborne. Once again Portsmouth was thrown into the midst of a great world and national event. For the next week every moment of the day and night was spent in perfecting the naval plans for the funeral on February 1st. Portsmouth's task was threefold. Firstly, to attend on the vast array of naval ships, both British and foreign, which came from far and wide and took their places in the long lines stretching from Cowes to Spithead. Secondly, to provide naval and marine guards and bands at Cowes and Clarence Yard and to arrange for the party of bluejackets who were to be the pall-bearers, and the massed bands of the Royal Marine Artillery and Royal Marine Light Infantry, and to assist the army contingents in getting to Cowes, including the gun-carriage and horses of Y Battery of the Royal Artillery, the Hampshire Carabineers and the Queen's Highlanders. Thirdly, to provide every facility for the great concourse of senior officers from all three Services and from foreign countries.

As the arrangements took shape, the drama of the whole

proceeding began to mount, and there was a feeling in everyone's mind that day, when it came, would be a difficult one to live through. The Queen had reigned for more than three score years. Much of her life had been spent within ten miles of Portsmouth, and it seemed as though the heart of the Empire had been in the Portsmouth Naval Command.

Friday, February 1st, dawned a perfect day. It was midsummer transplanted into midwinter. The Navy received the coffin on the Trinity Pier at Cowes. Alongside lay the yacht *Alberta*. As the funeral procession moved slowly through the square to the covered way leading to the *Alberta* the strains of the pipers' lament faded away and the Royal Guards of Grenadiers and Sailors presented arms. Reverently the bluejacket pall-bearers lifted the coffin from the gun-carriage and, followed by the King and the German emperor, placed it on board. Two Ladies in Waiting and the two naval principal A.D.C.s, Admirals Culme Seymour and Fullerton, boarded the yacht. Together with the King and Emperor, the remainder of the funeral procession then embarked in the royal yacht *Victoria and Albert*, lying off at the entrance to the Medina River. These included Queen Alexandria and members of the royal households, royal servants and six foreign princes and their ladies and their suites.

The time was three o'clock in the afternoon. Looking back towards Cowes the sun cast long shadows from the flagstaffs with their flags at half-mast. The little town was strangely still. Nearly all the residents were standing motionless along the sea board, dressed in full mourning. In the square and on Trinity Pier the military guards and the remnants of the procession stood silently watching as the *Alberta* slipped from alongside and began the slow journey at six knots from Cowes to Portsmouth. Picket boats patrolled to control the private boats, but there were practically none, and the glassy still water was broken only by the faint bow wave of the eight small destroyer escort.

As soon as the *Alberta* was in mid-channel the procession moved to the long line of naval ships. Led by the destroyers the *Alberta*, with the coffin under her awning, looked so small in contrast to the *Victoria and Albert*.

It was in some ways a simple scene which touched the hearts of every officer and rating in the ships lining the route. The lone officer in full dress standing in the bows, the figures on the bridge and the crimson-draped canopy aft under which lay the coffin covered by a cream satin pall across which was hung the royal standard, and at the head the Imperial Crown.

In the clear day the King, in the *Victoria and Albert*, could be seen standing on the bridge. Another lone figure of an officer 'in the eyes' of the yacht was all that could be seen of her ship's company, but the decks were crowded with figures in full dress. Both the royal standard and the imperial German ensign flew side by side at the main, while the White Ensign aft was at half-mast.

Next followed another yacht, the *Osborne*, and behind her the huge white hull of the *Hohenzollern* and lastly the Trinity House *Enchantress* and the *Elfin* following.

As the line of ships moved towards the channel formed by the men-of-war, the first battleship *Alexandria* fired one gun. This signal was repeated by the *Majestic* five miles away. From then on the whole fleet fired one-minute guns, the palls of smoke from the gunpowder lying like a blanket across the water, until from time to time a faint breeze cleared the line. This strange scene, the little line of yachts, the massive battle-fleet, the roar of the guns and the setting sun like a ball of fire making the green slopes of the backcloth of the Isle of Wight appear to be on fire, combined to make a picture which moved men's hearts. The only movement in the Fleet was when the ships' companies in turn manned ship. The smartness of the sailors was such that a battleship one minute appeared like a mass of grey steel without life, and almost seconds later the sides, masts and yards were lined with hundreds of men.

Along the eight long miles of sea across which the Queen was to be borne from her island home to the mainland, the great warships, emblems of her vast empire, paid their last respects in silence, except for the booming of their guns. As the *Alberta* passed along the lines, the ships' companies could hear the strains of Chopin's 'Funeral March' played by the band in the *Victoria and Albert* and echoed by the band of the *Hohenzollern*.

At Spithead the foreign men-of-war followed the procedure of the British flagship, the *Majestic*. First in order and opposite the *Majestic* were four grey-painted ironclads flying the German ensign at half-mast. Next, the dark and forbidding *Dupuy de Lome*, with her long ram showing above the water-line. Beyond her the massive Japanese *Hatsuse*, her flag almost touching the water, and astern of her the Portuguese *Dom Carlos I*. By now the sun was a red ball barely over the horizon, and the last rays picked up the *Alberta* just as she turned to port to enter the fairway to Portsmouth harbour. At this moment the guns ceased firing and, as though arranged for the climax of this unforgettable scene, the sun sank from view. Except for safely landing the coffin at Clarence Pier on the Gosport side of the harbour, the Navy's part was over.

No one present would ever forget that afternoon, and in the years to come grandchildren, many of whom had been brought from miles away to witness this historical event, crowding the front from Southsea to Point, kept alive the vividness of the most dramatic sea voyage ever staged.

During the nineteenth century when there had been war scares these had always been connected with France, but as the old century went out and the new one came in, the whole world picture was changing. Japan was building the largest battleship in the world, the United States was about to take up the challenge, but more ominous and much nearer home Germany was said to be laying down a ship of great size. France, the old enemy, had similar plans. The race for naval supremacy was on.

At the Admiralty the First Sea Lord, Admiral Fisher, brought his dynamic powers to bear on the problem. The result was the *Dreadnought*. Now, in 1906, unlike Tudor times when the principal building had gone to the Thames yards, there were no obstacles to placing the order with Portsmouth. Equipped with every skill needed to meet the First Sea Lord's requirements, Portsmouth built the answer to the Japanese in the record space of ten months. She was launched after four months from being laid down. *Dreadnought* was unique in every particular, embodying all the lessons learnt in the Russo-Japanese War. She was the first of the really big-gunned ships, her main armament being double that of previous ships. The greatest novelty was the adoption of turbine machinery in so big a ship. She was a success in every way, but in one respect the authorities made a mistake, and this was in the field of publicity. Although details of her construction were kept as secret as possible, her building was broadcast world wide, and the fact that Great Britain could build such a ship in ten months was acclaimed by all. This influenced other countries to follow the example, notably Germany.

The launching took place on Saturday, February 17th, 1906,

and the ceremony was performed by King Edward VII. But for the death of the King of Denmark, which had thrown the court into full mourning, the celebrations would have been far greater than actually took place. The King arrived the night before and went on board the royal yacht *Victoria and Albert* at the South Railway Jetty. Next morning he boarded a train alongside and was taken through the yard to the launching platform. Full guards were paraded, but no bands were allowed. There were extensive decorations along the route, but H.M. ships and official buildings were not allowed to dress overall or illuminate.

Attended by the Board of Admiralty and a vast concourse of dockyard officials and local civic heads, the King first christened the ship by breaking a bottle of Australian wine over the bows, and then launched her by tapping on a chisel, which severed the cord securing the weights over the dogshoes.

Amid tremendous cheering *Dreadnought* took the water perfectly. Portsmouth had certainly shown itself worthy of its great naval heritage.

11

Two World Wars

HM.S. Iron Duke

In the first half of the twentieth century the whole pattern of naval warfare changed as much as it had done in the second half of the nineteenth century, due to the advent of the submarine.

Portsmouth became the home of the submarines, and the first boat, built to an American design at Vickers, Son and Maxim, Barrow-in-Furness, arrived in the port in 1902 with its depot ship, H.M.S. *Hazard*. Two years later, the Admiralty designed 'A.1'. When she arrived, she berthed alongside H.M.S. *Latona*, which was lying in the northern and remote part of the harbour so that there would be as little damage to other ships and personnel as possible if she blew up.

In the early teething troubles of submarines there had been explosions from hydrogen and petrol fumes, but the fear of these dangers soon receded and in the same year, 1904, Fort Blockhouse was chosen to be the shore base of the submarine branch of the Navy. Shortly afterwards, when dived and carrying out the first experimental exercises with the Fleet near where the Nab Tower now stands, 'A.1' was hit by a merchant ship, the s.s. *Berwick Castle*, and was lost with all hands.

o

This disaster deeply shocked Portsmouth and the people found it difficult to understand why the salvage operations took a whole month, but this was no ordinary vessel and new techniques had to be worked out, apart from the fact that the weather intervened and blew a full gale, preventing any diving operations for some days.

August 4th, 1914, brought the greatest moment of change, this time at international level. Though there were people and places totally unprepared for war, where the years of peace had dulled the authorities into inactivity, with no thought for the future, this was not the case with the fortified town of Portsmouth and its naval arsenal. On all sides, naval, military and civic, the port was ready. Now the warfare of great battle fleets and big guns would be joined.

The Fleet was collected for the great Review in July through the foresight of Winston Churchill, First Lord of the Admiralty at that time. As this vast armada began to collect, the Commander of the military garrison felt that the Army should show itself as well. To do this, the largest *feu de joie* ever fired was arranged. Soldiers were stationed in lines stretching from the South Parade Pier on the Portsmouth side of the harbour entrance to Gilkicker Fort on the Gosport side. When the Fleet fired the royal salute, Brigadier Hire (then a captain), standing on the top of the Assembly Rooms, gave the signal to fire to the first man at the pier, and with perfect precision the whole line followed one after the other to the last man some three miles away at Gilkicker. This was carried out three times. It made the desired impression, both on the Navy and on all who had come to see the Review.

The first action was to convoy to France the expeditionary force which embarked at Southampton. In the sixteenth century King Henry VIII had placed a great chain across the harbour entrance; this time the underwater defence was taken further to seaward, and a concrete barrier with nets was put down from Southsea beach to the Isle of Wight.

Perhaps the most outstanding repetition of history was the conversion of merchantmen to ships of war, as in medieval times. Portsmouth was soon turning out armed merchant cruisers, converting yachts and trawlers to patrol boats and fishing vessels to minesweepers. King John and King Edward III had done much the same thing. Instead of fire-ships, there were now submarines and mines. It only remained to be at war with the French to complete the picture, but this time we were allied to them against the Germans, instead of being allied to the Germans against the French as in 1815.

In the dockyard, during the five years which preceded the war, the land which had been reclaimed was finally fully developed. The whole dockyard now covered three hundred acres. Twenty dry docks were available, a new floating dock for battleships had been constructed, and from 1906 onwards the whole equipment, machinery and power systems had been modernised. The yard was therefore poised to meet the conditions of a world war.

In the summer of 1914 the dockyard had just completed building H.M.S. *Iron Duke*, which was to be Admiral Jellicoe's flagship, and was fitting out H.M.S. *Queen Elizabeth*, which eventually became Admiral Beatty's flagship. The *Royal Sovereign* was being prepared for launching. There were one hundred battleships, battlecruisers and other heavily armoured ships available to the Royal Navy in 1914, and Portsmouth had built the major share. The principal task now was to keep these ships running, and to convert many of them from reciprocating engines to turbines, and from coal to oil. But the labour force was available, and with no interference from the enemy, the yard worked day and night for five years.

Within hours of the declaration of war, the town filled up with Naval Reservists in such numbers that there was no point in opening a recruiting campaign for the Navy. Volunteers were asked to join the Army and from this flood of young men Portsmouth raised three battalions and many auxiliary units as well, including the Red Cross. There were never less than twenty-five thousand soldiers on Portsea Island and Portsdown Hill, and sometimes as many as fifty thousand. When there was no room in the barracks or billeting, they were camped at Hilsea or on the hill and cheerfully underwent the rigours of winter in these conditions. The first volunteers had no uniforms and did all their training in civilian clothes or in hastily concocted suits like blue overalls.

Another innovation was bringing in the women. Before long Portsmouth trams were being run by women. There was a vast army of women tent repairers stationed at Hilsea, and W.R.N.S. and W.A.A.C.S. appeared. Admirals and generals came to inspect them, and some women were brought into the dockyard as riggers. A ship coming in to berth might find her securing hawsers being handled by a team of women, including two or three working the shore capstans. Bailey & Whites, the timber merchants, turned some of their machinery over to making munitions, and recruited women for the job. In the post office and at the banks women took over many of the jobs for the first time. Before the war was over, women were given the vote. Portsmouth held the first municipal elections under the new suffrage, and Miss Kate Edmonds was elected to St. Simon's Ward with a majority of six hundred.

Although attack from seaward was by no means ruled out, defence against this form of attack was felt to be in the sure hands of the Navy, and Portsmouth was not really worried on that score. Attack from the air by Zeppelin was, however, a distinct possibility, so every second street lamp was extinguished at night, and the remaining ones shaded. All blinds had to be drawn half an hour after sunset. Only once did a Zeppelin venture over the port. At eleven o'clock on the night of the 25th September 1916 an airship was held in the beams of the searchlights. It passed right up the main harbour and dropped four bombs, all of which fell harmlessly in the sea. The airship was at such a height that the anti-aircraft shrapnel failed to reach it.

Throughout the ages, the inhabitants of Portsmouth had learnt to bear the bad news of ships lost in battle, and casualties from both the war and peacetime service of their menfolk at sea, but the first news of the Battle of Jutland surpassed in tragedy everything which had gone before. Press releases from Whitehall were badly conceived, and a stream of reports came through giving total losses of the ships which had blown up or been seen to sink. It appeared in Portsmouth that not only were casualties terrible, but that the British Navy had suffered a major disaster. When it was realised twenty-four hours later that the Navy still commanded the seas, the blow was lessened, but not before women had been seen to collapse in the street with anxiety and near despair. The casualties were terrible and Portsmouth took the heaviest blow it had ever known. Of the six thousand officers and men who lost their lives, the majority came from Portsmouth. There was hardly a family without a relative or friend on the casualty list. Six days later, when the inhabitants were bracing themselves to attend a memorial service, news came through of the loss of the *Hampshire* with Lord Kitchener on board. The toll seemed to be never ending.

That Portsmouth had taken such a blow was partly due to the fact that the majority of the training for the Navy was centred on Portsea Island. The other principal Naval ports of Plymouth and Chatham had their own training establishments, but Portsmouth's were the largest.

The Gunnery School, H.M.S. *Excellent*, by this time had spread itself over the whole of Whale Island, including the land reclaimed when the convicts dug out the basin in the final enlargement of the dockyard area. In 1914 the school had been in operation for seventy-four years since Commander George Smith was directed by the Admiralty to select a suitable ship for a gunnery school, and to point out a position in Portsmouth harbour where she could fire a shot in practice without danger or inconvenience.

In Nelson's system of close quarters, the science of gunnery was neglected. The Admiralty then issued no orders on the subject and gunnery formed no part of the examination of a midshipman, nor of any commissioned officer. Now all had to be changed.

Commander Smith selected H.M.S. *Excellent* and moored her off the north corner of the dockyard. Captain Hastings succeeded Commander Smith two years later and held the appointment for thirteen years. In 1834 a new method of firing a gun was brought in by using a percussion cap and vent pin, instead of a quill tube and loose powder. Eight years later the first Ship Target Trial took place in Portsmouth harbour. This was to test the armour plate then being put round ships' boilers. The range was four hundred yards and the first shot struck the bull's-eye painted on the outer plate. The following two shots entered exactly by the hole made by the first. Everyone concerned was ecstatic with delight. But this was only the beginning. A better ship was required for the Gunnery School, so without delay H.M.S. *Boyne* was renamed *Excellent* and replaced the older ship. In 1859 the *Queen Charlotte* replaced the *Boyne* and she, too, was rechristened *Excellent*. Besides training with big guns, small-bore shooting had to be taught, so in the same year a rifle range was constructed on Whale Island. Five years later Mr. Reeves, Gunner, decided that too much time was being lost on the rifle range in ferrying men back for their meal, and on his own initiative, with a scratch working party, he built 'The House that Jack Built' at the range and gave the men their midday meal there.

By now another ship, the *Calcutta*, had been moored ahead of the *Excellent*, and even these two were bursting their seams. It was also becoming obvious that the teaching of modern gunnery and drill could no longer be carried out in two wooden ships. In 1879 a young lieutenant, Percy Scott, later Admiral Sir Percy Scott, mooted the idea of scrapping the ships and building the Gunnery School ashore on the island by enlarging 'The House that Jack Built'. The scheme was approved in 1884, and by 1891 H.M.S. *Excellent* afloat had come to an end. From then on improvements were added at a steady pace until in 1914, both in accommodation and for the training of officers and men in the rapidly changing field of naval gunnery, there was an establishment as ready to meet the trials of a world war as the dockyard had been.

In 1867 Their Lordships had directed the Gunnery School, H.M.S. *Excellent*, to compile a manual on the subject of the torpedo. The word 'torpedo' then meant any form of explosive underwater weapon. About this time the first locomotive torpedo was invented by an Austrian naval officer, who made it into a practical weapon by his collaboration with Mr. Robert Whitehead, the manager of an engine factory in Fiume. Mr. Whitehead brought two locomotive torpedoes to England in 1870, and in 1872 the *Vernon* frigate was brought to Portsmouth and fitted out as a torpedo instructional ship, being a tender to H.M.S. *Excellent*. Commander J. A. Fisher, later the famous First Sea Lord, Jackie Fisher, was appointed to the command.

From time to time as the school increased in size, more ships were added. These were *Actaeon*, *Donegal*, *Marlborough* and *Warrior*. World War I found H.M.S. *Vernon* not quite so well placed as the Gunnery School. The mining side of the school was expanding so rapidly that the ships were unable to house it. This section was transferred to the part of the Gunwharf which belonged to the Navy, and this makeshift arrangement lasted through the whole war. Then in 1919 it was decided to transfer the whole establishment ashore. *Vernon* acquired the remaining part of the Gunwharf owned by the Army and the ships were scrapped. From then on, what remained of the Mill Pond was filled in, and the whole developed as the Torpedo and Mining School. So the Pond of the Abbess, on the banks of which King John made his first 'dock', no longer existed.

There was also the new establishment, H.M.S. *Dolphin*, the

home of the submarine, across the water on Blockhouse Point, opposite where King Henry V had built his defensive tower. This property also had been acquired from the Army. The submarine was still the Cinderella of all navies, and its potential was not yet fully realised, but within a few months of the opening of hostilities, when the armoured cruisers *Hogue*, *Aboukir* and *Cressy* were all sunk in one day by a single German submarine, and later on when the enemy began unrestricted submarine warfare, all doubts as to the possibilities of this weapon had been removed. H.M.S. *Dolphin* now ranked with the other two great schools, nor in this case was there any rival establishment in any other naval port. To complete the picture, the navigators had begun their own school and had found accommodation in the old Royal Naval College in the dockyard.

The armistice in 1918 came rather abruptly and unexpectedly. In Portsmouth, with its tremendous war effort, both naval and civilian, at its highest peak, it was some time before the whole position could be put into reverse. Again, in many ways, history was repeated. The merchant vessels were disarmed and returned to their respective trades as in years gone by. This kept the dockyard busy for some time but, with the complete surrender of the whole of the German Fleet, the rundown of the Navy was soon in full swing. This was so rapid, and brought such distress in Portsmouth, that when the ships had to be manned again for a second time, recruiting was not on the scale of the 1914 call to the colours. The civic authorities did all they could to stand by the men and women who had served their country so well and whose homes were in Portsmouth, but much of the distress was not within their resources to relieve.

In these depressing times encouraging news for the future was timely, and this came in 1923 when the Royal Marine Artillery and the Royal Marine Light Infantry were re-amalgamated, and the Portsmouth Division decided to make Eastney Barracks their permanent home.

There had been marines in the Fleet since 1664 when Charles II ordained that a special regiment should be raised for sea service. They were called 'The Duke of York and Albany's Maritime Regiment of Foot', and thus had a link with Portsmouth from their foundation, as at that time the Duke of York, it will be remembered, was Governor of the town.

The regiment was disbanded from time to time until 1755,

since when it has remained in continuous service. In that year the officers and men of the Portsmouth Division were placed in billets in the town until 1765, when Clarence Barracks was built on the ground where Henry VIII's four brewhouses had stood since 1513. By now the regiment was already famous. When Rooke captured Gibraltar in 1704 they embarked at Portsmouth and took the principal honours in the fighting, and a few men had circumnavigated the globe with Anson in the *Centurion*, again setting out from Portsmouth.

More great deeds in the latter part of the eighteenth century inspired Lord St. Vincent, in 1802, First Sea Lord at that time, to recommend to King George III that the regiment should be given the honour of the style 'Royal'. This the King readily conferred, and at the same time the regiment became the Royal Marine Light Infantry.

Two years later a division was formed into the Royal Marine Artillery. From then, the artillerymen began a rather nomadic existence and in 1824, in their travels, they took over 'the premises of the late W. Turner Esq. in the High Street and St. Thomas's Street for the accommodation of officers', while the men divided into two groups and some went to the victualling store on the Gunwharf and others to Fort Cumberland.

The next to move were the Light Infantry, because the land on which Clarence Barracks stood was handed back to the Admiralty, so they, and some units of the Royal Marine Artillery, moved across the water to Forton on the Gosport side. Not long afterwards the artillerymen abandoned the Gunwharf and joined the remainder in Fort Cumberland. This latter move was not a rapid business and as late as 1879 officers were still going to and from the Gunwharf to Fort Cumberland, never neglecting to carry their sporting guns, as there was always a chance of a snipe on the Craneswater, in spite of the first South Parade Pier being opened in that year.

By now the ponderous construction of Eastney Barracks had been in progress some years, the first unit having been there since 1865. During the latter part of this century the barracks were steadily expanded and improved, so that when, in 1903, it was decided to form the Royal Naval School of Music, the organisers rather naturally chose the well-equipped Eastney Barracks, instead of looking for a resting place in either Chatham or Plymouth.

The decision to re-amalgamate in 1923 came at a time when

Forton Barracks were literally falling down, and the Royal Marine Light Infantry there were not sorry to have to re-cross the water and make their permanent home with the Royal Marine Artillery in Portsmouth under their new style 'the Royal Marines'.

Shortly after the Portsmouth Division of the Royal Marines had decided on their permanent home, two important events took place.

The first was civic, and of the greatest importance to Portsmouth. On 21st April 1926 the town was raised to the position of a City. This honour was richly deserved. Not only was Portsmouth the premier naval port in the Empire, but its contribution to the nation over the ages demanded that it should take a high place in the standing of the country's chief cities and towns.

The second event was partly brought about by circumstance and partly through the Society of Nautical Research. Since about 1880, H.M.S. *Victory*, at her moorings off Gosport, had given cause for anxiety. She was one hundred years old and on one occasion appeared to be sinking. Everyone who was near, from the Commander-in-Chief downwards, rushed on board and saved her by vigorous pumping. In 1903 the old ironclad *Neptune* broke away from the tug towing her to the breakers yard and collided with the *Victory*, with near disastrous results. Then, in the 1914–18 War, there was neither time nor resources to take proper care of her. By 1921, when the Admiralty were faced with making a decision as to the future of the ship, the Board were going through an economy drive, and could not possibly vote the money to carry out the necessary repairs to keep her in commission. An appeal for funds was launched by the Society of Nautical Research and the famous flagship was moved into the dock in the yard which was to be her permanent home. Surveyors and shipwrights then began the long struggle to preserve her. On the 8th April 1925 she was floated for the last time so as to bring her water-line level with the edge of the dock. Her keel was rested on a special stone base and the dock emptied. Next she was fully restored to her condition in every respect as she was at the Battle of Trafalgar. On the 17th July 1928 King George V came to Portsmouth and declared the *Victory* officially open to the public. His Majesty, a professional sailor in his own right, was the most fitting person in the country to perform this moving ceremony, and since that day the ship has been visited by young and old in their thousands, anxious to see this magnificent treasure which is Portsmouth's, both naval and civic, and which, through the years, has stood for all that is finest in the Royal Navy and its tradition.

The dockyard which Lord Nelson's flagship would now grace for all time had no slips big enough to build the great battleships of the inter-war period, but between 1928 and 1930 three County-class cruisers of nine thousand nine hundred tons were launched, and a variety of smaller craft were added to the Fleet. At the same time, the big battleships which were manned by Portsmouth crews made the port their base. At this time, in the army garrison there was at least one front-line regiment in residence in the Clarence Barracks, and co-operation between the Services was a matter of high military policy. The spirit of this policy sometimes took amusing forms, although on one occasion it was misplaced! H.M.S. *Nelson*, one of the largest battleships, and at that time flagship of the Home Fleet, was difficult to handle at slow speeds and one morning, on leaving harbour for exercises, just when she had cleared the entrance between the Round Tower and Fort Blockhouse, she failed to respond to her helm and ran aground on the Hamilton Bank. There was some play of these words in the clubs and messes which such a situation prompted, but in Clarence Barracks the Army perhaps took the fun a little too far, and sent a message to the captain and officers of the *Nelson* which read: 'Colonel and Officers hope you will consider yourselves honorary members of the Mess during your stay.' For a few hours co-operation between the Services was considerably lessened, but fortunately the ship got off the bank without damage, and time did the rest to restore relationships.

One building in Portsmouth which had witnessed all its history's stirring events of over seven hundred years was the cathedral church of St. Thomas à Becket. Since the first chapel was built by the monks of Southwick Priory between 1180 and 1196, the church had been enlarged, and the architecture spells out the passage of time, beginning at the east end with Early English style, and culminating in twentieth-century design at the west end. In 1927, partly because Portsmouth had been made a city and partly because the Diocese of Winchester had become too big and Portsmouth itself had become a diocese, the church was elevated to the status of a cathedral.

To complete the elevation of the city, on the 10th July 1928 the King conferred upon the Mayor, as Chief Magistrate, the honour and dignity of the title of Lord Mayor. There remained the question of a motto and in February the following year the City Council chose 'Heaven's light our guide' and registered it with the College of Heralds. This was a most fitting choice, as it was the motto of the Order of the Star of India, founded by Queen Victoria in 1861, the insignia of which includes a star and is very similar to the star in the badge of Portsmouth which for over seven hundred years had served as the seal for the borough and now the city. Portsmouth people also recalled that the star used to be seen frequently as an ornament on the troopships which conveyed the British troops to and from India and called regularly at Portsmouth.

Throughout its history Portsmouth and its dockyard had been the scene of innumerable events connected with kings and queens, but none quite like the one on the night of the 11th-12th of December 1936, when there took place the final act of a poignant drama.

While the city slept, King Edward VIII, by this time His Royal Highness the Duke of Windsor, drove through the silent and deserted streets into the dockyard to go on board H.M.S. *Fury*. Earlier that evening he had broadcast to the nation, announcing his abdication from the throne.

At 12.20 a.m. a small cavalcade of cars, consisting of a saloon car and two luggage brakes, crossed Portsbridge and drove to the Guildhall Square, from there down the High Street and into Broad Street, where it came to a halt on reaching the sea at the Portsmouth–Gosport floating bridge terminal. A driver got out and enquired the way to the Unicorn Gate from another motorist who had followed the cavalcade out of curiosity. Shortly afterwards the three strange cars entered the dockyard by the Unicorn Gate and went to where the *Fury* was lying. At 1.10 a.m. a single saloon car arrived at the main dockyard gate and, after a moment's conversation with an officer there, also drove to the *Fury*.

Hardly a word was spoken when the captain of the destroyer received his distinguished guest on board, accompanied only by an equerry and his dog, and within half an hour *Fury*, escorted by H.M.S. *Wolfhound*, which had come round in haste from Portland, passed between the Round Tower and Blockhouse Point. Silently the two ships slipped away into the darkness of the still winter's night on their way to France.

No doubt many people in Portsmouth recalled during that fateful week-end of December that only three months earlier Portsmouth and the Naval Command had welcomed Edward VIII, who had come to visit his fleet. At that time the streets were lined with cheering people and the Fleet spliced the main brace. Now everyone in Portsmouth sensed the depth of sadness in this historic event.

On Monday morning the mood suddenly changed. At the Guildhall, before a vast concourse of people and representatives of the Services, the Town Clerk, Mr. M. F. T. Sparks, read the Proclamation of the Accession to the throne of Britain of another sailor King, George VI, and the Lord Mayor, Councillor F. J. Spickernell, led the cheers. On board the *Nelson*, lying at the South Railway Jetty, the Proclamation was also read, the whole ship's company giving three cheers for the new king. As had happened so often in the past, the city and the Naval Command turned their minds to the future.

In 1936 the country was drifting on a policy of 'no war for ten years'. Yet in three years another world war was to break out, more dangerous to the existence of these islands than the Armada or Bonaparte's army at Boulogne. Unlike the time prior to the 1914 war, Portsmouth, the dockyard and the Navy were not ready. In the past Edward III, the Regency Council in the minority of Henry III, and other rulers in a lesser degree, had all laid up ships and neglected the Navy following a successful war, thus exposing this country to invasion and defeat. Yet this lesson had not been learnt. There was no talk of impending hostilities in the Jubilee Review of 1935, nor was there in the Coronation Review of 1937, when King George VI, another sailor in his own right, reviewed the ships at Spithead. Few heeded Winston Churchill's lone voice in Parliament, foreshadowing the war clouds on the horizon.

However, the dockyard had not been altogether idle during the last decade. Seven cruisers had been built, and there was a tremendous programme of reconstruction, due to the advance in the destructive potential of shells, torpedoes, mines and bombs. Also in consequence of these rapid advances, the dockyard was very busy working for the experimental establishments which were all centred in the local command. The dockyard slips were not big enough to have undertaken the construction of an aircraft carrier, five of which were by now with the Fleet, but all the services needed to keep these ships operational were the work of the yard. Converting machinery in all types of ships as improvements came along was a major operation, and some of the battleships were in the yard as long as four years.

After the Munich crisis a real sense of urgency prevailed, air-raid precautions were studied and protection arrangements were constructed for caissons and important installations. Both in the naval establishments and in the city, shelters were built.

When, on the 3rd September 1939, war was declared, once again the yard set about converting merchantmen, trawlers and yachts to war service. The protective boom from Southsea to the Isle of Wight was strengthened and the training establishments went into top gear. The depleted garrison set up anti-aircraft guns and made tank blocks. This time the City was completely blacked out and the dockyard did its best under shaded blue lights.

The Army followed the same plan as in the 1914 War and embarked at Southampton. Again Portsmouth provided the escorts, meeting the transports in the Solent and Spithead, as Henry V had done in his flagship the *Trinity* as long ago as 1415.

After the Battle of Britain, the enemy realised that sea power would now be the deciding factor in the war and that Portsmouth was the centre of much of it.

By 1940 the island population was a quarter of a million, and this had been raised by the influx of service men and women and additional dockyard personnel. In July Hitler resolved to destroy the naval might of Britain, and part of this meant the annihilation of Portsmouth.

Between July 11th, 1940, and the end of May 1944 there were sixty-seven air raids on the city, and three of these, on the 24th August 1940, the 10th January 1941 and the 10th March in the same year, were extremely heavy. In all the raids a total of 1,320 high explosive bombs were dropped, 38,000 incendiaries and thirty-eight parachute mines. As a result, the major part of the City was destroyed. Nine hundred and thirty civilians were killed, 1,216 admitted to hospital and 1,621 others injured. Considering the intensity of the three major attacks, it was amazing that more people were not killed. The comparatively small total was due to good shelter, excellent discipline (a quality second nature to a people wholly integrated with the Services) and the first-class state of the city's Civil Defence Services.

Historically, Portsmouth lost much, particularly in Old Portsmouth, where the famous 'George' Hotel was completely destroyed, and the city lost its Guildhall, apart from the bare shell. In many areas whole streets were razed to the ground, taking with them churches, hospitals, theatres and cinemas.

The night of Friday, 10th January 1941, marked the height of terror and destruction. Over 300 bombers kept up a continuous attack for most of the night, killing 171 people and leaving over 3,000 homeless. There were 2,314 fires all raging simultaneously, at one time.

This was perhaps Portsmouth's 'finest hour'. Never during that terrible night or in the days following did the people lose heart. At one time there was no electricity, practically no water and very little food, yet pictures taken next day show a people cheerful, utterly determined and never downhearted. When Their Majesties the King and Queen made a special visit to the 'Stricken City' they told the Lord Mayor, Sir Denis Daley, 'You are a wonderful people'.

The story was the same in the dockyard, where the work of fitting out ships, repairing the damaged and building new ones continued day and night without a break. At one time, over one-third of the dockyard had been completely flattened. Although a bomb exploded in the dock in which the *Victory* lay, mercifully the damage was only minor.

By a miracle the cathedral, too, escaped major damage. This was due in part to the presence of night watchmen from H.M.S. *Vernon*, who clambered over the roof of St. Thomas's putting out incendiaries at great risk to themselves. In the words of the Commander-in-Chief, Sir William James, who had organised the care of the cathedral at the request of the Provost:

What all who were at Portsmouth will never forget was that the Cathedral and H.M.S. *Victory* were untouched. The Cathedral stood like a lighthouse in a great sea of rubble and the *Victory* lay proudly in her dock with most of the buildings around her destroyed by bomb or fire. It was really something of a miracle and I have no doubt many people saw them, defiant and unscathed, as symbols of the righteousness of our cause and an assurance of final victory.

For four years Portsmouth endured attack, but with the increasing success of the Allied offences the great day was coming when the armies of liberation would cross the Channel to France.

Somehow it seemed inevitable that Portsmouth would be the spring board for the greatest expedition ever to make the crossing. Long before the time came for this armada to set sail, Portsmouth had been geared to the endeavour to the exclusion of all else.

It was Edward III who in 1346 camped his men on the common, made his headquarters at Southwick and landed his army on the Normandy beaches. History was about to repeat itself.

Admiral Sir Charles Little assumed the office of Commander-in-Chief Portsmouth Command in October 1942. From then on his mind was turned more and more to thoughts of the Second Front until the position was such that the whole of his Command was solely devoted to this enterprise. Admiral Sir Bertram Ramsay, commanding the naval forces of the operation, in a signal made shortly after 'D' Day, summed up the part played by Portsmouth when he said: 'The main burden of the operation, on the naval side, was perforce borne by the Portsmouth Command.'

But Portsmouth was not only a naval base full of ships and sailors. There were a large number of civilians resident on the island. 'They', wrote Admiral Little in his report, 'together with the people of Gosport and the towns and villages throughout the Command, learnt to be war-minded,' and he pays a very warm tribute to them 'for their helpful attitude throughout, which appreciably assisted in the success of the operation and particularly in the degree of security attained'.

To the residents, as 'D' Day drew nearer, more and more ships were seen to be arriving, more and more material was being dumped and more and more sailors crammed the streets (there were over twenty-three thousand accommodated in the barracks alone). Portsmuthians began to wonder how the enemy could overlook such a target. They remembered the terrible devastation of 1941 and dreaded the hour when the bombers would come again and try to complete the job. But never did.

To go from one place to another on Portsea Island meant showing identity cards and passes continually. Looking across to the Isle of Wight it appeared almost possible to walk to Ryde over the decks of the ships and landing craft. Everywhere ashore men and women in uniform hustled about, and it would have been interesting to have been able to enquire from each what he or she was doing. They were in fact dealing with such a multitude of things that the list would have been a long one, and would have included emergency meals, French currency, mobile bakeries, survivor's kits, reserve anchors and cables, the prevention of amateur fishing, the departure of E.N.S.A. entertainment parties, the passage of prisoners of war to cages, and the organisation of mails, to quote only a few.

Meanwhile at his headquarters at Fort Southwick the Commander-in-Chief and his staff were dealing with the wider problems. The 'hards' for embarkation had to be built; every ship in the vast concentration in the Solent and at Spithead had to have water. This service occupied nineteen water boats, supplied from three 10,000-ton tankers, all day and every day. Dredging was a problem, both at the hards and in the channels. There were nothing like enough dredgers available. Almost the most difficult task was the provision of moorings and anchorages. Seventy-two ocean buoys had to be laid to mark the channels to where the anchorages began and ended. On one day alone fifty-five pre-loaded coasters arrived. They were known to be coming, but every berthing place and anchorage had been strained already with the constant arrival of more bombardon[1] and whale equipment for Mulberry.[2]

Very careful thought had to be given to the provision of ammunition. Lighters had to be preloaded with expected requirements and tugs organised to tow them to the ships. By the evening of 6th June the first demands were made and during the first week of the invasion two battleships, ten cruisers, thirty-two destroyers and various lesser craft had embarked 2,173 tons of ammunition without a hitch.

Repairs and maintenance organisation were brought to a pitch where any ship, from a battleship to a small landing craft, could be taken in hand immediately and returned to the job in the shortest possible time.

The evacuation of Haslar Hospital to make way for the wounded had to be effected. There were special arrangements for the wounded who would be brought back to the hards at Gosport in medically fitted landing craft, to be rushed to Haslar, and further provision for the care of the wounded

1. Floating piers.   2. Artificial harbour.

arriving in craft of any sort, not fitted with any medical aids, and probably not going anywhere near the special hards at Gosport. Nor were the relatives forgotten, as an organisation was set up to bring them into the defended area to visit husbands and sons on the danger list and, if need be, to put them up for some days.

While all roads led to the hards, these would be crossed frequently by members of a strange party. The complete party consisted of 60 lorries and 400 trailers carrying 12,000 cylinders of hydrogen to replenish the 3,000 naval anti-aircraft balloons for use by the landing craft and other small ships. Sections of these replenishment units had to move from hard to hard wherever they were wanted, because none of these small craft could leave without sufficient hydrogen for their balloons.

Staff officers wondered where any more space could be found within the Command but did so even when faced with storing 960 buoyant mines and 750 ground mines for sealaying, and 1,850 for laying by the R.A.F.

In the very centre of all this stood the cathedral of St. Thomas of Canterbury where, as in the dark days of 1941, not a service was missed, special passes being issued to all who wished to worship there.

Portsmouth was without doubt the very core of this great undertaking, which after years of planning was about to be set in motion. The order to sail came from the Supreme Commander's forward headquarters at Southwick, where H.M.S. *Dryad*, the Navigation School, had been accommodated since the blitz in 1941. In turn, the navigators had temporarily moved out. There General Eisenhower and the principal commanders of all Services had collected.

General Montgomery, the Commander-in-Chief of all ground forces, was no stranger to Portsmouth, having previously commanded the garrison of the city in 1938.

On the 8th May the Supreme Commander decided provisionally that 'D' Day would be the 5th June. During May the weather had been fine, but on the 2nd June the forecast was not good and on the evening of the 4th Eisenhower postponed the operation for twenty-four hours. Next evening there seemed to be some hope of improvement in the weather, and having taken into consideration all the factors governing the choice of days which were suitable, Eisenhower named 'D' Day to be June 6th.

P

For years civilians in Portsmouth had not been allowed
near the beach or on the roads adjacent to it. Barbed wire
prevented access and buses had been diverted further inland.
Suddenly one morning the sky was filled with aeroplanes
towing gliders, and when the people went to the shopping
centre at Southsea, where business went on behind shattered
windows and temporary wooden walls, they stood on the
pavements amazed to see this great aerial armada. At the same
time they saw moving unhurriedly to the beaches thousands of
soldiers on their way to embark for the far shore. There was
no congestion as the operation kept to a perfect time-table,
although its roots began many miles away far beyond the
Portsbridge.

To the astonishment of all the spectators buses were going
along the road parallel to the beach and all restrictions had
been removed. For the first time many of the inhabitants were
witnessing men going to battle. Even those who had been
through the terror of the blitz in Portsmouth experienced a
feeling of being nearer the actual fighting than ever before, and
could not help wondering how many of those soldiers would
return.

'D' Day must always remain the greatest moment in the
history of Portsmouth. From the Command was launched one
of the decisive battles of the world and to some, at that time,
it must have been difficult to grasp the enormity of it all. That
we are free today depended on the success of the operation
and Portsmouth will always be proud that this city and naval
port was the hinge pin of the whole expedition.

To commemorate the embarkation from the beaches of
Southsea a stone was erected near South Parade Pier, and was
unveiled in 1948 by Field Marshal Montgomery. To provide a
fitting memorial to all officers and other ranks of all the Allied
Forces who took part in the invasion by sea, land and air, the
nave of the cathedral church of St. Thomas is to be completed
in a new and challenging design. This nave was under construction in 1939, but the work had to be stopped when war
was declared.

When after six long years the war came to an end, Portsmouth once again put itself in reverse, as it had done in 1918,
but this time both naval and civic authorities had profited
from the experience of 1914. Although there were inevitably
difficulties in running down such vast numbers of naval and

W.R.N.S. personnel, the transition this time was smooth and almost painless. In the dockyard once again a halt had to be called to construction and refitting work which would not now be required. It remained to repair the ravages of war, to build up industry and to house the people. This task has taken long to complete.

In Portsmouth for very many years there has been a unique co-operation between the naval and civic authorities. The appointments of both Commanders-in-Chief and Lord Mayors are generally rather short-lived, affording comparatively little time to get to know each other, but the two reigning Heads always work together for the common good of the Navy and the City. The Lord Mayor can be heard talking about 'my C.-in-C.' and the Admiral speaks of 'my Lord Mayor', indicating a respect for each other's position and in many cases a deep affection. The mutual help in their respective tasks which has resulted, has meant a very great deal to all who go down to the sea in ships from Portsmouth and who live in the city.

This relationship was finally cemented when the Honorary Freedom of the City was conferred on the Portsmouth Command of the Royal Navy. The day selected for the ceremony was the 7th May 1965, exactly two hundred years after the birth of H.M.S. *Victory*. Just before 8 a.m. the Lord Mayor, Alderman J. A. Nye, was greeted on board the *Victory* by Admiral Sir Wilfrid Woods, the Commander-in-Chief, in the presence of a distinguished gathering of naval officers, to witness the ceremony of colours and the hoisting of the flags to dress the ship overall. To mark the occasion Alderman Nye planted a commemorative tree on the dockside on behalf of the city. The scene then shifted to Southsea Common. Here over a thousand naval personnel and the Royal Marine Band of the Portsmouth Command were drawn up on the same ground where through the centuries so many expeditions had gathered to embark from the shore, culminating in the greatest of all on the 6th June twenty-one years earlier. After inspecting the parade the Lord Mayor presented the Freedom Scroll to the Admiral and, under the surveillance of the Town Clerk, Mr. John Haslegrave, both signed the Freedom Roll. Then the scene changed once more, this time to the Guildhall steps, where the Lord Mayor took the salute.

Now that the Naval Command held the Freedom of the City, it exercised it by marching with bayonets fixed, colours flying and bands playing. There are few more impressive sights in ceremonial than sailors on the march. All who stood on the steps of the Guildhall that morning felt intensely proud of the Navy and the City which is its principal home. As one naval attaché from a foreign country was heard to say, 'You have a way of doing these things which my country could not match.'

There followed a brilliant Mayoral lunch and the presentation of a magnificent silver model of the *Victory* from the Naval Command to the City.

The story of Portsmouth and its naval heritage does not end here. The port remains the largest and most important of our naval bases. All the principal training establishments are centred in the Command; foreign warships of many nationalities are constantly seen in the harbour; Portsmouth is still the home of the royal yachts. *Britannia* berths and refits here, and the Queen, the Queen Mother, Prince Philip and members of the Royal Family often join her and disembark at the South Railway Jetty in the dockyard. Here in the *Victory* the flag of the Commander-in-Chief still flies from the main.

For over a thousand years Portsmouth has played a leading part in our maritime history. Now we have entered the scientific, technical and nuclear age. The city and the dockyard are ready to accept whatever responsibilities are placed on them in this age and all that it holds for the Royal Navy in the years to come.

Epilogue

Two Portsmouths in the United States

C.S.S. Virginia

I

UNDER FOUR FLAGS, Portsmouth, Virginia

Those who have experienced the beauty of Virginia and its magnificent natural waterways, can easily understand why Captain Christopher Newport and his band of settlers decided to stay after they landed at Jamestown in 1607. They became the first permanent Colonists in America.

The area of water where Chesapeake Bay, the James River, and the Elizabeth River all meet is the Hampton Roads. Portsmouth, Virginia, lies in the southern region of this area and on the west bank of the Elizabeth River. It was settled as a plantation community little more than a year after the Jamestown landing.

In September 1608, Captain John Smith, with twelve men, set out from Jamestown in a small boat to discover country to the southward. Crossing Hampton Roads, they sailed up the Elizabeth River and saw 'garden plots' and other indications of Indian habitation. The river, which is actually a tidal arm of the sea, and which from the time of the first settlement has been the economic artery of the entire community, was originally called the Chesapeake, after the tribal name of the warlike and hostile Indians who dwelt upon its banks, and not until later was it re-named Elizabeth, after the eldest daughter of James I.

From this point the records are silent on what took place during the succeeding twelve years, but it is evident that the Colonists actually initiated a settlement. Proof of this is established by a petition from a shipbuilder John Wood who, in 1620, asked that his grant of four hundred acres of land be located on the Elizabeth River. It is to this beginning that one must look to find the roots from which in 1752 sprang the town, and finally, in 1858, the City of Portsmouth.

The numerous salt-water streams in the region provided a ready and simple means of transportation and communication for the settlers, who located their plantations on the shores of these navigable waterways. As a direct consequence, the building of boats and ships was from the first an economic necessity, and laid the foundations of the present vast maritime base with its naval shipyard.

During the next hundred years the Colony of Virginia was fully established with its own administration, and in 1752 a Colonel Crawford set aside some sixty-five acres from the extensive plantation he had acquired previously on the banks of the Elizabeth River. He called in the County Surveyor and laid off the little town, calling it Portsmouth, after the English naval port and dockyard. Several Scottish shipping merchants now settled in Portsmouth and local prosperity steadily grew.

Colonel Crawford died in 1762, and five years later, Andrew Sprowle, a wealthy merchant and shipowner, was the next to add to the development of the town. He purchased some waterfront lands south of the town and built a shipyard. The site was at that time separated from Portsmouth by a creek, and the situation being somewhat similar to Portsmouth and Gosport in England, he gave the name of Gosport to his new holdings.

When the American revolution broke out in 1775 Sprowle remained loyal to the Crown, and fled from the State of Virginia at the beginning of the conflict, with Lord Dunmore, The Royal Governor. All Sprowle's lands and property in the State were immediately confiscated, and the title to the Gosport shipyard was acquired by the newly independent Commonwealth of Virginia. The Union Jack was hauled down in Portsmouth and the Flag of the Commonwealth of Virginia hoisted in its place.

For the protection of her shores and the vast network of inland waters Virginia built a navy, and also operated the Gosport shipyard from 1776 to 1782. In May 1779, however, the operation of the shipyard was interrupted by the invasion of a British fleet under Admiral Collier, who was transporting troops commanded by General Mathewes. Disembarking his men from their transports anchored in the Elizabeth River, Mathewes occupied Portsmouth and burned the Gosport shipyard, against the advice of Admiral Collier. In the Admiral's own words, '.. . . the marine-yard was the most considerable one in America . . . large and extremely convenient. Five thousand loads of fine seasoned oak-knees for shipbuilding, an infinite quantity of plank, masts and cordage, and numbers of beautiful ships of war on the stocks were at one time ablaze...'

This was not the only time Portsmouth changed hands during the revolution, but these troubles came to an end when the French Fleet under Admiral de Grasse, supporting the revolutionaries, defeated the British, who were commanded by Admiral Graves. Sea communications on which General Cornwallis had to rely were cut, thus forcing him to surrender at Yorktown on 19th October 1781. There is a tradition that the bell of Portsmouth Parish Church was cracked in the celebrations following this victory.

With the close of the revolutionary war the Virginia Navy was disbanded, but in 1794 Congress passed 'An Act to Provide a Naval Armament'. This Act founded the Navy of the United States. Gosport shipyard was leased from Virginia to the United States and was chosen to build one of five vessels for the Navy, namely the *Chesapeake*, a 33-gun frigate.

The Flag of Virginia was then hauled down and replaced by the Flag of the United States.

The town of Portsmouth, together with the Gosport Navy Yard, narrowly averted capture and probably destruction in the second war against England in 1812–14. The harbour had been blockaded since February 1813 by a British squadron under Admiral Warren who, with 2,600 troops under General Beckwith, made his attack on Craney Island, which guarded Portsmouth at the mouth of the Elizabeth River. The attack was successfully repulsed by the State Militia, the Portsmouth Light Artillery, and some seamen from the frigate *Constellation*.

By now the town of Portsmouth was steadily growing. In

1790 it had about three hundred houses and a population of 1,700. Of these, 1,039 were white, 616 were slaves, and 47 free Negroes. Portsmouth's Parish Church had been built, the waterfront was alive with shipping, and by 1815 fifty-five sea captains were listed as residing in Portsmouth. In this year the first paddle steamer to be seen in Virginia, the *Washington*, steamed slowly up the Elizabeth River as the local populace stared in wonder. Also in the early nineteenth century, such prominent men as James Monroe, General Lafayette and President Andrew Jackson visited the town.

In 1819, now with a population of over 3,000, the town Trustees were created a body corporate. Shortly afterwards the Federal Government stationed the first lightship in the United States off Craney Island. More important was the launch, in the same year, of the 74-gun *Delaware*, the Gosport Navy yard's first ship-of-the-line.

A further event of national importance was the construction in 1827 of the first dry dock in the western hemisphere. Built of huge blocks of Massachusetts granite it was christened on 17th June 1833 by the reception of the *Delaware*, the first ship to be dry-docked in the United States. This dock is still in active use today.

Like the home town in England, Portsmouth, Virginia, had its share of plagues and troubles, and in 1855 a merchant ship named the *Ben Franklin* entered the Elizabeth River for repairs. Yellow fever mosquitoes, trapped in her holds, were released when the hatches were opened. In less than three months approximately one-tenth of the population were dead. Those who were able to travel fled the country, and only the bravest remained to care for the sick and bury the dead.

When civil war broke out between the Federal Government of the United States and the Southern States, the Federal Authorities, on the night of 20th April 1861, evacuated and burned the Gosport Yard, which they had held since 1794. All the buildings, workshops and eleven men-of-war were burned or sunk. Although Virginia had passed an 'Ordinance of Secession', she had not yet joined the Southern Confederacy, and for a brief interval the flag of Virginia was unfurled and the hastily re-created Virginia State Navy took possession again of Portsmouth and the Navy Yard. A few months later, on uniting with the Confederate States, the Virginia flag was hauled down and the Confederate flag hoisted.

Work was immediately put in hand to salvage everything possible from the destruction wrought by the Federal troops. The steam frigate *Merrimac* of forty guns, which had been under repair at the Yard, and had been burned to the waterline and sunk, was successfully raised. John Porter, a Naval constructor and resident of Portsmouth, converted the ship into the first armed vessel of the type ever built, and she was re-named C.S.S. *Virginia*. While on a trial trip in Hampton Roads she engaged some wooden vessels of the Federal squadron blockading the entrance, on 8th March 1862. Having sunk or driven them off, on the next day she drove off the Federal Ironclad *Monitor*. This was the first action between armoured ships ever to take place. These two actions immediately set in motion in the navies of the world emergency programmes of conversion from wood to iron, and the introduction of turret guns.

Not long afterwards, on 10th May 1862, the Confederates themselves, now on the retreat, burned the Yard, evacuated Portsmouth, and hauled down their flag. The Federal forces re-entered and ran up the flag of the United States.

The war ended in 1865, but Portsmouth's economic and social recovery took a long time. The cost of living had doubled, Confederates were refused work and of necessity were driven from the City, which caused feeling to run high for many years. Incidents were many, and when a newly-installed window in Trinity Church, given as a memorial to the Confederate dead, was inscribed, 'Died . . . in defence of their native State, Virginia, against invasion of the U.S. Forces', the church was threatened with closure unless the 'offence' was removed.

Reconstruction of the Yard on modern lines followed close on the end of the war, including an electrical fire alarm system, a telephone system and many miles of railways. Progress in building up the Yard and Portsmouth itself continued steadily, so that when war against Spain broke out at the turn of the century, and the first ships of the modern American Navy were built, the Yard was fully prepared to play a most important part. The *Raleigh*, a protected cruiser, was the first ship of the new Navy to be completely built by the Government, and the *Texas* was the Navy's first battleship. Public interest was fully aroused with the launching of these ships, and further increased when, in the same year, the International Columbian Naval rendezvous took place in Hampton Roads, an event which marked the completion of the second dock.

The success of the war against Spain, in which the Navy distinguished itself, ensured the future of the Yard, now styled 'The United States Navy Yard, Norfolk, Virginia'. In 1903 a third dry dock was constructed, and one year later the whole Yard was increased in area by 272 acres. By 1915, when it was clear that in due course the United States would be involved in World War I, the greatest Yard on the eastern seaboard was ready.

Events began by Portsmouth being the reluctant hosts of two interned German sea-raiders, the *Kronprinz Wilhelm* and the *Prinz Eitel Frederick*, the crews of these vessels numbering over 1,000 officers and men. With the entry into the war, both the Yard and Portsmouth had expanded, and by 1919 employment had reached a peak of 11,234, as compared with 2,718 in 1914. To accommodate the hundreds of workers and their families who had migrated to Portsmouth, two enormous war-housing projects had been undertaken.

Like most Naval Yards, when the war came to an end there was an immediate run-down, including the scrapping of the U.S.S. *North Carolina*, a battleship of 43,000 tons and over a third completed, due to the Washington Naval Limitation Treaty. Then, from the 11,000 mark in 1919, employment dropped by the end of 1923 to less than it had been in 1914, with all the hardship and suffering which such a crash programme inevitably imposed. However, those who remained in the Yard made naval history with the conversion of the collier *Jupiter* to the United States' first aircraft carrier, the U.S.S. *Langley*.

Fortunately the naval standstill and economic depression were alleviated by a battleship modernisation programme, six being allocated to the Yard, now styled 'The Norfolk Navy Yard, Portsmouth, Virginia'.

The part played by the Navy Yard and Portsmouth in World War II, with their services to the United States Fleet and to countless ships of many Allied Navies, surpassed all previous experience. From 1st January 1940 to the end of the war with Japan on 2nd September 1945, a period of five years and eight months, the Yard repaired, altered, converted or otherwise undertook work on 6,850 naval vessels. At the same time, 101 new ships and large landing craft were built, including 30 major warships.

To accomplish this huge task, the yard more than doubled its physical size, expanding from 352 acres to 746. A dry dock of 1,100 feet was constructed, and 685 new buildings put up. At the period of its heaviest working load, the Yard employed 42,000 men and women. Portsmouth itself was again hard pressed to accommodate all this increase in population, 45 public and private war housing projects were completed, housing 16,487 families.

With the close of major hostilities the inevitable recession set in, but, again like the home dockyard, this was better arranged than the rundown after World War I. Before the scheme had been completed hostilities broke out in Korea, and since then, with the war in Vietnam, the Yard has never fully run down to a peacetime footing, and is undergoing a vast technological change in building up a Navy electronically controlled, with nuclear power and guided missiles.

Today the traveller approaching Portsmouth is impressed by the vastness of all around him. The toll bridge across the James River eight miles long, the five miles of bridge and tunnel connecting Portsmouth and Norfolk with Hampton, and the twenty-one miles of tunnel and bridge spanning the entrance to Chesapeake Bay, illustrate the outlook and thinking by which the Yard is governed. Perhaps the most impressive comparison in this Yard, which is three times the size of the one in Portsmouth, England, is to stand looking down on the first dry dock, still in use, with its lovely stone from New England, and then drive the half mile along the Yard water front to the modern 1,100 foot dock, one of the largest in the world. This is typical of the state of development in two hundred years. Portsmouth, Virginia, certainly has its Naval Heritage from the *Delaware* to the most modern nuclear Navy, and the story is continuing.

The Raleigh

STRAWBERY BANKE, Portsmouth, New Hampshire

Portsmouth, New Hampshire, lies on the southern bank of the Piscataqua River which divides New Hampshire from Maine. The first European known to have visited these waters was Martin Pring, who describes them as 'a noble sheet of water of great depth with beautiful islands and heavy forests along its banks.' It is also ice-free all the year round.

Pring explored the river, but made no attempt to settle there. Other Europeans later made voyages up the Piscataqua, including Captain John Smith in 1614, who made a map of the coast, calling it New England.

Eight years later John Mason, of Portsmouth, England, obtained his patent from the Council of New England and the Royal Assent of James I, giving him a share of the land stretching from the Kennebec River in the north to the Merrimac River in the south. In 1629 a further patent confirmed Mason's sole ownership of the area from the southern bank of the Piscataqua down to the Merrimac, and he relinquished his share of the lands northwards. Mason named his own area New Hampshire in honour of his home in the old world.

From the time of his first patent Mason sent out settlers from England and when the first of these arrived in the Piscataqua they found a profusion of wild strawberries growing along the bank of the river and called their settlement 'Strawbery Banke'.

Mason was in every sense a model proprietor, despite the fact that he never saw his colony. He granted land to his settlers and appointed administrative agents. He sent quantities of arms, clothing, artisan's tools, provisions, cordage, and a large herd of Danish cattle, some pigs and goats. Concerned in creating a balanced and functional community, he saw to it that the first settlers included artisans, carpenters, coopers, smiths and masons. He even arranged for the passage of twenty-two women from England, who eventually married the settlers.

At the time of Mason's death in November 1634 his colony numbered about one hundred persons. A sawmill and water corn mill had been established in addition to salt works, but most of the population was engaged in fishing or boat maintenance. The river served as their main communication link with other colonies, and the harbour provided a safe mooring for ships. An inventory of the colony taken at the time of Mason's death shows that they had an abundance of food and ample means of protection against Indian raids. Although there was momentary disorder when Mason's death left the colony leaderless—two stewards driving one hundred yellow cattle to Boston sold them for twenty pounds ahead, keeping the money—the settlers met and made a Combination, an agreement to act together for the common good.

With the development of New England fast progressing, the settlement at Strawbery Banke came under the Massachusetts Colony from 1641 to 1679, partly due to the Cromwellian régime in England favouring the Massachusetts settlers. In 1653 the existing fifty to sixty families, numbering some three hundred and fifty persons, petitioned the General Court of Massachusetts, to grant them the right to change the name from Strawbery Banke to Portsmouth, after John Mason's home town.

After the English Civil War, Charles II sent Commissioners to North America to investigate the claims of the Mason heirs as well as the Massachusetts Colony's actions during the Parliamentarian régime. Although the Mason proprietorship was not restored, New Hampshire was declared a Royal Province on the 18th September 1679. In 1680 a Royal Council consisting of a President (the Lieutenant Governor) and six members was created to govern the colony.

Towards the end of the seventeenth century, shipbuilding gradually assumed a predominant position in the town's economy, because of the immensely rich fine timber on the mainland as well as the islands, and vessels were built for the British Navy. In 1697 Portsmouth was the home port for eleven ships, five brigantines, four ketches and four sloops. But this was only a start, and by 1771 Portsmouth and the nearby surrounding area produced seventeen per cent of the entire colonial output of ships.

Throughout all the wars of the eighteenth century, big and small, including the revolution, Portsmouth functioned as a military base and a centre of commerce. During the early eighteenth century the city flourished as a provincial capital because of its resident Governors. Also, during the revolution and subsequently, by virtue of the importance of many of its inhabitants, Portsmouth attained a position of influence in national affairs which it would never achieve again. Indeed, residents regarded themselves as something more important than a normal colonial society, and they attempted to emulate their counterparts in Georgian England. By the end of the nineteenth century Portsmouth was one of the richest towns in America. Its gentry wore fashionable wigs and fabrics imported from England and the Far East and they had more liveried servants and fine carriages in proportion to the population than any other town in America. Elaborate mansions were constructed on the outskirts, many of them with three stories and built of brick. As well, there were white frame houses, so delightfully typical of the colonial architecture. All this elegance reached a peak when George Washington visited the town in 1789.

As far back as 1705, when the defensive stockades were pulled down, Fort William and Mary was built. It was here that one of the first acts of rebellion against the British Crown occurred, when Captain William Pickering with a force of revolutionaries captured the fort on 14th December 1774.

Nobody really wanted a change in the local administration, or a disruption of the economy, for Portsmouth was enjoying a period of well-governed prosperity and had grown to a population of 4,590 inhabitants. A year later, when war with the Home Country became a certainty, many of the cultured and tolerant inhabitants who were Loyalists took their talents and skills to Canada.

On the outbreak of war the Continental Congress authorised the building of six ships at Portsmouth. The Hon. John Langdon tendered the use of his property, now known as Badger's Island, for the building and repair of ships for the new Navy, and work was immediately started on the first *Raleigh* of thirty-two guns, thus marking the beginning of the Portsmouth Naval Shipyard and heralding the foundation of the United States Navy. The *Ranger*, Captain Paul Jones' famous ship, was built two years later. It was the *Ranger* which, on 14th February 1778, in Quiberon Bay, received the first salute to the American Navy from a foreign country.

In 1798, shortly after the Navy was separated from the War Department, the new Secretary of the Navy, Benjamin Stoddard, decided that Portsmouth was the most suitable place for a Government shipyard in the area. The Yard was mainly developed on Badgers Island, one of the beautiful islands which had so impressed Martin Pring when he discovered the Piscataqua. The keel of the first ship to be built in the new Navy Yard, the *Washington*, a 74-gun ship of the line, was laid down in 1814 during the second war against Britain.

Though Portsmouth had taken on these extra responsibilities and had been the capital of New Hampshire since its foundation, it had to give up this position in 1807 to Concord on the Merrimac River, following numerous claims and counter-claims which formed one of the most famous legislative rulings in the history of Colonial America.

During the Civil War years, 1861–65, the Yard naturally increased in activity, and the labour force rose to 2,524 in 1864. With the end of the war there followed the inevitable recession, and in 1876 the question actually arose whether the Yard should be abandoned, but happily the decision was in favour of keeping it on. Shortly afterwards world attention was drawn to Portsmouth by President Theodore Roosevelt, who chose the Navy Yard for the discussion of the Peace Treaty following the Russo-Japanese War.

When World War I broke out and submarines began to play a vital role, the monopoly of submarine construction was still in the hands of two private companies, and the Navy

Department felt the need for a submarine yard of its own. The choice fell on Portsmouth to launch this new undertaking, from which the Yard became the principal base for submarine construction.

Portsmouth built 'L8', the first of this programme. She was completed in 1917 at a cost considerably below her contract price and was the fore-runner of a long line of Portsmouth-built submarines. 'L8' marked the beginning of the yard as 'submarine specialist' and it was officially designated as such. In this situation the number of employees in the Yard grew rapidly, so that, with surface ships as well to overhaul and repair, 5,722 persons were on the payroll in October 1918, including as many as 1,000 women.

In common with her sister city in England, Portsmouth, New Hampshire, suffered a local submarine disaster. In May 1939 the U.S.S. *Squalus* sank off the Isle of Shoals, only twelve miles from the shipyard, while on trial. The McCann rescue chamber was rushed from New London, thirty-three survivors were brought to the surface, and later the submarine herself. Her superstructure can be seen today, standing proudly in a select position in the Yard as a memorial to all who lost their lives in the disaster.

Entry into World War II initiated a vast building programme at Portsmouth and by December 1943 wartime contracts included the building of 104 submarines. A total of 32 submarines were completed in 1944, and on one day, 27th January, four vessels were launched, the time for building one submarine having been brought down from 469 days to 173. Portsmouth itself was overflowing, having to accommodate the families of 20,466 employees.

With the end of hostilities the shipyard suffered a phased rundown, which reduced hardship to a minimum, and this was helped by its being given the task of developing new and improved submarine designs. With its experience and modern facilities the Yard has had its full share in building and developing the nuclear submarine force.

Sadly, the 1960's are proving to be years of retrenchment and may even see the closing of the yard. But Portsmouth can be proud of its record. From the U.S.S. *Ranger*, with eighteen six-pounder guns, to the nuclear-powered ballistic missile-firing submarine *Abraham Lincoln*, it can point to an achievement in technical ability and efficiency second to none.

Portsmouth is equally proud of its history. Strawbery Banke will live again. A splendid scheme to preserve the history of the City has been taken in hand, whereby many of the original houses of the Strawbery Banke settlement still standing will be preserved for all time. The life of a bygone age will reappear with shops and craftsmen working at their trades as in olden times. Above all it is hoped that one day a full-scale replica of the *Raleigh* will lie off the Banke to remind the world that in Portsmouth, New Hampshire, the United States Navy was born.

Q

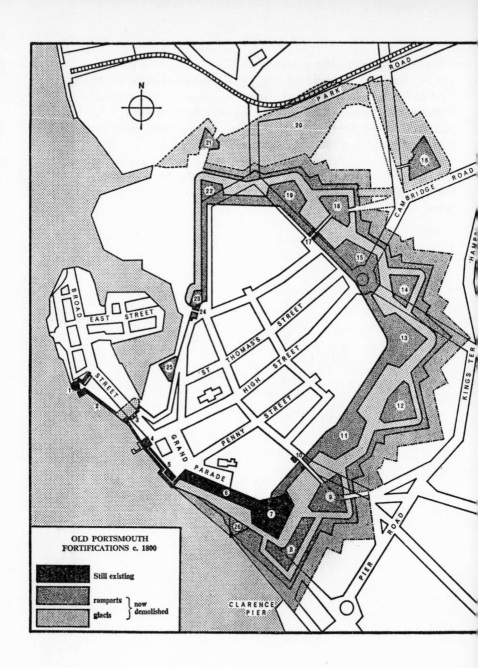

OLD PORTSMOUTH
FORTIFICATIONS c. 1800

Still existing

ramparts } now
glacis } demolished

Old Portsmouth

1 **Round Tower**
2 **Eighteen-Gun Battery,** part of Point Battery
3 King James' Gate
4 **Square Tower**
5 **Saluting Platform**
6 **Long Curtain**
7 **King's Bastion**
8 King's Counterguard
9 King's Ravelin
10 King William's Gate
11 Pembroke Bastion
12 Montague Ravelin
13 East Bastion

14 East Ravelin
15 Town Mount Bastion
16 Amhurst's Redoubt
17 **Landport Gate**
18 Landport Ravelin
19 Guy's Bastion
20 Mill Pond
21 Mill Redoubt
22 Beeston's Bastion
23 Legg's Demi-Bastion
24 Quay Gate
25 Camber Bastion
26 Spur Redoubt

Bold type indicates fortifications still in existence

NOTE:

Quay Gate = King George's Gate
King James' Gate = Point Gate
Landport Gate = Town Gate
King William's Gate = Spur Gate

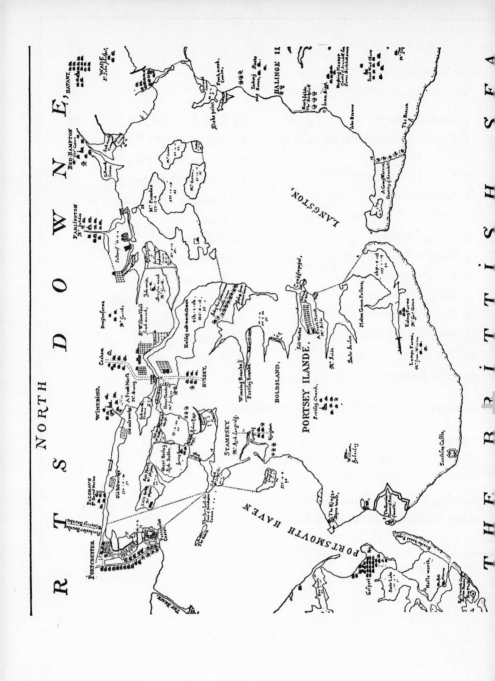

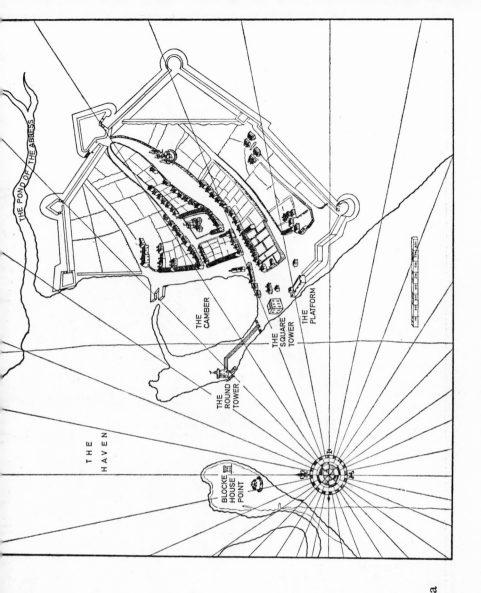

Overleaf: Portsea Island in 1833 showing fortifications around Portsea as well as old Portsmouth

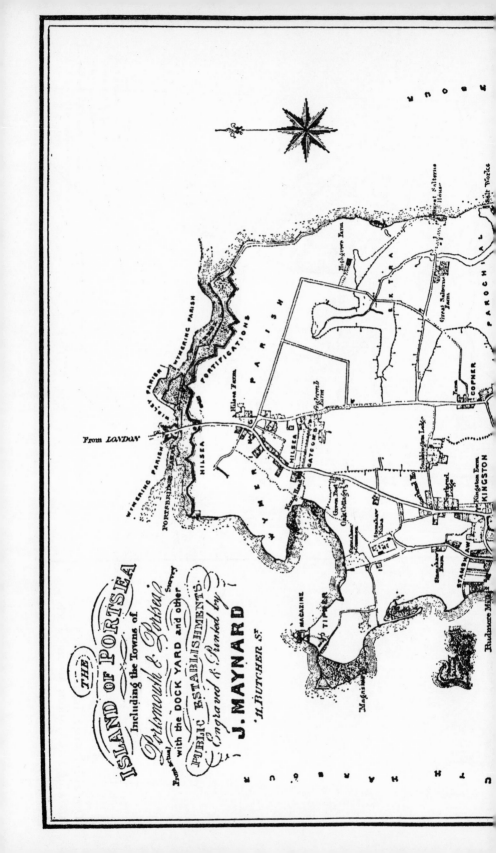

LANGSTON

HAYLING ISLAND

CUMBERLAND FORT.

LANGSTON LAKE

MILTON

Ramblers Joy

Eastnews of Farm

Milton Farm

Upper Milton Farm

PRATTON

Canal

Milk-and Cottages

DEADMAN'S LANE

Lump Hill

Jews Burial Ground

Rumpolt Farm

GREAT MORASS

LANDPORT

Old Dock

PORTSEA

ALL SAINTS

SOUTHSEA

SOUTHSEA COMMON

SOUTHSEA CASTLE

GUNWHARF

PORTS POINT

GOSPORT

SCALE OF ONE STATUTE MILE

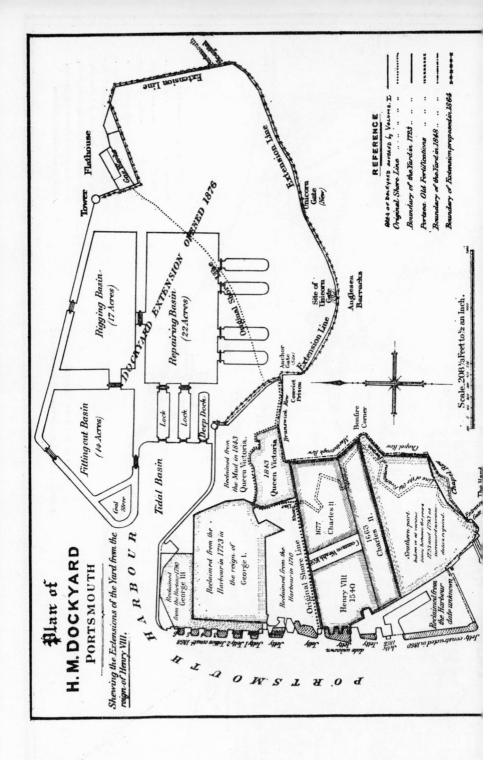

Portsmouth Dockyard showing extensions to the yard since the reign of Henry VIII (Note—Volume I quoted in annotations does not apply)

Index

No direct entry is shown for Portsmouth but all entries refer to the City